City Shapes

Rectangles

By Jennifer S. Burke

Welcome Books™

Children's Press®
A Division of Scholastic Inc.
New York / Toronto / London / Auckland / Sydney
Mexico City / New Delhi / Hong Kong
Danbury, Connecticut

Photo Credits: Cover © Alan Schein Photography/Corbis; All interior photos © Indexstock
Contributing Editors: Mark Beyer and Eliza Berkowitz
Book Design: Michael DeLisio

Library of Congress Cataloging-in-Publication Data

Burke, Jennifer S.
   Rectangles / by Jennifer S. Burke.
     p. cm. — (City shapes)
   Includes bibliographical references and index.
   ISBN 0-516-23077-8 (lib. bdg.) — ISBN 0-516-23002-6 (pbk.)
   1. Rectangle—Juvenile literature. [1. Rectangle. 2. City and town life.] I. Title. II.
Series.

QA482.B888 2000
516'.15—dc21

00-024036

5 6 7 8 9 10 R 05 04

Contents

1 Rectangles in the Dark   4

2 Rectangles on a Building   10

3 Looking Through Rectangles   14

4 Rectangles in the Park   18

5 New Words   22

6 To Find Out More   23

7 Index   24

8 About the Author   24

The city is getting dark.

Signs light up.

Can you find the **bright** rectangle signs?

5

It is winter in the city.

There is **snow** on the ground.

Can you count the rectangles in the fence?

Summer in the city is hot.

The **building** has a pool on the **roof**.

In the summer, you can cool off in the pool.

The pool is a rectangle.

9

Look up!

The building is covered in rectangles.

Can you find any other rectangles?

11

The buildings are in the shape of rectangles.

Some are big and some are small.

Which building is the biggest rectangle?

13

You can see through some rectangles.

There are many rectangles here.

Each window is a rectangle.

15

The **museum** building has many rectangle shapes.

How many different-size rectangles do you see?

The park is a good place to find rectangles.

Sometimes you can climb on rectangles.

Which rectangles are for climbing?

18

19

You can find rectangles by themselves or with other rectangles.

Some rectangles are big and some are small.

It is fun to find rectangle shapes in the city.

New Words

bright (**bryt**) lit up by light

building (**bil**-ding) lit up by light

museum (myoo-**zee**-um) a
    building that has art or history
    objects

roof (**roof**) the top of a building

snow (**snoh**) water that freezes
    in the air

To Find Out More

Books
Fun With Shapes
by Peter Patilla
Millbrook Press

Play and Discover: Shapes
by Sterling Staff
Sterling Publishing Company

Spot's Big Book of Colors, Shapes, and Numbers
by Eric Hill
The Putnam Publishing Group

23

Index

bright, 4

building, 8, 10, 12, 16

museum, 16

park, 18

roof, 8

snow, 6

window, 14

About the Author

Jennifer S. Burke is a teacher and a writer living in New York City. She holds a master's degree in reading education from Queens College, New York.

Reading Consultants

Kris Flynn, Coordinator, Small School District Literacy, The San Diego County Office of Education

Shelly Forys, Certified Reading Recovery Specialist, W.J. Zahnow Elementary School, Waterloo, IL

Peggy McNamara, Professor, Bank Street College of Education, Reading and Literacy Program

D0686673

"LOVE A   captivating,   ."

"A good story, full of warmth and pathos . . .
There are many amusing moments,
such as when Lyn takes four cougar kittens
into a beauty parlor and the cats
tackle the patrons under the dryers."
—*The Victoria Post*

"Most definitely entertaining . . . Often humorous,
with many accounts of the antics of the
kittens—in Ms. Hancock's fourth grade classroom,
riding in rubber rafts, entering people's homes and
generally romping about Vancouver and
Vancouver Island."
—*Westworld*

"There is laughter throughout."
—*BC Outdoors*

Bantam-Seal Books by Lyn Hancock

LOVE AFFAIR WITH A COUGAR
THERE'S A RACCOON IN MY PARKA

Love Affair
with a Cougar

Lyn Hancock

SEAL BOOKS
McClelland and Stewart-Bantam Limited
Toronto

LOVE AFFAIR WITH A COUGAR
*A Seal Book / published by arrangement with
Doubleday & Company, Inc.*

PRINTING HISTORY
Doubleday edition published October 1978
Literary Guild edition October 1978
Seal edition / May 1980

*The excerpt from the article "Natasha, a Tale of
Travel and Travail," which first appeared in The Victorian,
1971, is reprinted here by permission of Hilary Stewart.*

ISBN 0-7704-01579-2

COVER PRINTED IN THE UNITED STATES OF AMERICA
TEXT PRINTED IN CANADA

This book is dedicated to a dream
and to all those who share it.

Contents

Preface   ix
1 Cougars in the Kitchen   1
2 From the Salon to the Ski Slopes   12
3 Cougars in the Wild   23
4 Cougars in the Classroom   30
5 Now, Foster Homes   48
6 Sharing Cougar Experiences   71
7 Growing Pains   85
8 Two Go to Hollywood   100
9 Oola Makes Headlines   122
10 Cougars Cause Controversy   133
11 Last Days of Freedom   151
12 Imprisoned in the Zoo   164
13 And Now, Only One   181
14 Day Pass to Little Darcy   201
15 The Tragedy of Big Joe   221
16 And Then There Were None . . .   246

Preface

This book is about more than cougars. It is about love, love for an animal and love for a man. Both were built on dreams and both were lost without me knowing why. I have written this book more for them than for you, the readers, but perhaps you are the ones who will most understand—more than the man, the animal, or myself.

I have told you my story as it happened when so easily it could have been written otherwise. I have resisted the urging to omit the parts I would rather forget. Characters, like truth, are neither black nor white. They achieve their reality from being painted as they are, whether man or animal. Tom is not the romanticized cougar of modern film and fiction. He is a real animal, a wild animal subjected to the same pressures we are. And when he follows his own instincts can I love him, or his species, any the less?

I come to this book now with different awarenesses than I would have had if I had written it ten years ago, when cougars first came into my life. Then the words would have been wrung from me with anger and sentiment. My perspective in those days was no more than a huddle of maligned and motherless kittens. I lashed out at the media for daring to print that cougars did any harm. I silenced those who confessed they felt any fear. But time mellows emotions and learning helps me take the middle way.

Tom for me began an interest in cougars that continues to this day. Over the years there have been many stories and future books will tell of those; not of how I feel about the cougar but of how it is viewed by the naturalist and scientist, the guide and hunter, the farmer and rancher, the advertising man and the businessman, the media, the Indian, and the general public. But this book is Tom's story and my story.

As Lloyd Beebe of the Olympic Game Farm in Sequim, Washington, once said, "Cougars have given me the most enjoyment in my life." For the children in my class and their parents cougars have been important too. The magic engendered by association with them has lived long and fostered a friendship that still continues today. These then are the first to whom I express my appreciation.

To you my cougar foster families—Betty and Ramsay and David Barrie, Hilda and Basil and Jonathan Griffin, Sylvia and Stephen Miller, Hilary Stewart and Anthony Carter—and to you my friends Howard and Dorothy Smith and Fred and Sally Wolfe, I thank you all most sincerely for sharing so freely your love and your experiences with me.

To you the students in my classroom—particularly David Barrie, Chris Derocher, Jonathan Griffin, Carl Hall, Jane Hoel, Jeff Holm, Megan Horne, Robert Jackson, Gordon Kopelow, Sandra Lloyd, Heather McIllree, Stephen Miller, Billy Puckering, Sally Robinson, Barbara Sherman, Jennifer Smith, Tricia Smith, and Kathy Teghtsoonian—thank you for letting me share your world in prose and poetry. You are all grown up now but still we meet—at home, in the office, at university. And when one of you interrupts your busy day to phone an open-line radio show or come into a bookstore to express your own appreciation, I want to thank you now for remembering the times when cougars were our classmates. I want to thank you for caring. And when the roles are reversed and we meet in a newsroom where you are interviewing me or my animal companions who are probably rummaging through your drawers and filching your cigarettes and candy, thank you for your laughter and the light in your eyes.

And to you my colleagues and also my friends, Dr. Maurice Hornocker of the University of Moscow in

Idaho; Bill Robb and Lloyd Beebe of the Olympic Game Farm in Sequim, Washington; Mark Ferrari and Gary Bogue of the Alexander Lindsey Junior Museum in Walnut Creek, California; Richard Poelker of the Department of Fish and Game in Vancouver, Washington; Elaine Foisey of Cherryville, British Columbia; Elizabeth Guent of Seattle, Washington; Wade and Judy Warren of the Evergreen Game Farm in Snohomish, Washington; Bob Leslie of Camarillo, California; Dr. M. Bussanich, D.V.M., in Vancouver, British Columbia; and Donald Cowx of Vancouver, British Columbia. There are cougars in your classrooms too. Thank you for adding your knowledge to my own.

And thank you, Canada Council, for funding part of the research on cougars that continued long after the scenes that are encompassed in these pages.

And then there are those special patient people who endured me while this book was being gestated. Hilary Stewart of Vancouver, British Columbia, who messed about with cougars in kitchens, in cars, in cages, as well as while roaming the woods and along the beaches. Thank you for capturing those moments in your camera so the memories have life and permanency today. And Audrey Winterburn of Victoria, British Columbia, who steadfastly urged her elderly car northward along the Malahat on weekends when there was no other way so that I could keep my tryst with Tom. And Renée and Robert Jackson, wherever you are, you will know why I am indebted to you.

Finally, a very special thank-you to those who do not understand but still have faith: my parents, Ted and Doris Taylor, and my sister, Jan, and her children, Julie, Michael, and Jeannette of Western Australia who kept company with Oola and Natasha at the local zoo; to Ernie Perrault of Vancouver, British Columbia, who saw my story in a different way; to Jack Bone of Summerland, British Columbia, who also saw the story in a different way but who nevertheless gave me the peace and the perspective needed while it poured forth. Thank you for trying to understand.

And thank you, too, Tabasco, the raccoon who sat

on my knee while this book was being written—when you weren't filching my files, tearing up my typewriter ribbon, and chomping on my carbon copies—because, though not a cougar, you linked me to the wild and brought life to my memories.

And what of the cougars now? Oola and Natasha are alive and well in South Perth, Western Australia. Lara and Tammy were pursuing film careers in California when I last heard. Perhaps Pat Derby, somewhere in California, will reply to my pleas for information and share their present story.

And Tom, my special cougar, may you live long in these pages as you live still in my heart.

Lyn Hancock

January 20, 1978
Burnaby, British Columbia

1

Cougars in the Kitchen

It was well after midnight and I was alone in the house. A sudden scrape and rattle of a window being slowly raised and I was instantly awake. Above the bed the window curtains moved. Someone or something was climbing into the house!

I froze, too terrified to scream or turn on the light. David had left for Victoria on a photographic assignment the week before and wasn't expected back in Vancouver for several days.

Something lightweight flopped on to my stiffened legs. I bit the pillow to stop myself from crying out. The curtains wiggled, parted, and my husband's bulky parka-clad figure climbed awkwardly through the open window.

"Lyn, are you awake?" he whispered.

"No, I died two minutes ago when you first started opening the window," I snapped sarcastically, ready in my fright to launch into a tirade. "What's wrong with the front door?" Before he could explain about his lost key a small object on my legs moved to touch my hand. It purred.

"What is it? Quick, turn on the light," I blurted out in surprise. "Why, it's a cat. And you've got another one clinging to your lapel!" My anger was quickly dissolving into curiosity.

David grinned. "I thought you'd like to mother these little cougar kittens. Their own mother was shot. Don't you think they're adorable?" And the prospective father crooned fondly as he put a second furry blob on the bedspread.

I sat up to face the practical implications of these new arrivals into our already full household. "But what are we going to do with them?" I asked in bewilderment.

"Why don't we put them with these?" my husband replied. And out of his voluminous parka crawled a third and yet a fourth feeble-looking, spotted fluff ball.

I was speechless. "You're crazy! Absolutely impossible," I said at last, subsiding into the warmth of the blankets.

Indeed, right from the start David had been impossible. Certainly different. For instance, on our first date he proposed to me between counting eagles' nests as his plane skimmed the treetops. Our whirlwind courtship culminated in marriage three weeks later on the other side of the world in Australia. When we returned to Canada, he brought a fur seal into the house. And added a dog and a pool of sea birds although twice landlords had asked us to move.

It was now Sunday, January 29, 1967, and we were living in a small bungalow in Vancouver, and David was studying zoology at the University of British Columbia while I taught grade four not far away at Lord Kitchener Elementary School. Our landlord was a veterinary supply dealer. He got along well with Sam the seal and made only slight mutterings about the sea birds and the dog, but how tolerant would he be now of four cougars?

Oblivious to such potential storm clouds, Dave prattled on: "I went over to Vancouver Island to film a cougar hunt but I didn't like the guide. He shoots at everything he sees, including bald eagles. His American trophy hunter had shot the mother and these kittens were going to end up as bait for the hounds. I persuaded him to sell them to me instead. The Fish and Wildlife Branch gave me a permit to keep them six months. After that we have to apply for a zoo license. I've always wanted to study a cougar at first-hand. Now here's our chance."

Still dubious, I looked down at the four woolly balls of soft tawny fur, so sleepy and unseeing they looked inanimate. I was surprised to find that much of their body was black, in the spots, in the rings around their tail, in the ears that were still glued against the sides of their heads.

"Let's put them in Haida's box," Dave suggested. Translating thought into action he plonked the kittens next to our two-month-old Vizsla pup. Haida seemed too sleepy to notice her strange bed companions. We turned off the lights, closed the window, and went to sleep. It was 3 A.M.

Next day at school the children were aquiver with excitement to hear of their teacher being mother to four cougar kittens. Not so my colleagues, who were politely incredulous, mildly scoffing, and full of foreboding.

"How can you stand being married to that man?" one asked when I recounted the story of my mysterious midnight visitors. "I couldn't take it for a day, let alone three years."

"Watch that you don't get attacked," warned another.

"Cougars are dangerous animals. Several people have been killed by them."

"If you were a rancher you'd realize the amount of stock cougars have destroyed."

"Get rid of them before their eyes open," was the general consensus in the staffroom.

When I got home from school that night I found many innovations in our bungalow. Sam the sea lion still had the run of the back yard. The sea birds were still housed in the pool that once had been a flower garden. But the rest of the menagerie had taken over the kitchen. Not that I could get to it! The porch was blocked by a huge sandbox filled with sawdust.

With Sam bombarding me from behind trying to get in and Haida bombarding me from in front trying to get out, I leaped over the sandbox and entered what had been a small but perfectly adequate kitchen prior to the arrival of the cougars. Two boxes, one obviously for the dog and the other for kittens, stood by the oil stove. On either side of the refrigerator, beside the counter, and under the table were piled more boxes of evaporated milk, baby cereal, and different kinds of dog food. The remaining space was filled with a long plywood board that stood up from the floor. Four holes had been drilled and equally spaced along the middle of it. Obviously, Dave had not been to university that day.

"What's that for?" I asked a little testily, pointing to the board.

"Well, we put four bottles in these four holes and all four cougars can go up to the board at the same time to drink their milk while we take pictures of them," he explained enthusiastically. "Then Haida can go along the line and clean them up."

Suddenly I remembered Haida, a hunting dog. "And how is she getting along? Won't she have an innate hatred of them?"

"At first there were a few snarls and showings of claws but now she acts like their mother," David replied. "Look."

True enough, after her first effusive greeting on the porch, Haida had come back and dived into the one box of sleeping fluffy bundles and ignored the second box entirely.

"She pulls their ears and tries to drag them around the floor," David continued. "Then after they've been fed, she licks them all over and cleans their fur of any dried milk and droppings. That'll help your housework and keep them tame."

After the first few days we dispensed with the milk board because the kittens drank far more readily when the bottle was offered from a pair of hands. With four eager mouths tugging at the nipples, sixteen paws and eighty sharp claws groping, pushing, and pulling at the bottle, I had to wrap my hands in a towel for protection. We fed them from pop bottles about six times a day on a diet of two cans of evaporated milk to one of water, mixcd with a little brown sugar and baby cereal. To avoid rickets, a disease common in captive-raised carnivores, we laced this formula with plenty of calcium and multivitamins for the healthy growth of bones.

Bill Robb, from the Olympic Game Farm in Sequim, Washington, considers cougar bones to be quite brittle till about three years of age. He told me about Poorboy, a cougar who broke his legs five times. Perhaps such a vulnerability to bone injury has produced the sway-backed cougars that are seen sometimes in zoos. If we assume the same for cougars born in the wild, many animals hunting on their own at two years of age and attempting to bring down deer or elk much larger than themselves may be in a partially crippled state. Juveniles injured in this way may seek livestock as easier prey.

My first litter of cougars arrived in January 1967 from the wild. They spurred an interest that has intensified in the intervening years. Later, I was to raise several zoo dropouts, unwanted animals whose physical disabilities made them undesirable for public display. One of these was Chimo, a rambunctious, high-spirited cougar that had broken a leg twice merely jumping off a kitchen table. Each time the veterinarian inserted a steel pin inside her leg which was kept in position by a splint. But that didn't curb Chimo's boundless energy one bit. Swinging her splint like a tennis racquet or snowshoe and racing around on three remaining legs, she still chased bears and raccoons and a gibbon with such exuberance that I feared she would next dislocate her hip.

Different cougar owners devise different diets for their charges. With little information recorded in the literature, I had to experiment to find the right formula for the kittens' best growth and development. Natural cougar milk has six times more fat content than cow's milk, a concentration that is probably an adaptation in animals that leave their young in a secluded place and return to nurse at widely spaced intervals. Kittens in the wild may have to wait as long as eighteen hours to be fed, although four to six hours are more usual.

The formula for most hand-raised cougars usually consists of canned evaporated milk in various concentrations with additives such as lime water, cod liver oil, a dextrose syrup, raw egg yolk, whipping cream, cottage cheese, bone meal, even blood extracted from raw liver, and essential vitamins. Recently, an all-encompassing commercial preparation such as Esbilac with its 40 per cent fat content has been commonly used.

Our first cougars were fortunate because they had been raised on their mother's milk for the first ten days of their lives and thus had some resistance to disease. A kitten benefits from one to three days of natural cougar milk to build up such an immunity. If it is removed from the mother at too early an age, Wade and Judy Warren from the Evergreen Game Farm in Washington State suggest injecting 5 cc of the mother's blood into the kitten's veins.

Another zoo dropout I raised later, Chico, was sent to me within hours of being rejected by his mother. He seemed to thrive on a commercial formula, he gained weight and grew fat. A month later I agreed to take his two litter mates who had been kept several days longer on their mother's milk. Although they weighed less than Chico and their tails were bandaged after being bitten by the mother, their hair, whiskers, eyes, and ears were better developed. And being assured by the zoo that they were both healthy despite the rejection, I reunited them with Chico. Within the hour I realized something was definitely wrong with the newcomers and immediately put them on the other side of the house, well away from their brother. However, it was too late and by the following day little Chico, with no immunity from his mother's milk, died. His litter mates died a few days later.

In raising wild animals knowledge comes slowly, sometimes painfully slowly, with experience. When I became foster mother to my first litter I had no knowledge. I relied only on intuition, hard work, and good luck. Fortunately, they thrived.

For the first week the kittens spent all their time asleep except when they awoke six to eight times a day to fight over the milk bottles. In observations made at zoos, it seems that kittens compete for teats and some have been known to die of puncture wounds inflicted by the claws of litter mates striving for the same nipples. After each feeding, if Haida wasn't on duty, we massaged their rear ends, as their mother would have, to induce urination and defecation. Such a ritual continued around the clock.

Ostensibly, David was writing his thesis at university, but the practical novelty of raising cougars and their naturally insistent demands far outweighed the theoretical grind of textbook zoology. When he drove to town on business he carried the kittens in a cardboard box on the seat beside him. Every few hours he would park, rush into an available restaurant to inquire if he could warm up four bottles of cougar formula. Inevitably, when he produced the box of kittens, the cook, waitresses, and customers would compete to serve the cougars first.

Not that the cougars could return their stares! David figured the kittens to be about ten days old when they arrived. Their eyes were tightly closed, their ears flattened, but they responded to light and movement by climbing toward it. Their front legs seemed to develop earlier than their hind ones, enabling them to grapple for the life-giving nipples. The front paws were huge in comparison with the rest of their body and surprisingly strong. Their claws were still tiny but razor-edged.

When they were about two weeks of age their eyelids began to loosen and then, two days after that, parted to reveal an incredible blue. But you had to lie down on the floor at cat level to appreciate them because they were still covered with a cloudy film. They looked but didn't yet see. It was rather disconcerting. When they did eventually register to give you a full-faced stare, it was unforgettable. It was, at the same time, intense yet quizzical, a gaze framed by large upright ears like radar dishes and a contrastingly small snow-white mouth patterned like a butterfly.

Though eye contact was delayed, the cougars communicated in a variety of vocalizations. Their purr was constant and loud like a motorboat, especially when they were tickled behind the ears, under the chin, or when contented after a meal. When they were discontented they growled. Their most distinctive sound was a soft but high-pitched whistle or chirp, a short note something like a chick peeping. Hardly what you would expect from a cat! It was more like a bird call. It seemed a way of making social contact, of saying, "Hello, I'm here" or "Come here, I'm lost."

For the first week the kittens were mostly in their box, either in the kitchen with Haida or out in the car with Dave, so they hardly disrupted my school or household routine at all. However, this was only the calm before the storm. As soon as the word got around that cougars lived on West 13th Avenue, a steady flow of people knocked on both doors, front and back, and squeezed into my greatly reduced kitchen. Chaos reached a climax on weekends, when I was home from school and trying to fit in cooking, washing, cleaning, marking, typing Dave's thesis, and cataloguing his journals. I remember one Saturday afternoon there were so many people crammed in my kitchen, most of them strangers, that I found it impossible to bake a cake for additional visitors expected that night. As I retreated outside with my mixing bowl and threaded my way through the crowd, one lady asked, "Do you work here?"

On Sundays the pace intensified so much that finally we were forced to put up a sign on the front door: VISITORS AND FRIENDS—NO ADMITTANCE TODAY PLEASE. It was embarrassing but necessary. Everybody told us we should put out a tin to help pay for the cougars' food and pills, but that would have been even more embarrassing.

Looking back on the interest shown by absolutely

everyone else, it seems incomprehensible to me now that all those visitors were far more enthusiastic over the arrival of cougars than I was. I had fallen in love with our fur seal Sam at first sight of his velvety, golf-ball-size eyes. He was a personality right from the start. And hatching sea birds like puffins and murres under my sweater most likely appealed to my mothering instincts and sustained my interest in them when they grew up. However, I had never liked cats and it took me a long time to get adjusted to the cougars and share everybody else's enthusiasm. My attachment intensified only as they developed from nondescript blobs into personable little dynamos.

By the time they reached four weeks of age they had chewed up their sleeping box, crawled out, and set off around the kitchen. They loped in a peculiar manner with fat little bellies drooping on the floor and long tails curved upward and swinging rhythmically behind. Their rear ends were higher than their heads and I laughed at their lack of coordination. They now began to play, finding their feet, chasing their tails, making little leaps and jumps, taking their first run. When Haida in the excitement of puppyhood played too roughly, they retaliated by baring their teeth and growling. Their defense was more in their minds than their mouths because at this time only the upper and lower incisor teeth had appeared.

Solitary play gave way to group play, essential practice for growing up. They chased each other around the room, stalked, pounced, and pulled at the furniture, at Haida, at us. They climbed pant legs like trees. Then all at the same time, as if at some signal known only to them, they would find each other, stumble slowly around, close their eyes, and fall asleep in a tumble, relaxed and limp.

Their faces might be soporific but their dreams were active. At first they looked dead, then they would screw up their faces and snarl, their little bodies would wriggle and stretch, and their little tummies would pulsate up and down. As I watched, I wondered how they could dream when they had experienced so little of life. Haida still tried to cram herself in the cardboard box with them. Her long head and ears hung over the side but the rest of her body blended with theirs in one indiscriminate lump.

With limited time for things domestic, my cleaning problems increased with the cougars' desire to expand their territory. They squeezed between the stove and the refrigerator, climbed the pyramids of milk and dog food, and sent them crashing to the floor. After the second week the concertina-type gate we had fixed between the kitchen and the living room was no longer effective in blocking their entry to the rest of the house. The kittens soon learned to squeeze their heads and necks through the holes, but when their bodies wouldn't fit they pulled backward. This movement decreased the space and clamped their necks in the holes and then we had to extricate them. Although they couldn't go through the gate, they soon discovered that they could go over it by clambering up, tottering on the top, and falling flat on their whiskers on the other side. Once they learned to take a running leap to scale the gate, the house was theirs.

Now we had to keep an eye on all of them all of the time. No sooner would I return them to the legal bounds of the kitchen and the sawdust box on the porch than they zoomed back, up and over the ineffectual barrier, into the bathroom, the living room, the study, and storeroom, then into the bedroom and under the bed. In those days we slept Japanese-style on a mattress raised only four inches from the floor, and the cave underneath became their favorite hideout. As David was quite often away attending some meeting, giving talks, planning some new project, or occasionally attending classes, I had to run for some neighbor to lift the bed while I crawled under to get the cougars out.

In those early days of their growing up I found one kitten almost like another. But there was no doubting which was David's favorite: Tom, the only male, the largest of the four, the leader, the explorer, the one with the pudgy baby face, the bumbling awkward manner, the one who preferred our company to that of his sisters. I wanted to call him Marco, after Marco Polo, but David insisted on Tom, just as he had insisted on our seal being Sam.

"Names should be plain and to the point," he said emphatically. "You can name the other three but Tom is mine."

I had initially planned to give the cougars Indian names but I couldn't find anything suitable that was also easy to pronounce. The Kwakiutl called the cougar *put-e,* the Coast Salish *suw* or *sku-ti-su-mi-ye,* the Cowichans *htlak 'pnutsh.* Other Indian tribes called it *wahoo.*

As a compromise I settled on Oola for the first female. She was the beauty of the family, lithe, graceful, but a little aloof. The next female was an easy choice. David on a rare visit to the theater had just been smitten by Dr. Zhivago's sweetheart. So the skinny one, the one that looked more like a kangaroo than a cougar, the one that craved the most love, I named Lara. The runt of the litter was fearful and emotionally unstable. We should have called her Spitfire or Tigress, but by giving her the sweet name of Tammy we hoped to soften her bad-tempered tendencies.

Tom and his three sisters, Lara, Oola, and Tammy, were to have a permanent effect on our lives. I didn't know then as I found out later that Tom, far from being my husband's cougar, was eventually to become mine in a very personal way.

2

From the Salon to the Ski Slopes

I began married life with all the usual intentions, to teach till we had saved enough to buy a house and garden in suburbia, to have children, to cook three meals a day, to do the washing and the mending and the ironing, to give dinner parties, and go out to restaurants and theaters. I expected to join a local drama group and perhaps teach in the local Sunday school. I even worried that there wouldn't be enough meal opportunities left in life to try out all the recipes I avidly collected.

But right from the beginning things never worked out that way. The regular routine became getting up early to prepare food for ourselves and for whatever furry, finned, or feathered friends lived with us; doing a quick spit-and-polish run through the house and back yard to maintain some semblance of order; rushing off to school to devise a multitude of different projects with the children; coming home at suppertime to cook and clean, mark papers, prepare lessons, type, and catalogue. On weekends I collected food for ourselves and the animals, cleaned out Sam and Haida's houses, drained the sea bird tanks, baked the following week's supply of desserts for my husband's sweet tooth, and entertained the numerous visitors, friends, strangers, and children who came to the door.

David attended university and wrote his thesis (admittedly less and less after the arrival of the cougars); gave lectures around the country; picked up oiled seals and sea birds for our bathtub; planned summer collecting and study expeditions to the Arctic for falcons, to offshore islands for seals and sea birds, to interior mountains for sheep and goats; and dreamed up million-dollar projects like buying an island in the Fraser River for a wildlife exhibit. Regular job opportunities he turned down systematically. In the Year of the Cougars he was offered a public relations job at the local aquarium, a university position teaching an ornithology course he had taken himself two years before, and jobs as curator of birds at one zoo and curator of mammals at another.

Whereas I sparked off in many directions at once and tried with little hope of success to carry on all projects at the same peak of efficiency, David went through life with blinkers on, intense and dedicated to whatever was in front of him at the particular moment. Nothing else mattered. If one project failed he didn't waste time in picking up the pieces. He just put it out of his mind and went on to something else. He was a strong starter but a poor finisher. He is a true Aries, the pace setter, impulsive, dominating, and charming. I am a Capricornian, the goat, plodding along behind, practical, hard working, and security conscious. In the early days of our marriage David told me, "Planes fly both ways so if you don't like my way, you can leave." His way might make me cry at times, but it could also make me laugh. And it gave me variety, challenge, and purpose. His early aims and philosophy struck some sensitive chord in my soul and the reverberations set off as a result stayed with me long after he turned to other pursuits, and we began to lead separate lives.

In those days I did insist on one weekly self-indulgence. My Thursday appointment at the hairdresser right across the street provided, if not instant beauty, at least one hour of enforced sitting still. A few weeks after the cougars' arrival I headed for the salon carrying a cardboard box in my arms and a rucksack on my back. Rita, the hairdresser, met me at the door.

"Hope you don't mind me cougar-sitting through the appointment," I said tentatively. "Dave's away, they have to be fed, and I can't give them free rein in the house."

Rita was delighted with the cougars, which she never had been with the sea birds she'd seen at my place or with Sam who had sauntered onto her back lawn one Grey Cup night in search of his own fun and frolic. Most people like animals that are soft and furry and cuddly. But sea birds and sea lions can't be cuddled. Young cougars can.

So she scorned my suggestion that we first line the floor with the newspapers I'd brought and assured me they could have free rein in the salon. Nor were the customers worried by the appearance of a quartet of frisky cougars around the room. Young animals first introduced into a strange room will keep their distance from people. While Rita shampooed and set my hair, the women under the dryers vied with each other to see who could attract the kittens to come closer. The cougars scampered around, first slinking along the walls and then bounding out into the open to grab at the movie magazines, rolled-up balls of paper, knitting, and other objects dangled before them. Sometimes they grabbed an ankle. But torn stockings would be a status symbol—at least a talking point—when the ladies got home to tell the tale of encountering cougars in a beauty salon. I had to shout my answers to their questions and comments in order to be heard over the noise of the dryers.

"Are they really cougars?"

"Is that the same as a mountain lion?"

"Why, they look just like cats."

What's in a name? A lot, when it comes to cougars. *Felis concolor,* the Latin name for this member of the cat family, probably has more names than any other American carnivore—not only a variety of Spanish, Mexican, French, and both South American and North

American native names but a wealth of English names as well. In western Canada it is called the cougar, a corrupt form of the Brazilian Indian name for the jaguar. In eastern Canada and the southern United States it is called panther, a name that sends chills and thrills down the spines of those who remember their fairy tales. In the early days of settlement "panther" was turned into "painter" by the uneducated. Some pioneers thought the stealthy, little-seen, long-tailed yellow cat was a lion that lived in the high mountains and gave it the name mountain lion or cat-of-the-mountain which later became catamount. The Incas called it a puma, which at least is an original and distinctive name for an animal unique to America. But it is also called wild cat, Indian devil, ghost cat, mystery cat. Old-timers call it a varmint and some officials still call it vermin.

To the ladies in the beauty salon, however, the cougars were cuddly cats, just like their own back home except for the funny black spots and the over-sized paws. They wanted to put the kittens in baskets and tie ribbons around their necks. They wanted to touch. Fear subsides when you touch. The vulnerability of the orphaned cougars awakened the nurturing instinct that is in all of us and not just the females of the species.

By the time I had joined them under the dryer one lady had been back home for an old blanket and a couple of bath mats for my cougar "layette." "Sorry about the cigarette holes," she apologized profusely.

"I doubt the cougars'll mind." I laughed as I wondered if it would be right to filch a mat for my bath-room. Considering that through the kindness of my vice-principal I had spent only thirty-five dollars to furnish our whole bungalow, the cougars seemed to be getting a good deal in comparison.

Rita warmed the milk in a pan on her hot plate for the four o'clock feeding, but I was under the dryer and it was impossible to balance all four kittens on my lap at the same time. Tom disappeared up my arm and into the warm dark cave above my head, but the other three shoved and pulled themselves into competitive positions for the best bottle. Ouch! Tammy dug into my knee with her claws as Tom pulled on a curler and I feared we'd all be electrocuted.

Within seconds three other ladies joined me at the dryers, each with a cougar and a bottle, and the conversation centered on formulas, temperatures, burping, and colic. Meanwhile, others went home to get their children. The place was rather crowded by the time husbands began to appear. They'd come home from work, found their kitchens deserted and their suppers still between the pages of the cookbooks. However, complaints evaporated under the magnetism of the cougars and a couple of husbands even helped me home with my armfuls of animals.

David was still keen on making a film of a cougar hunt, but I was more interested in keeping a photographic record of the kittens' development. Filming in our small bungalow became impossible. No sooner were the lights set up for one sequence than the star performers scurried off to another part of the room or another part of the house. And we would have to set up the lights all over again. Weekdays were hectically busy and weekends were complicated by Dave's regular job at the aquarium. One sunny weekend we decided to compromise and try to take both our film requirements amid the natural forest setting of Stanley Park, the home of the Vancouver Public Aquarium.

Our friends Hilary Stewart and Tony Carter, themselves excellent camera artists and avid animal lovers with the necessary sense of humor and patience for animal photography, came along to help. The plan was to set up a scene where we find a litter of kittens that have been orphaned by a cougar hunter, as indeed ours had been. It took a good deal of looking around for a suitable location that was free of spectator disturbance, open enough to provide some sunlight, and yet close enough to the aquarium so that David could dash away to give the talks at the killer whale and dolphin shows and then dash back again to continue filming the cougars—on the hour every hour throughout the day.

Finally we found a suitable spot. A thick cedar log sweeping upward from its skirt of protruding roots stood in a little clearing that was fully bathed in sunlight. Though amputated at the waist, its gauntness was softened by a delicate layer of green moss and algae.

Cougar kittens, like raccoons and bears, can climb before they can walk and always upward. En masse the scramble of cougars, still uncoordinated on level ground, clawed into the trunk and made their way up to form a perfect still picture on the level table at the top. Perfect, except you couldn't program them to look at the camera all the time. Exposed, they blinked in the strong light, the first sunshine we had experienced after weeks of rain, and made no attempt to explore farther than the top of the log.

They felt more secure in the shady depths of a hollow horizontal log nearby. This fallen tree made an ideal cougar den and one from which they soon started exploring, first following Tom, then scrambling individually in and out of the adjacent thickets. Their dark spotted coats and ringed tails formed a perfect camouflage against the mottled greenery.

But they didn't stay around their log den for long. It was lucky that we took the still photos first because before half an hour had elapsed, they were exploring a rapidly extending territory at a rapidly increasing pace. We found even though we were taking movies that it was impossible to keep the actors within camera range. Helter-skelter, they would scramble up on stumps, down into holes, over logs, under roots, and through bushes. We would set up an ideal location and try to keep them within it by plugging up potential escape routes and hiding places, but it was a panic. Dave or Tony would be at the camera, I would be trying to keep all four cougars in sight of us and in particular the lens, and Hilary, putting into play her talent as art director of a television studio but with far less cooperative subjects, would attempt to arrange them in attractive positions. We got very few shots of the four of them together, and even less with the camera on a tripod. It became essential to belly along the ground on our elbows with the camera in hand amid the shrubbery and try to follow one or two of them.

Then right in the middle of a pose or a sequence David would glance at his watch, realize it was ten minutes to the hour, rip off his old clothes behind the nearest tree, throw on his uniform, and dash off to the aquarium about two hundred yards away. As soon as he was gone, Tony reached for his cigarettes, Hilary pulled out a flask of coffee, and I rounded up the camera lenses strewn on the ground. The cougars were left in peace to practice their coordination. Twenty minutes later David would return, change his clothes again, and ask how many pictures we'd taken. Shamefacedly, I'd confess to none.

As this frenzied activity continued all day long, it was no wonder our producer made a slip in his efficiency while narrating the show at the aquarium: "Good afternoon, ladies and gentlemen, here in the B. C. Tel pool today. we have four young cougar kittens . . . [then as the crowd tittered] no, I mean two dolphins and a killer whale."

On the way home we stopped at the docks to pick up the week's supply of animal food, called at a friend's place to collect Haida who was being "dog-sat," and were tearing along the highway trying to make it in time to take some long-suffering neighbors out for dinner, when the tire blew. There we were, stranded on the main highway with a car full of frozen fish, all the camera equipment, a dog, and four cougars. And we hadn't yet joined the automobile association. At such moments I usually look for a man who doesn't mind helping a maiden in distress. Our plight soon attracted attention and a friendly but puzzled spectator offered to give us a lift back to our house.

Waiting there for our ministrations was an oil-slicked seal we later named Esso. Victim of an oil-spilling tanker in the harbor, he was cleaned, fed, and relegated to the bathtub—which meant we had to content ourselves with "a cat's lick and a promise" before dressing for dinner. Needless to say, we went in our guests' car and solved the problem of our own stranded vehicle much later that night. Fortunately, the cougars were tired after their own long day and they went to sleep immediately, curled up with Haida in their orange box on the back porch.

Two weekends later we were filming the cougars again, this time in the snow at Manning Park about 125 miles east of Vancouver. One of my pupils from school, nine-year-old David Barrie had asked me to go on a ski weekend with his family. At that early time in our marriage I still managed to fit in a few activities independent of David's instigation. With my grade-four companions I had already gone skating at the University of British Columbia ice rink and hiked on Hollyburn Mountain. Since Dave didn't ski and worked at the aquarium on weekends, I decided to leave him with the cougars and go holidaying with the Barries.

David had other ideas. "Let's all go," he said. "It'd be a great opportunity to take the cougars out of the kitchen and into the wild to film them against the snow."

I was horrified. "Daaaavidd! The Barries are a very respectable family. When people ask you to go on a ski holiday, they don't expect you to bring your menagerie too. They are a normal family. We're not."

"Go and ask them and see what they say—or I will."

Better that I phone them than David! With great trepidation I lifted the receiver and broached the subject. "Mrs. Barrie? It's Lyn Hancock speaking. About that ski holiday. Well, it's like this. Dave wants to come too and there's nobody else at home to look after the cougars so . . ."

I could hardly believe my ears when she interrupted me quite unconcernedly. "Not to worry. Bring the cougars too. We'd love to have them. I've never yet been on a ski holiday with four cougars."

When Friday came we all piled into their car, Ramsay and Betty Barrie, their son David, and the two Hancocks with their family of cougars. Bob and Joanne, the Barries' teen-agers, and their friends drove to the park in a second car. With the exception of the driver, each of us had a cougar on our lap. Between our feet, taking up the rest of the space, were the lights and camera equipment and enough groceries to last a week. As we drove out of the city, I seriously wondered how long we'd enjoy our friendly relationship.

There was no room in the car for a sandbox, so it was only a matter of time—precisely thirty minutes for each of them—that IT had to happen. The kittens must have been suffering from motion sickness because they all developed diarrhea at once. Progress was considerably slowed by having to stop and dip cougar bottoms in roadside puddles and wipe them off on leaves. Such a natural approach saved on paper towels in the crowded car. But four messes to stop and clean up in the first half an hour was not my idea of how to cement a blossoming friendship. Fortunately, for the rest of the weekend we had no problems in that regard. Maybe it was the change of water that affected them, but they went for another day without relieving themselves at all.

Being wild animals in a provincial park was no advantage for our cougar kittens. Anybody so far who had actually seen the cougars had been smitten immediately. Not so the manager of Pinewoods Cabins, who refused us admittance as soon as he glimpsed our furry traveling companions. When you travel with animals you learn fast. We chose a place outside the park boundaries, registered the human members of our group, and conveniently forgot the feline.

Ramsay and Betty Barrie, David and I, and little David all crammed with the cougars into the one cozy cottage. When the sun went down, while other ski parties sipped hot mulled wine in front of a roaring log fire in the main lodge, we thought ourselves lucky to be feeding, cuddling, and playing tag with cougars— even if one did pee on Betty's pillow.

Raising cougar kittens was a natural extension of her normal duties for Betty, a nurse. To make housekeeping easy, we kept them in the bathroom, a boon of a room for anyone addicted to animals. There's little in the way of breakable furniture and what there is cleans easily. Messes can be washed down the sink or flushed down the toilet.

The kittens at five weeks of age acted pretty much as an indiscriminate bundle; their vastly different personalities had not yet shown themselves to any great degree and they did things pretty much together, except for Tom, who didn't look like a cougar at all. It was Tammy, the runt, who acted the role of the traditional cougar in fable and fairy tale. Much of the time her ears lay flat, her eyes narrowed to slits, and she snarled at imaginary terrors. Admittedly, whenever anything untoward happened, it happened to Tammy. On the first night in the ski cabin she crawled into the corner of the chesterfield, got accidentally squashed, and just stopped breathing. Betty, used to practical solutions in emergency situations, was at her side immediately to administer artificial respiration and in a few seconds Tammy was back in the land of the living.

I was hoping that David could have spent the first day photographing the cougars himself while the rest of us skied, but this proved impossible. So we settled on a compromise solution to combine both activities. While big David pointed the camera, little David Barrie and I balanced a gyrating squirming bundle of cougar kittens on our knees and took off down the toboggan run.

The next day, to my embarrassment, David roped the whole family into forsaking the slopes and taking their positions as film crew. Slithering, slipping, and sliding around in the snow after the cougars in Manning Park was infinitely more difficult than traipsing after them in Stanley Park had been two weeks earlier. The only advantage was that the cougars clambered around more clumsily than we did and their slower movements enabled us to keep them in camera range more often. Their warm fluffy coats were ample protection against the cooler interior temperatures of the park and this particular day was unusually bright and sunny. Still, I couldn't say the kittens appeared as if they really liked their surroundings as much as they had obviously done in their wanderings in Stanley Park.

Ramsay Barrie must have been the only person in his office on the following Monday morning to have taken four cougars skiing for the weekend and, what was more, to have thoroughly enjoyed it—despite his stint as part of a camera crew.

3

Cougars in the Wild

With the comments of my teaching colleagues still ringing in my ears as to the nature of cougars, I began a search for information. One study had been done on the food habits of cougars in Utah and Nevada; another on mountain lion predation in New Mexico; and another on reproductive and vocal behavior in zoos. The only two books available were based on information obtained largely from hunters and ranchers. Ten years later, one of these, *The Puma* by Stanley Young and Edward Goldman and aptly subtitled *The Mysterious American Cat*, still remains the standard text on cougars.

The cougar may not have been studied by the serious student of biology, but it had certainly captured the imagination of the headline writers in newspapers and magazines. "WANTON MAN KILLERS," "INSATIABLE MONSTERS," "VICIOUS, CUNNING AND BLOODTHIRSTY," "EXTERMINATE THEM," they proclaimed with high moral fervor. Reporters tried to satiate the appetite of adventure-starved readers with descriptions of "hunger-crazed cats terrorizing towns on an annual rampage." Accompanying illustrations showed the cougar snarling, its wicked mouth wide open, its evil fangs bared, and its malevolent eyes blazing.

Man has long decreed that some animals are "good," e.g., his dog, his horse, a fluffy white-coated seal pup, or a floppy-eared, soft-eyed doe or fawn; and some animals are "bad," e.g., the big bad wolf or the cruel,

23

cunning cougar. In 1967 the cougar was still a varmint and on the "bad" list. Its aesthetic value was not yet appreciated and in most places it could be shot on sight. British Columbia was one of the few places where the bounty had been lifted and the cougar was seen as beginning to have a dollar value as a trophy animal. It seemed ironic to me at the time that for the cougar to be given some protection it had to be declared a big-game animal. This meant it was allowed to be hunted with set seasons and bag limits.

At the turn of the century Teddy Roosevelt, a big-game hunter and a noted conservationist, described the cougar as "a big horse-killing cat, the destroyer of deer, the lord of stealthy murder, facing his doom with a heart both craven and cruel." How did the cougar come to have such a reputation even from the so-called conservationists of the day?

Men fear what they do not see and this elusive, powerful, and generally silent cat gradually acquired a reputation for being dangerous. It was hated as well as feared because as a predator it competed with man for the same prey. The cougar is the most adaptable of all the cats. It is capable of making its home in many kinds of habitats—jungle and temperate forest, pampas and prairie, sea beach and alpine meadows. Once its range extended from the Yukon to Patagonia, from the Pacific to the Atlantic. But as the vast wilderness became crisscrossed by roads, splotched with settlements, and filled with people, the cougar was eliminated in most areas of North America east of the Rockies by about the turn of the century.

In the last ten years a few cougars have been occasionally reported in all provinces in Canada except Prince Edward Island and Newfoundland. But only in the south of British Columbia and, to a lesser extent, Alberta can they be called common, though still not often seen.

The information I pieced together in 1967 about the life history of the cougar was based on reports from hunters, ranchers, and zoo keepers. Even today little has been studied of the animal in the wild and even less published.

It is generally assumed that cougars are polygamous. Between two and three years of age, the usual age of sexual maturity, the female signals her mating condition by a bloodcurdling caterwauling, something like the scream of a Siamese cat but louder, harsher, and more prolonged. The sound has been described traditionally as "the demonic cry of a woman in labor." I was to first hear it myself several years later from Chimo, the only cougar I have raised to come into season. She crouched in the cage, rubbed the area between her anus and genitals against the ground, brushed against the wire, and allowed people to approach and pet her more than she usually did. At such a time she liked to be scratched and caressed. And it seemed to me, more by men than by women, though the fact is that more men than women were willing to pet a full-grown cougar! For about two weeks there was relief, then the indescribable yowling would start again and keep us all awake. My mother-in-law was staying with us then and she threatened to leave unless we could make the cougar stop.

Since we didn't have a male at the time to satisfy the lovelorn Chimo, I have never been able to parallel the experience of Bill Robb, who looks after the cougars at the Olympic Game Farm in Sequim, Washington. Bill says that a female makes a slightly different sound when she is actually being mated. "The first sounds like she's saying, 'Where are you?' and the second is a terribly pained sound when her mate gets there," he told me.

"I guess it can be regarded as pain or ecstasy, depending on your point of view," I replied, laughing.

Though zoo keepers hear the female's scream fairly frequently in captive situations, very few people have heard it in the wild. The cougar has a reputation for being a silent creature and some hunters, even wildlife researchers, go so far as to say the cougar doesn't scream at all. To them it is against the cat's shy and solitary nature. Perhaps the female comes into heat and the male catches up to her scent trail and mates with her before much vocalization occurs.

It has been found at the Olympic Game Farm— probably the place where more cougars have been bred in captivity than anywhere else—that if a litter is removed before twenty-eight days, the female will come into heat again, but if the kittens are left longer and then removed, she will not mate again till the following year. Bill says it is possible to recycle a female to get three litters a year, though, being too hard on her, it is not usually done.

The cougar seems to be much the same as an ordinary house cat in its courting habits. Nobody to my knowledge has ever observed the mating behavior of cougars in the wild, but by reconstruction of tracks in the snow and from the stories of hunters, it is possible to make a few guesses. It is probable that a male must fight off other males before he successfully copulates with the female. Then they wander together for a week and separate. One recent observer found that a mated pair stayed together for sixteen days.

After a gestation period of between ninety and ninety-six days, the female gives birth to a litter of between one and six kittens, with the average litter size between two and three. The litter is equally divided between males and females, although statistical evidence gives a slight edge to the females.

The mother seeks complete isolation from her kind at the time she gives birth to her young but chooses a den area near an abundant supply of prey such as deer, rabbits, birds, and beaver. A cougar's lair is often located under an uprooted tree or in a shallow cave on a mountainside. If there is no natural hole the cougar mother builds a crude bed of sticks, leaves, and grasses in a dense thicket. The opening is protected by thick bushes, projecting roots, or windfalls. Most of the dens one cougar hunter has observed are close to water. Cougar observers on Vancouver Island have found cougar families being raised near beaver dams, satisfying the need for both food and water.

While the female cougar chooses thick brush as a protection for her kittens, she likes a rocky ledge nearby for sunning and resting herself. Ideally, it should provide a vantage point for observing things passing below yet be as inaccessible as possible for things passing behind.

It is the female that tends the young and protects them from other males. That males sometimes kill and eat kittens is thought to be an important factor in preventing overpopulation. Strangely, one of the male cougars at the Olympic Game Farm showed such an interest in caring for young kittens, licking, fondling, and playing with them, that he was given a job of acting a female cougar film role in a recent TV production of *Grizzly Adams*. This is definitely the exception, not the rule.

In the Pacific Northwest cougars are born usually in late spring or early summer, when temperatures are warmer for the young kittens and when there is a greater variety of food available. In Utah and Nevada where winters are more severe, the most common month of birth is July, with a general peak between June through September.

Still, cougar kittens have been found during every month of the year and at altitudes ranging from sea level to seven thousand feet even in areas with pronounced changes of climate. My first kittens were born in the wild on Vancouver Island west of Campbell River in January, as were two other litters I raised later. The Island enjoys a mild marine climate with a low snowfall in winter.

Young cougar kittens stay with the female until they are about two years of age, by which time the male kittens may far outweigh their mother. The average adult male in British Columbia weighs about 125 pounds and the female, 100 pounds. The heaviest recorded cougar was in Arizona. It weighed 276 pounds.

It was coincidental that I should raise my first cougars in 1967 because that was the year one of Dave's fellow students at the University of British Columbia, Maurice Hornocker, presented a thesis on "An Analysis of Mountain Lion Predation on Mule Deer and Elk in the Idaho Primitive Area." At that time Dr. Ian McTaggart Cowan was the big drawing card for students of wildlife and U.B.C. had a wide reputation for its focus on wildlife management. Dave was studying eagles, Mike Bigg was looking at seals, Val Geist was living with mountain sheep, Fred Zwickel was counting grouse, and Maurice Hornocker was collaring cougars. Most of the students I knew then are the big-name biologists in their respective fields now. Being curious about my adopted province and its wild animals, I often went on field trips with the boys or sat around asking questions in their tiny university offices that were crammed to the ceiling with books, papers, hides, skulls, feathers, bottles of formaldehyde and jars of such unsavories as reproductive tracts.

Although Maurice Hornocker was registered at U.B.C., his field work was in Idaho where conditions were better for studying cougars. The trees were not as high, the forests were not as impenetrable, the greater amount of snow made tracking easier, and money was made available there for an expensive project that entailed hiring cougar hunters with dogs, buying radio transmitters and receivers to collar and follow marked cats, transporting personnel and equipment into wilderness areas by plane, and living for months at a time in tough winter conditions. Also in the Idaho Primitive Area the cougars were not as disturbed as they were on Vancouver Island after so many years of bounty hunting.

In 1967 Maurice was just beginning to explode some of the myths that had long surrounded the cougar. He was accumulating quantifiable evidence to prove objectively what a few cougar devotees had observed subjectively. He showed, at least for Idaho, that cougars eat mostly deer or elk, but not one every week throughout the year, as irate hunters had been saying.

Cougars were more likely to eat one deer every ten to fourteen days in winter and at considerably longer intervals if elk were killed or in summer when ground squirrels were more abundant.

While writing this book I talked to Maurice again, this time in Hungry Horse, Montana, where he was studying wolverines. He had wound up his ten-year study on cougars in Idaho, but other biologists in Arizona, California, Colorado, Nevada, Utah, and British Columbia had begun their own research on cougars and were using similar methods to those used by Maurice about the time my four cougars came tumbling through the bedroom window.

An outdoorsman writing in a naturalist's magazine in 1912 said that "After 31 years of more or less constant association with the beast, I have arrived at the conclusion that the cougar is the most incongruous mixture of courage and cowardice, boldness and stealth, wisdom and imbecility of any animal that runs wild."

What were cougars really like? In raising these four soft, spotted, woolly cushions that seemed more like Persian kittens than wild animals, would I really find out?

4

Cougars in the Classroom

When David couldn't help me hold a milk bottle I knew he had to go to hospital. As a teen-ager he had broken his elbow several times and it had been mended with bones from other parts of his body. But over the years he had strained it further by hauling heavy boxes around sea bird rookeries, fighting to force-feed belligerent, unappreciative sea lions, climbing up into eagles' nests, and climbing down into falcon eyries. Slowly, it had been getting worse and now he had reached the point where he had no feeling in his left hand, the one he used most. The surgeon suggested changing over nerves to give him back feeling, but he couldn't promise strength, which spelled doom to our future plans in wildlife work.

Sam and the sea birds needed my attention only in the morning and evening, but the kittens at six weeks were still on a two-hour feeding schedule. Thus when David went to hospital I had to take the cougars to school.

I have never been the typical teacher—whatever a typical teacher is. My first years as a teacher in the largest high school in Western Australia, trying to be Professor Higgins to a thousand Liza Doolittles, were understandably hectic. Most of my students were brawny, boisterous teen-age he-men who could hardly be expected to prefer elocution and "culcha" to their more usual pursuits in the surf or on the "footie" field. Especially when their speech and drama teacher was a "sheila"—a girl—and this was the first time some-one had dared to teach this subject with this age group! Maybe for some of my students the fact that I was only two years their senior helped. Certainly, my hyperactive level of energy and enthusiasm did. I remember running from one class to another between periods on the hour every hour, five days a week across school grounds that covered fifteen acres. As well as the usual accoutrements of a teacher, I lugged a heavy old-style tape recorder. Before school, at recess, lunchtimes, and after school I had the crazy idea of taping the voices of my twenty-five classes and then playing them back to show hopeful improvement as the term wore on and I wore out.

Four years later I took on a whole school again. It was for the educationally subnormal in the east end of London. My room was sandwiched between a factory on top and a warehouse below, with no facilities whatsoever. My students, ranging from six to eleven plus, were dropouts from all the other teachers' classes. At least my kind of Cockney matched theirs. I'm sure I didn't teach them anything that year, but Capricornian persistence at least made me stay for my punishment. All of their previous twenty-five teachers had given up.

This stint in the purgatory of an English blackboard jungle was open sesame to a position on the other side of town the following year. In the 1960s the west side of London was the mecca of all Australian teachers living in Earl's Court. (Arabic or Hindi is more of a passport now than Aussie-type Cockney.) I guess the school board thought I could withstand anything because once again it gave me the class nobody wanted. This time it was a group of West Indians whose parents were rioting on Portobello Road. The rest of the staff thought me madder than a mad dog or an Englishman when I dared to take the children out of the four walls of the classroom and arranged the curriculum around field trips in London. But I found discipline easier to maintain in a subway to the Tower than in the schoolroom. Besides, I could meet my friends and touring relatives at the Elgin Marbles in the British Museum while my West Indian children were sketching Egyptian mummies.

When I came to Canada one year later, I decided to look for an easier job. But as I was a landed immigrant the job came looking for me. A fatherly employment supervisor in Montreal packed me off to a hotel in eastern Quebec to be a waitress in a resort hotel with quite a questionable reputation. I found out why that first night. As I walked in, the owner was being carried out—in a straitjacket en route to a mental institution. The barman had just tried to commit suicide in the lake. The guests were helping themselves to liquor and food. The accountant was mumbling that the place should be burned down and the insurance collected to pay the bills. And the owner's wife offered me the job as manageress.

Wanting to be early in the office the next morning, I scrawled a large notice on the door of the kitchen to the cook—"KNOCK ME UP BEFORE 7 A.M."—and I went to Room 12 to unpack and sleep. But not for long. I was kept awake the entire night by people hammering to get in. In desperation I shoved the wardrobe, the dresser, the chairs, the table, and finally the bed against the door and wondered how long I would last. Next morning my indignant questions were answered by a lesson in the Canadian language. At the end of the summer I settled for a job producing the school play for a province-wide competition in the footsteps of a professional Broadway director. And that winter the hotel burned down.

Plunging into marriage with its accompanying menagerie meant looking for a job that was routine. I didn't want to take too many books home. Once again the job was different. I was assigned an experimental class called the major work class and that was exactly what it meant—major work. My students came from all over the city, specially selected for their academic potential though it didn't always mean they were high achievers. In fact, some didn't want to learn at all.

But if you introduce an owl, a sea lion, a couple

of eagles, a trio of tortoises, or a quartet of cougars into the classroom, someone is going to learn something. The trouble was that the children were learning too much. One parent complained to the school board that his daughter talked about nothing else at the dining table but schoolwork. Another protested that when the children came around on Saturdays to look at the animals in their teacher's back yard, she insisted on asking them questions.

I expected the class to be as interested, as curious, as enthusiastic about life as I was. If rushing them along on the same wave sometimes caused problems, I think it all worthwhile now, more than ten years later, when some lanky young man with a deep voice comes up at an autographing session in a local bookstore and asks to look after the animals as he used to do in the classroom. Or an eager biology student at university says that he got his start from measuring feather growth in grade four. Or a budding young poet thanks a sea lion for stimulating him to write his first poem.

It was fun and it was a lot of work. But work when you are interested is play. Whatever it was, we all did it together, the teacher, the children, most of the parents, and of course the animals. We had no set curriculum. We just got in a bus or the mothers' cars and took trips—to the zoo, the aquarium, a printing press, a research station, a museum, a magazine, all around Vancouver and other towns as well. We asked a lot of questions, took a lot of notes and pictures, then came back to the classroom to put it all together.

Or we just stayed at school and observed the animals. Sam, the fur seal, made Megan Horne's day.

> One day I felt like dying
> I was so sick of school
> I had been in a stuffy room
> And I wanted to be cool.
> It was time for language
> And sometimes it's fun

But I was in a bored mood
Sick from the hot sun.
Waiting in line outside the door
I heard a lot of noise
It sounded like a seal's bark
But I wouldn't believe the boys.
We all crowded into the classroom
And quickly shut the door
We couldn't let Sam the seal out
Or he'd cause a great furore.
We were told to sit down
But Sam did so excite
That we just clustered around
Even when he did bite.
Then Mrs. Hancock tried
To get Sam on her desk
But he was being bad
So we tried a test.
Our teacher went out to her car
And brought in Scarlett Macaw
Sam was 'sposed to calm right down
He didn't. So we cried "Aww!"
Finally we got the seal
To pose on a chair
While we wrote poems and stories
And tried to take much care.

But for everything there is an end
When its time has come.
Language ended and we were sad
For it had been much fun.

Billy Puckering was a chap of few words. He came straight to the point.

Mrs. Hancock has a pet
Which is usually very wet
It is a seal
Whose name is Sam
And if he hits you with his flipper . . .
Wham!

I learned as much as the children did. At a time in my life when a Townsend's Solitaire meant not a bird but some kind of diamond ring, I welcomed each orphaned creature that landed on my doorstep as an opportunity to learn something of the species as a whole as well as to rehabilitate the individual animal. I became the constant recipient of a steady succession of swallows that dive-bombed windows, owls and hawks that toppled from nests, grebes and seals that swam through oil slicks. They were learning experiences every one, even though one mother reported me to the S.P.C.A. for giving her daughter a trauma by keeping a pickled one-day-old naked nestling robin on my desk. It had died the day it was brought to school, one of nature's rejects whose short life taught us that not all birds are hatched with feathers.

Before the cougars came to school we had been visited by Sam, the fur seal, who was really a sea lion, the rhinoceros auklets who weren't rhinos, the puffins who weren't parrots, the eagles and falcons who didn't look at all dangerous, and as fulltime residents of the classroom, a turtle and two tortoises.

The stuff of learning should not be crammed into compartments to be taught as science today and geography tomorrow. When we looked at the animals we studied not only them but where they came from. Sam taught us about Alaska, where he was born, and California, where he was heading when he washed up instead on a British Columbian beach. Sam taught us about the explorers who came to our coast to shoot seals and sea otters and stayed to settle.

There was much in the books about all the other animals that came to school, but scarcely anything about cougars. Mention the very word and everyone had something to report from what he had remembered about other people's experiences, but if we were to find out anything about cougars from firsthand experience, the kittens would have to come to school.

The teaching staff couldn't understand why I was spending so much time and effort in keeping the cougars alive when less than ten years before their tax money was being paid to make sure cougars were dead. My colleagues warned me of the dire consequences if I let the cougars loose in the classroom. For my own part I couldn't see how Tom, Oola, Lara, even Tammy, could inflict more damage than Sam herding the class into his harem. But seals enjoy a good press. Cougars don't.

Every morning I had been giving the class a running commentary on the kittens' progress, and some students would walk home with me after school to see them, but I avoided bringing them to the classroom until David's going to hospital gave me no choice. I warned the children to wear gloves and sweaters and took a chance that all would be well.

The day the cougars came to school I should have taken a taxi as our clunker of a car was a real death-trap. Its doors, windshield wipers, electrical wiring were all about to expire. David had the annoying habit of glimpsing a three-figured reject on a lot, driving it once around the block, and handing it over to me. Luckily, I had just joined the automobile association and very soon I was to be its best customer.

School was less than a dozen blocks away and usually I walked. But on a morning of suddenly cold temperatures after a month of rain, I piled the exercise books and reference materials in the front of the car, the box of cougars in the back, and tried to defrost the windows. Ancient Hillman Minxes are not noted for their defrosting ability, so my normal method was to pour hot water over the glass to melt the ice and pray my guardian angel would prevent a sudden splintering. With temporary vision till the next freeze-up, I then opened the windows and turned up my collar.

My other problem, and the more annoying one, was that the cars Dave picked out for me never wanted to start. After a long warm-up with the windows open, which only the engine enjoyed, the car finally spluttered into action and we were away. But not for long. It died at the next stop sign at a busy intersection. On this important day I wasn't going to waste any time on my own efforts, so I dashed into the nearest house and called the emergency road service.

The man didn't take long to come and to my relief

he had never met me before. He gave my car a quick once-over, pronounced it a lost cause, and suggested I send it to the junk yard.

"But the bell has gone and I have to get to school," I pleaded. "It isn't far. Could you give me a lift?"

"Sorry, lady, it's against the rules," was his stern reply.

Fortunately, the kittens nestled angelically in a sleepy lump in their cardboard box on the back seat had more persuasive power than I did and the kind gentleman shall remain forever nameless. He fixed up a towline, dragged my car home, and telling me to lie low, drove us to school in his own vehicle.

It was a little difficult to be inconspicuous when accompanied by boxes of scribblers and reference materials, not to mention Tom, Oola, Lara, and Tammy. And as the second bell had gone, the children were agog at the window waiting when we drove into the schoolyard. I had no lack of eager helpers to carry in my boxes. The children scuttled to their seats ready for the opening of the most important box of all—the cougars. There was a sudden expectant hush as the lid was lifted then:

Aaaaaaaaaaaaaaaahhhh-h-h-h!!!"

It is always the same sound—the anticipatory intake of breath, the long drawn-out expression of delight, fascination, of appreciation for things small and vulnerable and sweet. It echoes the charm of babies, of flowers, of sunsets—and cougar kittens. It finds expression on the faces as furrowed brows and tight lips flower into openmouthed wonder and smiles of joy. Then as always, "Can I touch it?"

But gently, they are babies. You are giants. This is a strange place. Let them come to you. Let them take their time. It'll be better that way.

First Tom edged over the box and stared at the circle of faces. Anxious hands reached forward. Ssh! Back! Don't scare him. Then Oola and Lara took tentative steps onto the table. Only Tammy crouched nervously at the bottom, then snarled as she caught

sight of Paul with glasses. Cougars' feelings are mir-
rored in their faces just like children's, whether of fear
or anger, joy or sorrow, hunger or satisfaction, fatigue
or exuberance. It is anthropomorphic but true. More-
over, they are aware of human expression as well. If
you smile at them, they smile back. If you frown, they
will lay their ears back and hiss.

Barbara Sherman saw them this way:

In early February Mrs. Hancock brought four
cougar kittens to school. Everybody clustered
around their box. All I saw at first were four
long tails sticking out. Finally I got to see and
touch them. They are bigger than the little kittens you buy in the pet store. Their coats are
light brown with black spots. Their big feet are
flat and they have sharp claws. They wobble
when they walk. Their ears are quite small and
pied in colour. Their back feels bony but their
fur is soft. They sound a lot like birds. When I
heard them before the box was opened that was
what I thought they were. I like the cougars very
much and would love to have one at home. Still,
the classroom is the next best thing.

Kathy Teghtsoonian preferred verse to describe her
reactions:

> They're fuzzy, so fuzzy,
> Little balls of fur.
> Sometimes they growl
> Sometimes they purr.
>
> Spotted little fuzzy balls
> Orange, grey and black,
> Looking for a cuddle
> Spotted on the back.
>
> Their tails are short and striped,
> Blue eyes look so cute,
> Brown and orange coats
> Make a fitting suit.

> Screaming like a blue jay
> Making noisy sounds,
> Having pictures taken,
> Trying out large bounds.
>
> Backs up, heads down,
> Lots of furry hair,
> That's what it's like
> With our Cougar Affair.

We tried putting the kittens in the sandbox by the window which housed Himie, the box turtle from Florida, and Gomer and Ludwig, the gopher tortoises from the Mojave Desert in California.

> Eating in the sandbox
> Walking on the floor
> Ambling here, pacing there,
> Plodding out the door.
> Rolling in the sandbox
> Yet still keeping clean
> Himie small, Aggie big,
> And Gomer in between.
>   Chris Derocher

But as soon as the cougars caught sight of those cold, hard, primeval-looking reptiles, they jumped out smartly and scurried for the darkest corner. The resident animal occupants were quite content to lumber around their sandbox and leave the rest of the classroom for the temporary visitors.

In contrast to the formal rows and single spacing of the traditionally arranged classroom, our desks were placed in groups of four, surrounding a table that supported a huge papier-mâché relief map of North America. We covered the map with a large pink blanket and it became the kittens' home base. At feeding times the cougars stretched up from the Central Plains to suck on their milk bottles. At sleeping times they nestled down in the folds of the Rocky Mountains.

At other times they roamed the room at will while

the children observed them. Jennifer Smith wrote in her journal:

> Mrs. Hancock let the cougars wander around, so every so often you would see a little animal walking past your desk. No one brought news clippings because we were all so anxious to play with the cougars. Besides, the kittens were news enough.

It took a lot of patience for the students not to grope and poke, to press and pull, but it paid off in the long run because the cougars felt relaxed enough to behave at school as they did at home. They seemed to delight in the sheer joy of new-found movement. They leaped and pirouetted in mid-air, they ran and chased, they stalked and pounced.

> Baby cougars here and there
> Baby cougars everywhere
> Baby cougars in and out
> They cry, they purr, they growl, they pout.
> Little tiny balls of fur
> Pat them, then they're sure to purr.
> Yawning, always bugging you
> Especially when they go "poo-poo,"
> Swishing around his long, long tail,
> Crash! Alas, he knocked over the pail.
> Water and soap all over the floor,
> Around the room they race and roar.
> And when you say, "Oh, go away,"
> Then they whimper and seem to say,
> "Well, if you want us to, we'll go, okay?"
> Sally Robinson

Even adult cougars will play, a behavior pattern noted often in captivity but only once or twice in the wild. A naturalist at the turn of the century enjoyed such a rare occurrence. He described a cougar chasing imaginary objects and pretending to catch and devour them, making leaps and bounds like those of a kitten chasing an erratic and elusive butterfly. Another observer maintained that she looked outside her cabin to see her two-year-old son tossing sticks at a cougar which, to her utter amazement, was leaping playfully aside and purring pleasedly. It ran off to the woods when she appeared.

And then there is the story told in the back woods of Idaho about the little girl who made friends with a cougar. But when her parents and older brothers discovered that she was seeing this varmint, they declared that the cat was responsible for stock disappearances and would have to be killed. One stormy night the little girl went to warn the cougar. Neither she nor the cougar was ever seen again. Stories differ but the little girl and the cougar may have been on a bridge when it was washed out by the storm. Such a tale may be farfetched but it is certain that the cougar is playful in captivity, possibly also in the wild, and curiously, sometimes *does* seek out human company.

After a period of rambunctious play, the kittens climbed up on the children's laps or sought caves in dark desks. To facilitate this, some students emptied their desks of books to attract occupants. At a vulnerable time like sleeping, all young animals want the security of a warm dark place close to mother or litter mates or else some substitute. The kittens might look as if they were killing each other one minute, but when suddenly they relaxed, usually all at the same time, they huddled together if they could, closed their eyes, and fell asleep.

Baby cougars, fat, skinny, bright,
Cute, stripey, short of sight.
Black dotted little things,
About to fall, then tight they cling.
Four sharp little claws on each paw
Scratching up and down your skirt
Like a little saw.
Running, crying, taking little bounds,
Messes, ripped dresses but hardly any sounds.

Little blue eyes stare at you
Like some little stars.
Romping all around the room like four little cars.
Oh, cougars are fun to have in your room
Don't you hope you get some soon?

Tricia Smith

The rumor that cougars were in a grade-four class-room spread quickly around the school after recess, so sleeptime was a good time to invite in the other classes. The children could file past, even touch, and for the first time see a cougar in some other activity than glowering malevolently, ready to spring. I was constantly worried about one of the children getting scratched and going home to complain bravely to mother that he or she had been attacked by a cou-gar. A couple of boys took off their sweaters and hoped for some scratches in order to impress their families at dinner that they had been in contact with mountain lions—or worse still, panthers. The kittens were only about five pounds, with their back teeth just erupting and their canines not yet in sight, but they used their well-developed claws to good advantage to cling, to climb, and to defend themselves. Luckily, the children saw any scratches as status symbols and a chance to show off to the other students that, yes, they had cougars for classmates. I wasn't sure if their mothers would see ripped dresses and torn cardigans in the same light. The staff continued to warn me dourly that I was probably in for trouble. And not even sleeping kittens belied their fears.

The children were conscious of the cougars' claws, but they paid far more attention when, speaking euphemistically, the animals went to the bathroom in the schoolroom. Such an event featured prominently in their poetry.

They run around on padded feet
I think their spots look really neat.
With ears of pink and eyes of blue

That stare inquisitively at you.
They love to play but bother you
When on your desk
They go "poo-poo."
Their fur is nice, as nice as silk.
The only thing they drink is milk.
In play they spring into the air
And of their claws, you'd better beware!
                                    Jennifer Smith

Learning cannot always be conducted in a carefully guarded and antiseptic society. I have little patience with either grownups or children who smirk and put a peg on their noses at an animal's perfectly normal functions. Mine is a practical approach. Without any ado, I carry lots of paper and clean up quickly. Carl Hall didn't seem to mind either.

The lovely little cougars
Nestle on my chair
And when they "go" in my desk
I don't even care.

"Cougars, cougars, cougars,"
Are the only words said.
"Cougars, cougars, cougars,"
Go swelling through my head.

They are furry, soft and lively,
Lovable, huggable and such a surprise.
When they come to the classroom
The room is full of delighted cries.

The cougars slept twice as long as they were awake. Now in the second month of their lives, they did sleep less and play more than in their first month, but it wouldn't be till their third month that their play periods would exceed those of sleep. Fortunately for the curriculum in general and the attitudes of the staff in particular, the schedule of the six-week-old cougars allowed the children a little time for a few disconnected activities—not many but some!

It didn't matter anyway. Biology might be the subject that initially motivated us, but in the process of discovering the cougars we found we had covered the rest of the curriculum as well. Mathematics were accounted for when we weighed and measured both the kittens and their milk; when we accumulated the numbers of cougars killed for bounty money and calculated the cost to the government. Social studies were taken care of when we looked at where cougars used to live and where they might live now. Art was covered when we concocted our own cougars in paint and crayon, in cloth and metal. And nobody could say we omitted music. Not when David Barrie instructed us to sing his song to "John Brown's Body":

Every now and then I have to feed some seals and birds!
Every now and then I have to feed some seals and birds!
Every now and then I have to feed some seals and birds!
I love to feed those birds!

There's a pigeon guillemot and then there's murres and
    puffins too!
There's a pigeon guillemot and then there's murres and
    puffins too!
There's a pigeon guillemot and then there's murres and
    puffins too!
And sometimes a rhino auklet!

And sometimes when I'm there I have to feed the cougars!
And sometimes when I'm there I have to feed the cougars!
And sometimes when I'm there I have to feed the cougars!
And sometimes I feed the dog.

English of course permeated all.

My role was as a catalyst. I merely stimulated the children with a desire to learn and provided some of the materials to fulfill our objectives. I did show the class a few practical techniques: how to pick up the kittens by the scruff of the neck as their mother and house cats do; how they immediately go limp and dangle till deposited. I showed how to feed and how to burp, how to extricate claws that get entangled in shirts and sweaters. But everything else was taught by the cougars themselves.

Perhaps the cougars taught communication more than anything. As teachers we shove a blank piece of paper in front of a child and tell him to fill it by the end of half an hour, this time a poem or next time a story. We expect him to be an instant writer when most of the time we ourselves cannot be. Without experience a child has little to communicate. Having a live animal in the room is certainly one way to provide experience for communication. If someone wants to say something badly enough, the words will come. The problem is how to help a person *want* to say something badly enough.

Trying to make the reason for writing as practical as possible, I took the class to visit local magazine and newspaper production rooms, to printing presses; I invited several friends who were writers and reporters into the classroom; and we produced newspapers and magazines and novels for distribution to an audience of staff, other classes, parents, and friends. Everyone contributed and it was heart-warming to see the improvement in children who had shown little interest in self-expression before their introduction to animals.

Take eight-year-old Stephen. That isn't his real name but I'll call him that. Stephen was sent to the major work class as a last resort. Nobody else wanted him. He had tuned out the world of parents, peers, and teachers and was a dropout in grade three. He sat at the back of the room in silence and obstinately refused to do anything. I'm not known for my patience and it became the bane of my life to see everybody working except Stephen. Especially as his I.Q. surpassed all of ours! It wasn't any use trying to bludgeon him into activity by putting him outside the classroom door or reporting him to the principal. That had been tried before. Coax him to prepare a project and his eyes asked why. Because you're the student and I'm the teacher? Because everybody else is doing something and you're not? Because you're going to need this when you grow up? It would have been easier if Stephen fought back but he didn't. He just sat and looked at you with those round brown eyes and made you feel disconcerted, embarrassed, unequal. And you questioned your motives.

I tried to enter Stephen's world but I didn't have the key. The other children either ignored him or, with the cruelty of youth to anyone or anything that is different, ridiculed him. They called him Poker Face. His mother, a psychologist and a social worker whom I'll call Sylvia, was divorced. Stephen's father, a university professor and also a psychologist, lived in another country. Stephen sometimes wrote to him.

He rarely spoke and he never smiled. The day the cougars came to school Stephen smiled. It was like the opening of a beautiful flower. It looked like the beginning of a whole new world. He made contact with something outside himself and it was good. He observed like the rest of us. Perhaps he saw more. He wrote:

> With eyes wide open, his ears pricked,
> The cougar cub explores the room.
> At first he does not seem to notice
> That he is not in a cave
> But then he sees the children
> Who just will not behave.
> He starts to walk toward them
> But at once he is picked up
> He's shoved inside a desk
> With no room to crawl about
> Then he sees a crack
> And through it he creeps,
> He gives a jump
> And he is away
> Now to the dark places
> He will always stay.

It was Tammy who left the rest and came to him. She climbed onto his lap and crawled inside his desk. The other children probed and pressed. Stephen, softly, delicately, passed his fingers over the tips of her fur as she disappeared. His face, pale and controlled most of the time, relaxed and softened. Tammy had made contact too.

5

Now, Foster Homes

Several parents came to collect their offspring that first afternoon and of course to see the cougars. It provided a bonus for me because it solved my transportation problem home. One parent even volunteered to drive me to school till David was out of hospital.

The next day a reporter from one of the two major papers appeared at the door to take pictures of the teacher's pampered pets being cuddled by their classmates. Jennifer Smith wrote in her journal,

> I was one of the four people who held a cougar in the pictures that were taken. The cougar I was holding was wild and was screaming. We couldn't figure out why until after the pictures were taken and then we discovered she had gone to the bathroom on my lap. Mrs. Hancock sent me to the washroom to get cleaned up.

A parent had phoned in the suggestion and the paper had grabbed the opportunity to get a cute photo of animals and children to attract attention to page one. I let him take it, but I worried all day long that David might disagree. And he did. I caught a bus to the hospital that night to see him after his operation and tentatively mentioned the picture. He was furious. He wanted nobody to know about the cougars until we were ready to present our own film on the subject.

Free-lance photography is a precarious and competitive business and he didn't want a picture coming out now in the paper when it could be timed to better advantage later.

"But," I pointed out to him in my defense, "that doesn't guarantee that the paper would publish it then when you want it. They'd probably not publish it at all if they thought someone would get any advantage out of it."

"The 'Klahanie' program on CBC-TV wants to do a half-hour feature on the cougars and the 'Seven O'Clock Show' news program wants to do several sequences showing their progress. Neither one is going to be happy now that the newspaper has come out with the story first," he continued angrily.

Though the surgery had been successful, I didn't want the patient upset so soon after the operation, so I tried to do what I could to stop the paper from printing the ill-fated photograph. "No way," pronounced the photo editor on the phone. "It's really a great picture and you have no valid reason for suppressing it."

I should have known better than to try. I was to have more disadvantageous dealings with the press later.

The intricacies of handling the big media being beyond me, I felt more secure in returning to my own little medium in the classroom over which I thought I had control. The children and I were just reporting on the visit of the photographer from the newspaper for our own class magazine when the principal came to the door waving a copy of that morning's paper. Fortunately, his remarks were not heard by the class.

I was in hot water again. I hadn't asked his permission to bring the cougars to school in the first place. He had only permitted them to help me out while my husband was in hospital. I hadn't asked his permission to allow a reporter in the classroom. There were other teachers doing just as good work in town as I was. He didn't want one of his teachers or her class singled out on the front page of a newspaper. The other classes would be envious and it wasn't good for staff morale.

I honestly had no idea of such ramifications. It hadn't even occurred to me that I should have checked with him first. I had been worrying about my husband, not my principal. The following morning he received a phone call from the school board who saw an advantage of their own in publicizing one of their special programs such as the major work class. Some of the most important and politically influential people in the city had children in my class. Not only did the school board approve of a front-page picture such as had been taken, but they wanted their own staff reporter and photographer to do an official story for their own publications. In addition, they asked the principal for permission to have the story told on television.

Meanwhile, down in our basement classroom, the children and I continued to study cougars. I felt the crisis that ensued that afternoon was ill-timed. It was all much ado about nothing, but it resulted in some frantic moments before calm was restored. The children had just filed out of the room for their library period when I noticed an icky yellow patch on the floor outside the door leading to the corridor, a door that had been kept closed and guarded since the arrival of the kittens.

Did a cougar do that? If so, how did it leave the room without being noticed? And if so, where was it now? I stared sternly at the class but in shocked tones they assured me they hadn't done it. I asked the last straggler in line to go back into the classroom and count the cougars now sleeping in the corner of the coat cupboard.

"How many, Carl?" I ventured anxiously to the class extrovert.

"Three, Mrs. Hancock," called out Carl in hollow tones from between the coats and the lunch pails.

"Oh no," I groaned, looking quickly up and down the corridor. "Make sure. Check again."

"Only three, Mrs. Hancock."

After the last two days I was mentally prepared for disaster. Not wanting to incur the ire of the librarian by having the class late and the word getting to the rest of the staff, I told the children to go. Then I shanghaied into the search some straying grade sevens who were standing around in the adjacent washroom during their private study period.

"I've lost a cougar," I told them, trying to appear calm and not dramatic, as if it was something that happened every day. "I'd like you to help me find it. Go quietly around the school in pairs and see where it is. Pick it up by the scruff of the neck and you won't get scratched when you bring it back to me."

Everybody disappeared upstairs.

I ran to the other end of the basement where some workmen were painting. "Have you seen a kitten around here in the last half hour?" I blurted out.

"Yes, ma'am, there were two cats in here a little while ago," one of them replied, putting down his paintbrush.

Oh no. Now there were two cougars missing and loose in the school. Not wishing to go into details about the difference between a cougar kitten and a domestic one to check out their story, I jumped to the worst conclusion. Quickly, I scanned the playground and the nearest trees through the window. They weren't there. I bet they'd been picked up by someone out on the street and were on their way to getting their second pictures in the papers. Being an ostrich at times like these, I didn't dare go upstairs.

The children had no such qualms. Their jobs were not at stake.

I dashed back inside the classroom and made for the coat cupboard. Before I got to the racks to count for myself, the principal appeared at the door, even more formidable than before. He was the last person I wanted to see at this particular moment. He already disapproved of our cougars. He was sure to disapprove in these circumstances of two cougars less. Carl, obviously enthusiastic about his participation in such an important event, appeared behind him.

"What's all this furor about cougars escaping in the school?" the principal exclaimed grimly in more of a statement than a question. "Your class and the grade sevens have been galloping up and down the corridors knocking at every door, screaming their heads off, disturbing the classes. Carl's just barged into my office and interrupted a very important meeting."

I leaned against the coat rack for support and waited for his next words when he caught his breath. They would surely be a suggestion or an instruction that my services were no longer indispensable.

Something furry brushed against my stockings. I looked down and out from the corner of the coat cupboard, stretching and yawning after an hour's solid sleep, wobbled one, two, three, *four* innocent cougar kittens.

The principal was so nonplused, perhaps even magnetized by those four sets of quizzical, inquiring blue eyes looking up at him, that he must have forgotten to serve me notice. He grunted, turned on his heels, and returned to the more normal world upstairs and the other staff members he could understand. I was so relieved that I didn't even tell Carl to count to a thousand by fours.

Jonathan Griffin wrote as his version of the incident:

Carl and I were just about to go to the Library when Mrs. Hancock came in saying, "Count the cougars." She thought she saw puma business outside. Once we had counted the cougars we found one was missing. We checked the classroom, we checked it again but didn't find the missing mountain lion. We checked the corridors and asked people there if they had seen a catamount in the hallway. Three boys said they had seen a panther entering the boys' basement. Outside the boys' basement, workmen said they hadn't seen anything like a cat go through the back doorway. By now Mrs. Hancock had quite a group of students (who were supposed to be in class) following her and confessing willingness to help find the painter. So she sent three people up to the top floor, four to the second floor and three to the bottom floor, with the rest looking over the ground outside the school. Then Carl and I went back to the classroom and we found the missing cougar that wasn't lost after all. Mrs. Hancock called off the red alert and thanked everybody for helping. Finally, I got to Library period, half an hour late.

Jennifer Smith added to her journal, "This is the queerest day I've had all year."

Perhaps Jeffrey Holm said it for the principal:

Mrs. Hancock had a little cougar
Its fur was black and white
And everywhere that Mrs. Hancock went
That cougar was sure to bite.

He followed her to school one day
Which was against the rule,
It made the children laugh and play
To see a cougar at school.

And so the principal turned him out,
But still he lingered near,
And waited patiently about
Till Mrs. Hancock did appear.

"What makes the cougar love Mrs. Hancock so?"
The eager children cry,
"Oh, Mrs. Hancock loves the cougar, you know,"
The principal did reply.

A couple of days later, David unexpectedly appeared at the front door of our house. A rebel by nature and even more of a free and independent spirit than I am, he just got up from bed, signed himself out of hospital, caught a taxi, and with his complete arm from the shoulder to the wrist still in a cast, came home.

"I've had enough of an all-liquid diet, mostly hot milk and cold soup, and they discovered I was exchanging meals with the guy in the next bed," he said as he wolfed down a couple of cinnamon buns with his one good arm.

It appeared he had investigated all of the nooks and crannies in the huge hospital complex, invited himself to coffee with the doctors in the cafeteria, flirted with the nurses, and now with nothing else to keep him occupied, was thoroughly bored with unaccustomed inactivity.

"How's my favorite cougar?" he asked, going to the box to get Tom after he satisfied his appetite with home cooking.

It was definitely noticeable that Tom was different from the other cats. Whereas his sisters had the small, narrow, pointed face and alert eyes of the typical female cougar, Tom's head was large, almost square with fat puffy cheeks. His expression was stupefied most of the time, startled at other times. Oola, Lara, and Tammy, even as kittens, showed the streamlined grace and nimbleness of the adult female cougar. Tom looked more like an overgrown tabby cat. He sought out human, not feline companionship. When Dave came in, his eyes lighted up and his purr rumbled from a vibrant dynamo deep down inside. He seemed to prefer man's company, Dave's anyway.

"Let's split up the cats," David said suddenly. "Tom is obviously going to be the tamest, the one most imprinted to us. He should be the one we take to schools for lectures. He's special. But he won't stay that way if he is always with his sisters, especially that Tammy. We want Tom to relate to us, to people, not other cougars. They'll all stay tamer that way too."

"But how can we do that? Keep three outside and one inside?" I asked, thinking immediately of the practical consequences in our small house with a back yard that already was fully occupied with other members of the family.

"No, we'll keep Tom here and you can give the other three to your kids at school to take home; then every week or so we'll have them back, check on their progress, and see how they get along with each other...."

I stopped him. "You're joking! I've been worried enough just keeping them en masse in the classroom under my supervision. Anything could happen if the kids took them home. Their parents wouldn't allow that anyway."

But I was wrong. Almost all my students volunteered the services of their families as soon as I breathed the merest whisper of wanting foster parents for the cougars. I quelled the forest of hands and laughingly suggested that it might be a good idea if they asked the heads of their households first.

Realizing my head was the one that would end up on the chopping block if anything went wrong, I chose very carefully.

The Barrie family was an obvious choice, having been initiated in cougar care and having survived a weekend in Manning Park.

"David just about burst his buttons to get home to ask us," Betty told me over the phone. "He's got a real crush on his teacher and he loves animals anyway. But we do have an irritable and ancient spaniel called Topsy. And Bob and Joanne are allergic to cat fur. Maybe we could try it for a while."

David's story tells how he proudly carried away Lara.

Once upon a time there was a baby cougar called Lara. She lived with her two sisters and brother, a fur seal, a dog, and Mr. and Mrs. Hancock.
One day Lara and her two sisters were at school but her brother was at home. Mr. and Mrs. Hancock were absent too.
Then Mr. Hancock came home and Tom, who was feeling lonely and would be happy to see anyone, ran to Mr. Hancock and licked him.
That night, Mr. Hancock was talking with his wife. He said "Today Tom was left alone and when I came home he started to lick me. Further-

more, I think we should give each cougar to a separate family."

So they set about asking all their neighbors and friends if they knew of anyone who was capable and willing to take one. They only wanted someone who loved animals to take one. So all the neighbors set about asking if they could have a cougar.

Some thought they were too big and others didn't like the expression on their faces. Some thought they were the cutest things, but they didn't know the first thing about taking care of them. Two days later when I came to feed the murres I asked Mrs. Hancock if I could take a cougar for a month. I knew how to take care of them and I wanted to take one of them. Now the only thing to do was ask my mother if I was allowed to take one. I went home and asked my mother. She said she would ask my father. My father said, "Yes," and I was very excited.

Finally, the big day came when we were to go and get a cougar. Everyone was all excited, especially me. We jumped into the car and rode off to Mr. and Mrs. Hancock's house.

When we arrived we knocked on the door and waited. Presently, we heard footsteps. The footsteps were silenced for a second and then there was a loud thump as Mrs. Hancock jumped over a gate. More footsteps and the door opened.

I was silent for a second. Then I started pouring poor Mrs. Hancock with questions. After I had been silenced, we went into the kitchen. Mrs. Hancock apologized for keeping us waiting, but she had been feeding the animals.

Mr. Hancock then showed us the cougar we were to take. It was Lara. Mr. and Mrs. Hancock and Mom and Dad stood talking while I familiarized myself with Lara.

After a while, Lara was put into her box along with the pablum, concentrated milk, and vitamins. Lara was driven to her new home. When she

arrived the box was opened and a little cougar
nose popped out and a slightly larger dog nose
poked in. Lara climbed out to snoop around a
bit. The first thing she hid behind the stove. The
second "shelter" was behind the chesterfield. The
third was the bird cage (we had no worries about
the bird because Lara didn't like raw meat).

Many happy days followed. My brother Bob
liked to hear Lara playing "Kitten on the Keys"
when she was in a musical mood. One of her
favourite activities was to race through the house
at top speed in her evening playtime. She would
come around corners so fast that when she turned
a corner she would not have enough traction and
would smash into tables and chairs, banging her
head with a loud crack. We would expect her to
have at least a fractured skull. However, she
would simply get up and shake her head and
run some more.

Mom was her favourite person when she was
tired. With a pitiful little cry she would pull her
hand into position, grab her thumb with her
mouth, and suck until she was asleep.

Lara slept in the bathroom in a little box. When
she decided to get up she would try to open the
door by smashing against it, then she would pull
all the washcloths and towels onto the floor.

We all loved Lara very much and we knew that
she loved us. She taught us a great deal about
animal conservation.

There was no dearth of parents who wanted cougars
for their children, but I anxiously waited for Stephen
to ask. Maybe this would be the key. With a little
trepidation I asked if he wouldn't mind walking home
with me and perhaps helping me feed Sam when we
got there. He nodded casually, more noncommittal
than enthusiastic.

I curbed my natural tendency to carry on a nervous
animated conversation, especially in tense situations,
and we set off down the road together. He didn't speak

but then in a way he did. He seemed to know all the dogs and cats on the block. They came to him, waddling, running, leaping, scampering, and scurrying. They bowled him over and he fell down with them in a heap and a laugh. He opened gates of what must have been perfect strangers' houses and while I looked the other way in embarrassment, he walked up the path and patted a dignified Siamese sunning himself on the porch or pressed his nose against the face of a furry Persian sleeping on the window ledge.

> "It was long ago," they say,
> For long ago it was,
> When the hound had no bay
> And the bee no buzz.
>
> Then a strange beast was made
> Who could make many noises.
> All the animals came to him
> And begged him for voices.
>
> He gave the hound his bay
> And the horse his neigh.
> Without him, we would not be
> Who we are today.
>   Stephen Miller

It was a long walk home. I had never seen Stephen so happy, so animated, and with such pink cheeks. He didn't speak and neither did I. "Like to look after a cougar?" I broached nonchalantly as I bent down to pick up the fish heads that Sam was slinging across the back lawn.

Stephen threw the seal another fish and said, "Okay." No emotion, no excitement, just a calm acceptance.

"I'd like you to have Oola, Stephen; she's the nicest female, I think. But will you wait till next week as a friend of mine wants to borrow her to take some pictures? In the meantime you'd better check with your mother." It was my longest conversation since school had got out.

Tony Carter offered room and board to Oola while

Stephen was adjusting his family to the idea of giving a cougar a home. Tony had a sense of humor that got along well with cougars, as we found out when he helped us take photographs in Stanley Park. We had first met Tony a couple of years before at the Indian fishing village of Klemtu where he was packing fish for the local cannery. Almost the first words he'd said after we'd been introduced were "You just call on me if I can do anything to help." Often that summer he'd offered warm socks, dry bunks, and pots of hot coffee to a pair of drenched rubber-boating eagle watchers.

There was only one person we could dare ask to take Tammy home and that was Hilary Stewart. Artist, amateur naturalist, herpetologist, archeologist, she was the kind of friend who was always there when you needed her. I remember well the first day I met Hilary. It was the same day our second landlady in two months gave Sam a month's notice. From attic to basement, "No children and no pets" had been the recurring cry and now we were to move again. Our spirits were pretty low. Dave's university exams were the following week and any more distractions might jeopardize them. Hilary came around to play with Sam after being introduced to us by Anne, her sister-in-law, who taught next door to me at school. Seeing Hilary enjoy a hilarious romp on the floor with the seal soon had us all laughing and we knew Sam was definitely worth the trouble of once again looking for another place to stay.

If anyone could overcome a cougar kitten's fear and bad temper by love and patient understanding, it would be Hilary. Certainly Tammy, or Tigress as we sometimes called her, was difficult. As the runt of four in a litter, she might not have survived in the wild. In captivity, she was the only one who had suffered illness. One night, suddenly and unpredictably, she went into an epilepsylike seizure for no apparent reason and we felt sure she would die. On the vet's suggestion we injected her with a dextrose and water solution for several days, but her condition seemed to worsen. I prayed it wasn't infectious because we had spared no time or expense to raise as healthy a litter of cougars as possible. We gave her a last, seemingly useless injection, put her in a box by herself on the kitchen table, then left her for dead. In the morning we were astounded and elated to find the box open and empty with Tammy, as lively as her sisters, scampering on the floor. We welcomed her back into life, although both her sickness and her recovery remained inexplicable.

A friend of mine once had a similar experience with Tina, a female cougar about the same age as Tammy. In each case the symptoms and diagnosis were the same. He reported: "Tina stopped eating, became feverish, had convulsions about eighteen hours later, and seemed to suffer from a bad headache. She tried to pull the hair off the top of her head with her front paws and back feet. I gave her a tetracycline dose which completely knocked her out. Though her heart was still going, I gave her up for dead. I put her in a box and took my wife for a car ride for a couple of hours. When we got back there was Tina at the door purring and ready to eat."

Tammy's normal behavior was as unpredictable as her illnesses. We couldn't get close to her, as we could to the other three kittens. She was always fearful and on the defensive. One particular evening she stretched out along the back of the chesterfield, eyes closed, purring peacefully. A guest, a rotund gentleman with a bald head and, fortunately, a patient and tolerant disposition, nonchalantly leaned back against the covers just a few inches away from the purring pussy cat. Suddenly, Tammy woke abruptly and lunged with all four paws onto the man's shiny, unprotected pate. Sharp, razorlike unsheathed claws clasped down hard on his skin. "Owww!" His hand shot to his scalp at the same instant mine pulled away the offending kitten. We stared in disbelief as Tammy, no trace of her vindictiveness of the minute before, crouched calmly on the floor at our feet. Nevertheless, our guest wore a turban of towels for the rest of his visit.

It was with considerable misgivings that we delivered

Tammy to Hilary's NO PET penthouse apartment in Point Grey with full cloak-and-dagger subterfuge—smuggled under a coat and with surreptitious glances around for the landlord. I hoped that Hilary's shelves of pottery and carvings, her original paintings, her own amphibian and reptile pets would survive the experiment and that Hilary would live to tell the tale. Ever optimistic, she thought she could manage and even have fun in the process.

When David took Tom with him over to Vancouver Island for one of his fortnightly eagle-censusing flights I was alone. For the first time in an unbelievably busy seven weeks I was in the kitchen with only Haida for company. I even thought of letting Sam in. Poor Sam had been totally ignored. He had his pool and the children used to come at lunchtime from the adjacent school, but since the arrival of the cougars he had definitely taken a back seat. Instead I swept up the sawdust from the sandbox on the porch and cleared the newspapers that lined the floor—a necessary precaution during the house-training process. I realized I'd almost forgotten what the pattern on the linoleum looked like.

A couple of nights later Hilary phoned. "Hi!" I greeted her dubiously. Her voice sounded bright and cheerful enough. She often told her friends, "Just brush by the Hancocks and you'll bump into adventure." Well, now she was right in the middle of one.

"This is Tammy's mother calling. I took Tammy to Kitsilano beach yesterday. She had a wonderful time and so did all the people who came to watch. She is very spirited and active. She loves running and leaping and jumping in and out of the water, not like a house cat at all. But with all the people there trying to play with her she always comes running back to me with that peculiar chirp of hers—the "eep, eep, eep"—it's like a mixture of pleasure and recognition of something familiar, a greeting."

So far so good. "But what about inside the house?"

"She has the full run of the apartment except for the kitchen, which is on a swing door. I didn't think she would have the strength to push against it but I was wrong. This morning I was awakened by a crash in the kitchen. I opened the swing door and ran into the most frightening and heartbreaking sight you ever saw. Tammy had swung open the door and trapped herself in the tiny kitchen. She sat on the counter amid the shambles. She'd bowled over the garbage, knocked down all the potted plants, opened the cupboard, and let all the dishes out, smashed the saucepans off the stove, tipped over the sugar bowl, and gone to the bathroom in the sink—it must have been the cold that did it. What a mess! There was sugar and soil and soup and crap all mixed together and everything footprinted over everything else. My instant breakfast!"

At this point I gurgled something between apology and commiseration but Hilary prattled on:

"I'm not complaining though. She really is a dear and when I'd cleared a place to find some breakfast I got dressed, hid her under my coat again for the journey downstairs, got in the car, and drove to work."

Hilary was then the art director for a television station in Burnaby, half an hour's drive from Point Grey.

"Have you ever tried to drive with a two-month-old cougar on your head and a great paw draped across your face when you're trying to see the traffic? It's an absolute nightmare. Tammy was wandering in and out of the gas pedal and through the steering wheel. She wouldn't stay in her box at the back. I realized I couldn't drive home like that. So Henry, my carpenter, made her a box with a wire mesh in front, but all the way home she cried and screamed and clawed and pawed at it. Then I got a glimpse of blood so I panicked and let her out. She'd only nipped a paw but she was out, and we had another nightmare journey. Next day I put a tall vertical box in the car and put her in the bottom of it. She can only just climb up onto the dining chairs, so I didn't think she'd get up the slippery smooth sides of the box. I was wrong again. She popped her head out the top and we endured a third nightmare trip. But today

I put a hot-water bottle on the passenger seat beside me and got her settled on it first, and she slept all the way. I realized she wanted a cuddly warm place because she kept coming to my lap, but there's just not enough room between the steering wheel and me for an eight-pound cougar. It should be okay now. At work Henry has arranged a real log cabin for her with chicken mesh doors, one of the studio props, and Tammy loves it."

Next I heard from Tony about Oola, or as he called her, Squeak, after the distinctive birdlike chirp that is the most common vocalization of cougar kittens.

"Well, I've just had a week with Squeak. She's fine and has the run of the house and gets on well with all the dogs. She rides on my clutch in the car and likes to watch me as I shave. She did try jumping into hot soapy water, but she soon came out of that. With all four paws flying in different directions, she finished upside down in the wastepaper basket. By the way, she doesn't want the bottle any more. I have her on solid fish."

"That's great, Tony, that's the first cougar to be weaned. And we should adapt them to fish and then chicken to give them the whole animal rather than raw beef, which is too expensive anyway. Then it's easy because Sam and the sea birds and the cougars can all eat the same."

Tony continued. "Yes, she has a can of sockeye salmon in the morning and another at night. As a variation I give her moose."

I exploded into the phone. "Tony! You must be kidding. That's okay for you, you're a hunter and fisherman, but we'll never be able to afford a moose and salmon diet. You'll spoil her."

Oola was obviously the most advanced female, but I was glad the other cougars were still on the bottle. As long as they were healthy and continuing to put on weight, nursing on a bottle would keep them dependent and tamer for longer.

As Betty Barrie was my image of the perfect mother and nurse, I was less apprehensive when she phoned.

"Oh, Lyn, Lara is the sweetest thing. As soon as she spies the bottle she leaps four or five feet in the air to grab it, then she lies on her back in my arms and sucks noisily and I swear she has a smile on her face. She burps like a baby too, but more satisfyingly, wet and milky and peaceful.

"You know from the first day she has loved us all. She smiles and purrs on our approach and if she can't find us, she thumps about the house—it's incredible how much noise those big padded feet make—and whistles piteously. All she needs for reassurance is an answering whistle and then she adds a great rumbling purr to her smile. And she comes when you call her."

I gave a sigh of relief at such good news, and Betty continued: "Her theater is the living room and she delights in putting on a performance. She sits placidly on the back of the chesterfield, smiling and purring, then with no change of expression, she leaps gracefully right across the living room in mid-air, cracks through the evening paper into Ramsay's face as if to say, 'Pet me, please.'

"She doesn't always smile though. She's very much afraid of strangers, especially very young children, and runs to her cave behind the stove. If they come near, she spits and hisses.

"She slept on David's bed for the first few nights, that is till she went to the bathroom on the covers. You know it went right through to the mattress."

I steeled myself for the usual apology. But I didn't need to make it.

"So now at night we lock her in the bathroom. As I'm the first to get up in the morning her welcome to me is the most obstreperous. She jumps and pours forth that motorboat purr, clutches and hugs me with those massive paws till she pushes me on the toilet. She then grabs my left arm till she maneuvers my thumb into her mouth and sucks it till it starts to dwindle. That's the ultimate of cougar cub affection, purring, smiling, and sucking my thumb. And despite my old flannelette nightgown and my hair still in curlers, I feel a queen sitting there on the toilet. That's love. Perhaps we won't be friends when you want her back."

Well, that sounded encouraging. Even David phoned from the Island. A further interruption to his university career was our acquisition of six acres of breezy flood-land on the Saanich Peninsula beside beautiful Island View Beach about ten miles from downtown Victoria. For David and later for me, the farmland of the Saanich Peninsula spelled Paradise. I remember his enthusiastic comment on our first date as the ferry wound through the maze of Gulf Islands on its way to Vancouver Island:

"See the sun shining to the west. Next stop is God's country."

As we still lived in Vancouver he had persuaded his folks, the most accommodating parents in the world, to move out of their house and live in the rambling old beach cottage at Island View Beach till we could move ourselves and our animals there at the end of the university year. He wanted them to clean up the property and run the coffee shop that came with the place. I hated the thought of leaving Van-couver and the friends I'd made from my class. But David insisted I teach for only one more year. He said he needed me to work on his projects and look after the animals full time. "You can be Slushy Number One and we'll hire Slushy Number Two," he said with the laugh that usually got me to do anything.

The cougars in the city were quickly outgrowing their kitchens, their bathrooms, and their living rooms, so David was planning to house them in the country in an extensive landscaped enclosure behind our house at the beach. It was to be over one hundred feet long, but I hated the thought of our tame, personable, house-raised cougars kept in an impersonal pen like zoo animals. How I wished to own an island not too far from the advantages of civilization but far enough for us to be able to roam freely with four cougars as companions, to watch them explore the world of the wilderness and not the world of four square walls. Perhaps David could study a family of cougars after his eagle thesis. Dreams. His voice brought me back to reality.

"This is going to be no ugly zoo cage, Lyn. A friend of mine with a helicopter is flying about a hundred logs from the beach to the back of the property. The pen'll be a real beauty and fit in perfectly with the rest of the landscape. I've got Mother out every day raking sawdust and gravel flat to raise the surface level of the place. It used to flood here."

"How's Tom?" I interjected.

"He's simply great, a real hit with everyone. He goes everywhere with me, even to the neighbors. He's such a calm cat, he's practically stupid. I've been taking him around to schools, so you'll be pleased to know he's continuing his education."

David's return to Vancouver coincided with National Cougar Week. Local car salesmen were mounting a big advertising campaign to sell the new Lincoln-Mercury Cougar XR$_7$. Great minds, I guess, do think alike because at the same time, but without each other's knowledge, the Ford Motor Company in the States planned to use a live cougar to advertise their new car for 1967 at the same time David planned to pay some of our cougars' food bills by offering the "untamed elegance" of our own cougars for the local promotion.

His negotiations fell flat when the car salesmen were only prepared to pay twenty-five dollars for a day of cougar appearances in their showrooms. As this offer was scoffed at by various local public relations men, David didn't go to the bother of having the cougars earn part of their keep. Later, but not because we wanted it, two of our cats did become intimately connected with the Mercury campaign in the States. Now, ten years later, when the word "cougar" means "car" not "cat" to many city people, I often wonder how much money that company has put out for advertising since the time they said they could afford only twenty-five dollars.

Tony's wife began to find cleaning up after a cougar too time-consuming, so Oola came back and went to the Millers. I hoped that in taking on the responsibility of raising a cougar kitten, Stephen would become more responsible for his own learning. Raised by older parents and sisters in a free, unstructured environment where he was expected to discipline himself, he faced a totally different world when he went to school and met children who came from families more devoted to the "white Anglo-Saxon Protestant" work ethic. It left him apart and alone.

I Like to be Alone

I would like to be the first star out
But not a star in a shining crowd.
Or a single drop of dew
But not a raindrop in a cloud.

For if I was but one in a crowd
And I left, none would care.
But if I was the only person
And I left, there would be no one there.

I would like to be a single splinter of wood
But not part of a log.
Or a single tuft of grey cloud
But not a fragment of fog.

I would like to be a grain of sand
Blown by the wind from the reach of the sea
But not in a crowd where no one saw me.

Stephen Miller

To impose discipline on Stephen was to run into a stone wall. Perhaps by imposing discipline on Oola he would learn it himself. Trouble would come when he didn't.

Split Personality

If I were you and you were I
We would not be two.
I would not be just I

And you not just you.
We would have many troubles
   from the start
For none would be able to tell us apart.
                 Stephen Miller

I continued to walk home with Stephen and sometimes he talked, in short phrases that were as enigmatic as his poetry. But he smiled more often. I was learning to let him be in the classroom, to let him work if he wanted and at his own pace. Slowly, sometimes exasperatingly slowly, when he withdrew into a world I dared not follow, he continued to write poetry. He wrote when he didn't do anything else. And he expressed himself in a way far beyond his years.

Beady-eyed
Evil-beaked
With white down feather.
Hunchbacked
Wings spread
Lying flat together.
Black-clawed.
Weak-winged
With white down feather,
The falcon chicks here lie comfortable
Safe from all the weather.

Most eight-year-olds still echo the jingles of their nursery rhyme days and view their subject from the outside. Stephen not only wrote to a rhythm of his own but he was able to feel from the inside.

Predation

The cold blood is running
It is running in my vein
And I want to kill
And to kill again and again.
I feel a great urge to run
And to catch my running prey.

The cold blood is running
Running in me today.

And

Migration

Someone is calling
Whom I do not know
But from where the waterfall is falling
Out across the snow
I hear a wild voice
An old voice
And I know that I must go.

Stephen read avidly, especially from history and
the classics. Echoes from his solitary life style were
heard in his poetry.

The sea ghosts are coming
They will rip my corpse apart.
Their wings' soft thrumming
Makes the blood throb in my heart.
And now I hear their startling cry
And to the world I say good-bye.
But no, I hear a voice outside
"To the poor Apane I still abide."
And then I knew it was Orbon
Defying the ghosts outside my door
And all at once I feel safe again
Safe from the worlds of ghosts and men.

I waited for the time Stephen would feel safe in
the world of the classroom, when he would stop running, when he would trust people as well as animals.

It was once written that no-one but people who run travel
    this way,
But no-one knows that on this day.
They knew it. They knew of wolves running behind,
Running to catch the human dinner they had in mind.
And lions and leopards chasing their human prey.

But we have forgotten it
As men who live in the future will forget things that
  happened on this day.

Sometimes Stephen was disconcertingly direct. While
the rest of us saw love in the eyes of a cuddly, still
blue-eyed cougar kitten, Stephen saw something else.
"Don't look into Oola's eyes; they're horrible." Oola
never did get close to any of us. She was never
frightened like Tammy nor did she throw temper tan-
trums. She remained aloof, independent, in control.
Like Stephen. And Stephen saw it first.

6

Sharing Cougar Experiences

Two or three times a month the cougars' foster families came around to the house for an evening of friendly discussion. It was a tight squeeze in our tiny bungalow, mothers and fathers and children and Tom and Oola and Lara and Tammy, not to mention Haida. At the first meeting held in the latter part of March the cougars had only been separated a couple of weeks, yet so closely did they identify with the various foster families that they kept their distance from us and each other.

For a few minutes they sniffed each other very carefully. Tom went "prrt?" in a questioning tone and lifted a paw. Tammy hissed. Oola raised a paw and batted Tom gently. Lara did the same. Soon they were all down in a bunch scuffling and flinging themselves into a boisterous rough-and-tumble at full force. Then Haida frolicked on the rug with them. We were squashed to the sidelines and felt very neglected. Except David and me. Dear, distinctive Tom still paused in his play to rub against our legs with a purr as he passed.

To add to the confusion, David allowed Sam into the living room to see how the cougars would react to such a different species, one they would never encounter at close range in the wild. Poor Sam felt sorely neglected too. Once used to the run of the house and to being the center of attention everywhere he went, he had not once been past the porch since the arrival of the four cougars. To make matters worse it was spring and approaching the time on the Pribilof Islands when male fur seals round up their harems. The year before he had herded our tabby cat around the yard. This year Haida was his victim. The dog would enjoy his playful antics for half an hour and then, bored with being guarded in a corner, try to plunge through the doorway and into her box, now free of the four squirming cougar kittens. Invariably, I had to act the part of the bigger bull sea lion and with an intimidating rolled-up newspaper and a loud voice help Haida to escape.

Sam would never charm the cougars. The sight of his long, gray, unfamiliar shape in the doorway struck terror into each of the cats, including Tom. They hissed and snarled like traditionally posed, cornered adults. They continued growling even when Sam flippered quickly outside. Tammy lost all reason and even when she fell asleep with ears laid low, she kept up a stream of growling and hissing till we gave her a tranquilizer to settle her down.

While our charges slept by their old box in the kitchen, we talked about their reactions to the animal members of their respective households.

"Oola and our cat have worked out a relationship, distantly friendly," Sylvia Miller began. "When the cougar first saw the cat she walked all around him and studied him curiously. The cat hissed but that didn't stop Oola, who was interested in playing. Eventually the cat relaxed and just watched. Oola came within two feet and lay down beside him. It looked as if they were accepting each other. But when Oola started to wash herself the cat seemed suddenly frightened. He growled and backed up. His whole perception of the cougar changed as if there were an enemy in the house. They now eat close together without caution but the cat hisses to make sure Oola stays a few inches away. With the dog it's a different matter. He wants to play with Oola but she growls, chews on his tail, and hisses if he as much as turns his head to her."

"Lara sure wants to play with our dog, Topsy," Betty Barrie said. "She just loves to stalk and leap, then land smack on Topsy's back when the dog's least suspecting it. Poor Topsy. She's an old maid and likes everything in its place. I think she only likes Lara when the cougar's asleep."

Later I was to meet a couple from Idaho, Howard and Dorothy Smith, who had a remarkably gentle male cougar that not only hunted with a dog but helped to raise its pups. The Smiths showed me films of a litter of pups all trying at the same time to get inside the cougar's mouth. The dogs resembled pet raccoons in the way those bandits are always trying to prise open the mouths of humans. The pups licked the cougar so much that my friends had to build a ladder up to a barn so the cat could escape from such canine affection.

Cougars in captivity have often been raised by dogs. As Bill Robb from the Olympic Game Farm puts it, "We like to keep our cougars with other animals so they don't use their excess energy on us. If we don't have other cougars we find a dog to act as mother to them. This mother-son relationship continues between the dog and the cougar even when both are fully grown. And with the dog taking the play out of the cougar, there's less chance of having the cat leaping on us when he gets big enough to hurt us."

Even Cougar Brown, a nonagenarian bounty hunter from Vancouver Island who prides himself on the large numbers of cougars he's killed, used to have his hunting dogs raise cougar kittens prior to selling them to zoos after the mother was shot.

It is often assumed that the enmity seen between cats and dogs is hereditary: that they have an inborn tendency to be aggressive toward each other. But such tendencies may be overlain quickly by the power of imprinting to the mother figure soon after birth and the power of environmental learning made possible by close contact during the growing period. Perhaps the reason for such hostility is not instinctual at all but simply that the two animals get their signals crossed.

When a dog wags a tail and lifts a forepaw it means he's friendly. When a cat does it means just the opposite.

Haida's role, now shared with the different families, was more that of a playmate than a mother. The kittens were now nine weeks old and a little over ten pounds in weight. Soon they would outstrip the dog in size. And then only time would tell if they remained as friendly to her then as they were now.

Tammy, in living alone with Hilary, did not come into contact with pet cats or dogs. She was more acquainted with toads.

"I'm keeping some pollywogs in a big round bowl by my telephone," Hilary interjected. "Tammy jumped onto the cabinet and put her paws on the rim of the bowl. She was bending down when I immediately shouted, 'No!' That's one word she had to learn very fast, so she jumped down again and ran away. Then I thought, Wow! That'd make a tremendous picture, so I tried to entice her back. But of course with that 'no' ringing in her ears she wouldn't do it. It took a few days before she jumped back to the bowl. Then I found that it wasn't the pollywogs she was after but the water."

"How are you managing with discipline?" I asked apprehensively, wondering how much damage was being done to the well-furnished rooms that now housed three of my cougar kittens.

"Well, we'll have to buy new drapes and a chesterfield suite when Lara leaves," said Ramsay Barrie, laughing. "Not to mention a couple of bathrobes, innumerable towels, and toilet paper. She just loves toilet paper, she pulls it from the roller by the yard. If you see her doing it and you yell, 'no,' she'll stop. The trouble is how to keep a straight face while you're yelling."

"Oola is very dignified," countered Sylvia. "She's never been rough or destructive."

"What about the jade plant?" interrupted Stephen from the doorway.

"Well, a bit of that is missing, but that's all," admitted his mother.

"I read somewhere that a mother cougar bites her offspring in the back of the neck when it gets unruly," I said with a laugh. "I don't know if you're willing to go that far, but you can train cats to sheathe their claws by squeezing their paws till they hurt, just enough till they withdraw the whole claw in."

"That's what I do with Tammy," added Hilary. "I give the paw a real good squeeze so she winces. It only took five or six squeezes and she soon learned to put her paw out but her claws in. Of course, she also responds to the word 'no.' She hasn't done much damage yet to the apartment, but you'd think she'd damage herself the way she bangs against the shelves and chairs like a rubber ball."

The others nodded knowingly as Hilary continued: "The funniest thing happened the other day. Tammy has the free run of the dining and living rooms, which are separated by a sliding door. They are too heavy to keep opening and closing all the time so I keep them ajar, just enough so I can squeeze and Tammy can run through. On this particular day Tammy started to make her usual mad dash through the rooms, but this time she picked up a stick about eighteen inches long that I had been using to wedge the kitchen door shut after that first frightful night when she locked herself in. I could see what was coming but she was so fast I couldn't stop her. She went flying through the air, hit the partially opened doors, did a double somersault right through the opening and hit the floor on the far side of the living room. It's fantastic the knocks she takes without any apparent damage to herself."

"What do you do with her at work if she is that hyperactive?" I asked in astonishment after our laughter subsided.

"Well, the studio wanted the log cabin back so I have to keep her in my office," Hilary answered unconcernedly. "Most of the time she sleeps on the shelves above my drawing table or on the window ledge where she watches the people come and go. She pees on newspapers in the corner and romps with me on the lawn outside the studio at lunchtime."

"But what about your art supplies?" I exclaimed in wonderment. "Even quiet old Tom has torn out the stuffing from my Egyptian pouf."

"Well," admitted Hilary hesitantly, "she likes watching my pencil move and tries to catch it just when I'm trying to do my most careful work. But the only real damage she did was to do an ink walk over some grand and glorious designs I'd completed for an oil company in Calgary. There wasn't time to do the drawings again so I scribbled, 'These are cougar tracks, sorry about that,' and luckily the executive thought it a great joke. He probably didn't believe me!"

All the foster parents commented on the kittens' attraction to moving objects like pens and pencils, cars, people walking on the street, a ball of wool unraveling on the floor. In later years other cougar owners told me how their pets pounced upon objects that were extended parts of people, like long straggly hair, floppy hats, or baggy clothing. Insufficient evidence has been collected to determine which of a cougar's senses is the best developed. Although no one has yet made such a study, the only references available both then and now emphasize the importance of smell as the major factor in helping a cougar locate its prey. We cougar parents had only limited experience, but to us it seemed that the sense of sight was the best developed. The three females especially seemed to use their eyes a lot; to catch movement before sound and smell.

Everyone agreed that the cougars liked sitting in high places, a shelf, a dining-room table, a window ledge, while they followed movement below them. However, there are few, if any, observations to support the theory that cougars in the wild lie in wait on the limb of a tree ready to pounce on some unsuspecting prey that might chance along underneath. A cougar stalks its prey, covertly if possible, to within two or three jumps, then leaps onto the neck and shoulder of its victim. If cover is scarce it may have to make a short dash before it leaps. And if the prey escapes it rarely follows but repeats the stalk on a different animal. The cougar kills most effectively when it holds down the head of its prey with a fore-paw and bites down through the base of the neck.

Cats in general have a better developed collarbone than most other carnivores such as dogs and wolves. We all commented on the fast development of our kittens' forelimbs which were already strong and powerful, enabling them to catch and grasp even large, heavy objects.

Stalking in response to a moving object was something that kittens did often, especially Tammy. "When she catches sight of something like a glove on the end of a string," said Hilary, "she hides behind a table leg or a chair, then stalks it slowly, her belly low to the ground. Suddenly she springs on top of it and grabs it with her front paws. Lately, she's been hiding behind a door literally waiting for me to come in. I forget she's there and walk through the doorway. Kapow! She pounces on my ankles and on this prey kind of pounce she forgets to keep her claws in, though she's pretty good at other times."

"I got a phone call from a hunter today that was interesting," I volunteered. "He said he'd been sitting in the bush, leaning against a tree and dozing. When he opened his eyes there was a cougar lying crouched a few yards away, watching him. He guessed the cougar had been staring at him for fifteen minutes. Cougars, of course, are very curious and that may be why the animal stayed around, but as soon as the hunter made eye contact it bounded away. It seems that a cougar doesn't fear man unless it knows it's observed.

"Eye contact seems to be important too, as well as movement, to stimulate a cougar to pounce on its prey," I added. "The kids at school were playing a game of I Spy with the cougars. One of the kittens would be sitting on the center table looking down at someone working. It kept watching as long as the child wasn't watching it. But as soon as the kid looked up and caught the cougar's eye the cougar pounced."

Years later Gary Bogue and Mark Ferrari, two researchers from the Alexander Lindsey Junior Museum in Walnut Creek, California, noticed similar behavior in cougars they raised. "This is a case where looks can kill," said Gary. "I started things out by staring at a sleeping kitten. They seem to sense your eyes. One eye quickly opens, it makes hard contact with yours, then suddenly the cat is up, crouched and ready for the game. It looks straight into your eyes. Only you really don't want to play, so you break contact and glance away. The cat simply walks around to the side you are facing and you can actually feel those eyes trying to pull yours down to meet them.

"One time I had trouble trying to introduce a young female cougar to a male. Up till then he had at least given me some grudging respect, but when I brought in the female cat he seemed furious with me. Instead of instantly charging me he tried to make eye contact. But man, oh man, let me tell you this wasn't any little old cub game. He tried everything short of running up and grabbing my face to get me to look him in the eye. I looked up at the sky . . . over at the house . . . at a tree . . . the grass . . . bushes . . . anything. The cat's whole body was in a tense, ready-to-attack position. Every move I made, his head slowly swiveled and followed. I finally even moved carefully within the restrictions of his chain, approaching as close as ten feet, close enough so I couldn't have gotten away. But even with his intense dislike at that moment he respected my not making eye contact with him. Incredible! Finally I withdrew beyond the end of the chain and made eye contact with him. Instantly he visibly tensed all over, his hind feet quickly moving under his body in readiness, the black tip of his tail flicking back and forth. His glance sent hot and cold flashes down my back. It was a moment of utter fear for me. I'd never felt a thing like that in my life and I never want to feel it again. I couldn't help myself.

I broke eye contact. He didn't charge. He knew I was far beyond the limits of his chain. But to the last day we had him, I couldn't trust myself within his range.

"But I want to make it clear that this eye control ability only applies to people who have already worked out a special cat/human relationship," Gary went on. "The cougar has to consider you as 'people' or his parent, partner, sibling, whatever before he'll respect you enough to allow you the privilege of ignoring his call to attack by your not making eye contact with him. Don't ever try controlling a cat with your eyes if you don't have this relationship. Hard eye contact on a strange cat may provoke instant attack, one that can't be stopped by glancing away. Don't look them square in the eye. It may be taken as a direct challenge."

During that first evening of discussion everyone agreed that all four cougars disliked glasses. Perhaps this was because eyes behind glasses are made to appear larger, different. Perhaps the animals are confused by seeing four eyes or their own reflections.

"My boss wears glasses," said Hilary. "Tammy doesn't like men at all, especially ones that wear glasses. When the boss came in to my office one day Tammy lashed out at him with her paw and gave him a scratch down the side of the face. Well, he went home and showed his five-year-old kid. Wow! The boy was most impressed. His dad had been mauled by a cougar! Father couldn't lose face in front of a kid, so when the scratch healed over he came back again for another 'mauling.'"

"Lara's like that too," Betty told us. "But I don't know whether her dislike is caused by the glasses themselves or the situation in which she first encountered glasses. One day I made vegetable soup and hot biscuits for lunch. Our own three children as well as some friends were in the kitchen trying to cram as much food as possible before going back to school. Mike, who wore glasses, got up from the table for a moment and Lara, seeing her chance, jumped up and thrust an inquiring paw into his soup. From then on she associated her burned paw with a six-foot, four-eyed monster. She never did like him or anybody else that wore glasses."

"How are the cougars getting on with other people?" David asked with an offhandedness that belied the anxiety that both of us felt regarding the continued tractability of the cougars.

"I've had to let some of my neighbors into the secret," admitted Hilary with a smile. "They were asking about the clump, clump, clump they could hear above their heads as Tammy zooms around the living room, springs up on the chesterfield, tears around the tadpole bowl, or jumps up to catch a fly on the wall. Then once as I was putting my groceries into the car I had to get a couple of them to help me entice Tammy back after she scuttled under the other cars in the parking lot."

"What about Merle? Does she know?" I interrupted.

"The girl next door? She's met Tammy but she wouldn't tell the landlord. I was about to knock on her door the other day when I heard that little whistle a cougar makes when it's lost. Ahah! I thought, Tammy must have got out when I came out of my apartment. I dashed down into the lower stairwell and found her wandering around looking up at each door but not knowing which one was hers. Making the same cougar sounds as she was doing, I scooped her up and brought her back into the apartment. This time I made sure Tammy didn't slip out as I shut the door, and then went over to visit Merle. But the dear sweet old lady from the back apartment was there on the landing. 'I could have sworn I heard a bird. Did you hear it?' she asked. 'A bird, Mrs. Jones?' I echoed innocently. 'Yes, it was a whistling kind of sound made by a bird.' she went on. 'I assure you there isn't a bird in the hall.' I said emphatically as I sidled into Merle's apartment. She wouldn't have believed me anyway if I told her the bird was a cougar!"

Two years after Hilary recounted those experiences

something similar happened to me, only this time Mrs. Jones stayed in her apartment and didn't come out to investigate. I was keeping three cougars for a week in Hilary's bathroom, probably the only bathroom in Vancouver at the time where you could sit on the toilet and pet a cougar. Not that these cougars were the cuddly type! They were wild terrors and far too old at three months to be tamed by imprinting. A cougar hunter had shot the mother and phoned to say that if I didn't want to buy them for seventy-five dollars apiece he would "bump them on the head." He assured me they were tame enough to be carried in his shirt. He must have been wearing a bullet-proof vest. The night they arrived, I tried to make the house cougar-proof, which meant barricading all the corners to eliminate all possible places of retreat. If I hadn't done so they would have continued to wedge themselves between the gas stove and the hot-water heater and obstinately died there. I was sure I had lost them one morning and I just couldn't believe it when I finally found them squashed in a narrow crack behind the refrigerator. Cougars do have long, lithe, and pliant bodies, but before that incident I had not believed the biologist who reported that an adult female cougar with a body diameter of nearly fourteen inches passed through an opening into a small cave measuring only six inches across.

While I had the three cougars in Hilary's bathroom they huddled behind the toilet and wouldn't budge till the room was empty. Then, snarling and spitting, they would emerge from their retreat to go on a rampage. I had to strip the room of its breakables and hold the door shut by a rope tied to a drawer outside the bathroom.

When the day came to leave, I packed all three into a tall wicker laundry basket in order to carry them to the car. When I turned around to put the lid on I found the basket empty. They had knocked it over, tumbled out, and run helter-skelter out of the apartment. Inadvertently I had left the door open! Contrary to their usual custom, which was to stay together with such ferocity that it was impossible to prize them apart, they had separated and disappeared. But where had they gone? Up the stairs? Down? To the back landing on the same floor, where Mrs. Jones lived? Oh no, not down the three flights and out the front door? I hurtled down the stairs in panic to stop one just as it was about to make a flying leap through the well-polished glass. Oblivious to scratched hands and arms, I grabbed the clawing, snarling cat and tried to bundle it under my sweater as I carried it upstairs. All the while I kept thinking of a dozen other doors opening in this no-pet apartment building before I got to Hilary's door on the top floor. Later I thought of the Spartan warrior enduring pain in silence while a fox tore out his guts. As soon as the first cat was safely back in the basket with an encyclopedia on the lid to ensure that it stayed in place, I raced into the corridor and down the stairs for the others. I scooped up one on the stairwell below and found the third one prowling a few feet from Mrs. Jones's door. It wasn't till all three were securely inside the wicker basket that any of the residents opened their doors to inquire about the commotion. And it wasn't till then that I suddenly felt any pain from my scratches.

However, I had to laugh because it reminded me of the time in my London bed-sitter when the landlady came to give me notice. She said she'd endured six weeks of some animal hopping and jumping and clumping around above her head and that both I and the animal had to go. I put on a Stravinsky record and showed her the animal: me miming a kangaroo for an exam the following day at the Royal Academy of Music. Honestly, even if you don't have animals, you still have problems.

But people who like animals seem to have a more tolerant nature than many other people and manage to survive the day-to-day problems they encounter. The Barries told us about some of theirs while living with a cougar.

"I lost Lara once," said Betty. "I was getting ready

for a meeting, so while I took a bath I put Topsy, the dog, out and thought I'd shut the back door. When I got out of the tub, Topsy was in the kitchen and I knew by her face she was just dying to tattle. Lara was gone. Obviously, I couldn't call the police because I didn't know how they would view the situation and some of the neighbors were afraid of cougars, so I dressed hastily and crept like a criminal down the sidewalk, whistling and *prrrrt*ing! It was only about five minutes, but it seemed much longer before Lara came galloping out of a hedge and threw herself into my arms. She was ecstatic and so was I. I never did get to that meeting."

Ramsay broke in with another story: "Remember the postman? Lara often sits on the back of the chesterfield looking out at the street and the people walking by. She loves it. Her ears thrust forward and her eyes flatten into slits. You can see her intensity in every inch of her body. One day the postman came up the walk to deliver a registered letter. I yelled, 'Postman,' for Betty to open the door and then lunged for Topsy who lunged at the postman while Lara lunged outside. At the last minute I grabbed her by the tail and got her inside again. Delivering mail at our house is always a hazardous experience anyway, but this was too much for the postman. 'My God,' he said, 'you got a cat too? What in the hell breed is that? Beats the biggest cat I've seen.' I agreed that it was a big cat, but then, as I told him, his parents were big too. I wonder what the poor fellow would have done if he had known *how* big. Probably we'd never have got our mail again."

We could have gone on talking cougars all night but by now the kittens in the kitchen were awake and joining the children and Haida in another free-for-all, which made holding onto our coffee cups and continuing conversation in our crowded quarters impossible. The Barries bore Lara away, the Millers took Oola, and Hilary cuddled Tammy in her coat, ready to sneak her back to the apartment. I whipped up Tom into my arms and said good-bye to them all from the steps.

David and I went to bed that night secure in the knowledge that the cougars were educating not only us, the pupils, and their parents, but an ever-widening circle of people who came into contact with them.

7

Growing Pains

The cougars, now officially the "Seven O'Clock Show" cougars, appeared regularly on CBC television. Oola, Lara, and Tammy all lived within a few blocks of each other, so it was a simple matter to round them up whenever the station wanted to film them. Our own cougar footage lapsed under the pressure of too many other things to do. And too few hands, though we didn't need as many as the CBC, whose unions specified two lighting men (in broad daylight?), two soundmen, two cameramen, a producer, an interviewer, and sundry others who appeared in our back garden in their big portable studio to tape a ten-minute progress report. There were so many people scurrying around in an ever-diminishing space that I didn't blame the cougars when they piled over the fence and tore down the lane. Only Tom could be persuaded to stay on my lap against a background of roses while the interview took place. And I hoped the landlord saw the show even though the roses belonged to the neighbor. The last time he came he was greeted by Tom and Haida playing tug-of-war with my new woven peasant bag from Guatemala.

There must have been many people who did follow the exploits of the cougars on the "Seven O'Clock Show" because we were flooded with invitations to speak at dinners and show slides and introduce our animals. Spring was the season for banquets—Girl Guide ones for mothers and daughters, Boy Scout ones for fathers and sons. Sometimes the pace was so hectic that we accepted two invitations for the same night. David would speak at one banquet and I at another. We'd have to halve the slides and the animals. Perhaps I would take a puffin and a murre, Lara and Oola, while David would take Sam, Tom, and Tammy. After it was all over, sometime after midnight, we'd return the cougars to their respective homes and compare notes. Once I had four turkey dinners in one week. David may have eaten well, but time for finishing his university work was again interrupted.

One of the hazards of showing slides or movies in public is the breakdown of equipment while hundreds of people are waiting and watching. At times like these, while the gentlemen and janitors are fixing power points and machines, I rely on the animals for diversion in addition to their educative roles. Sam loved chasing anybody that ran and this always produced screams and laughter and something to talk about the next day at school or work. Sam was the only ham. The cougars, when faced by crowds, would either cling to our necks or run to the nearest corner of the room or stage where they stayed for the entire show. However, there was one banquet at which I was certainly glad to have a cougar stand in for Sam.

My hostess said she would collect me at five o'clock. I decided to take Tom as Sam's companion. With Tom the only cougar now at the house, I had gradually introduced them in the back yard and they were on sniffing terms.

A shiny new white convertible pulled up outside the front door. Tom was already tied up at the gate. I called Sam. But still considering himself neglected, he was at times disobedient. I called him into the kitchen, through the hallway, and into the living room —rooms that had been out of bounds to him since the arrival of the cougars. But nothing, not even herring, would entice him past the front door. I resorted to a leash. We have invented all kinds of harnesses over the years, none of which have worked with any degree of efficiency; Sam has always slipped his wily neck through the lot. With one flip of his concertina-like neck he slipped through this one.

It was now six o'clock. My hostess phoned the banquet hall to tell them we'd be a little late. A little late? Fifteen minutes later Sam followed the fish as far as the street but obstinately refused to go farther. By now a group of neighbors had congregated to see the outcome and Sam was enjoying once again being the center of attention while his mistress, with one eye on her watch, was becoming increasingly mortified.

It was almost seven o'clock. I glanced at the hostess. She was probably wishing she had rescinded the invitation. Tom sat patiently on his haunches, waiting. The hostess was waiting. The onlookers were waiting. Sam was waiting—but I didn't know for what.

I cajoled, wheedled, threatened, and commanded. But he knew that with me he was always chief bull. I made one approach with grit and determination. He could see I meant business. He galloped off past the crowd but in the opposite direction from the waiting car. I tore after him, chased him across the road, and back down the other side of the street. He stopped momentarily by the convertible.

"Into the car, Sam," I ordered and by a stroke of instinctive luck he climbed in. I collected Tom in my arms, made a final phone call to the waiting banquet, closed the doors, and thankfully proceeded to the car.

Oh, no! Whether through fright or excitement or the glamour of a new car in dazzling contrast to ours, I'll never know, but Sam had made a horrendous mess over the back seat upholstery. The crowd of course thought it hilarious. I rushed into a neighbor's house for paper towels and a rubber hose.

Both apologizing and cleaning up at the same time, I ordered Sam out of the car. It was one command he obeyed with alacrity. In fact, he flippered off across the road, pushed open the front gate, cantered around the side of the house, pushed open the back gate, and climbed into his enclosure before I could pick up the paper towels—a return journey at a record speed of two minutes compared with the outward journey of two hours. Sam had made his point, and stayed behind.

Sheepishly I climbed into the convertible with Tom and a coldly irate hostess.

But Sam had not yet performed his *pièce de résistance*. That was the night I returned at midnight to find he had got through the back door and wreaked havoc in the house. Everything that was up had been pulled down. Everything that was down was pushed up. Everything here was now there. And where nothing had been were things everywhere. Tablecloths and towels, cushions and rugs, curtains and dresses, sheets and blankets were strewn and crumpled all over the house. But the bedroom was the scene of Sam's greatest upheaval. In contrast to the other overflowing rooms, it and the bed were denuded save for Sam, complacently waving a flipper from the sodden mattress. If animals wink, he did. The cougars, despite their playful rambunctiousness most of the time, their runs, leaps and jumps, had never inflicted such damage. But even Sam could never match a raccoon for disorder in the home, but that's another story—or book.

House training in the usual sense was comparatively easy with the cougars. Cats as a species are noted for being clean and fastidious. Tom and Tammy were trained to a paper-lined box, Oola to kitty litter, and Lara trained herself to go in the tub.

The bathroom was nearly the undoing for Lara. Betty phoned to tell me the details: "Lara's just started on fish and probably gorged herself to produce the inevitable result, diarrhea with a capital D. I phoned home from the office at the hospital today, a noisy place with busy nurses and doctors milling about, and asked Ramsay innocently over the phone, 'How's everything?' An enraged bellow burst out: 'That—— cat's got to go. She's——on the wall, on the ceiling, all over the bathroom and floor, then wiped herself on all the towels.' The words were so unprintable I had to hold the receiver away from my ear. As a result, the nurses couldn't help overhearing the gist of the story. They're still probably wondering what kind of creature we keep in the house. It would take too long to tell them."

The kittens were about seven weeks old when they moved to their foster parents' homes, an age when it has been noted that captive-raised cougars stop drinking milk and start eating solid food. From observations made in sparse zoo records, I learned that hand-raised cougars start to eat meat about two weeks earlier than ones that are mother-raised. Perhaps this difference can be accounted for by the fact that the kittens raised in the zoo nursery are fed ground meat in their milk from one month of age.

Nobody knows for sure when or how wild-raised cougars are weaned. However, many stories depict two-month-old cougar kittens being transformed into ferocious bloodthirsty monsters at the first whiff of their mother's kill. This was not the case with the cougars we raised. I remained in close contact with their development during this transition period by phone and by regular visits to deliver their food.

Oola, Lara, and Tammy had to be weaned gradually to solid food. We started the process by mixing dog-food pellets in their milk and baby cereal. Later we added chicken and herring. We didn't accustom them to red meat in case there was any truth in the old tale that it would make them more aggressive. We knew a dog showed wilder enthusiasm over a juicy bone or a chunk of steak then dry dog food and that zoo cougars were more lethargic on a commercial preparation than a raw-meat diet, but this didn't necessarily mean that the temperament of the animal was being altered more than for the moment. Still, we decided to be cautious and did not feed them raw red meat. Chicken and herring were better, too, in that they were more easily available, economical, and being fed as whole animals hopefully provided better nutrition.

The cougars were about nine weeks old when they began to twist their heads sideways as they drank, spilled their milk, and ripped the nipples off the bottles—signs that they should be weaned. Oola was the easiest to wean, probably as a result of her gourmet introduction to solid food by way of salmon and moose at the Carters'. Lara and Tammy started lapping milk and dog food in a saucer, then graduated to pieces of chicken and herring within a week. But I thought Tom would die of hunger before he recognized that meat was good to eat. He'd jump up for the milk bottle, chew a new nipple to shreds, but drink nothing even when I'd break down in the face of his hunger and give the bottle to him. When I offered him dog-food pellets soaked in milk on the end of my finger, he'd lick the milk but not touch the solids. I'd sit on the floor for hours and coax him with chunks of fish, even raw beef. For two weeks Tom purred, whistled, romped around the room, looking for something to satisfy his hunger. One night he spent the entire dark-ness hours in bed, licking and chewing on my face as I tried to sleep. I endured it, thinking it was a hopeful sign that by morning he'd start to eat solids. Finally after three weeks of near starvation he began to lap milk from a saucer, then accept other food.

Do female cougars in the wild bring meat to their kittens first or do they bring their kittens to the meat? Most people think the mother drags in a carcass while her young are still drinking milk and lets them gnaw on it to habituate them to the juices. One friend who kept a cougar in captivity told me he had nearly killed his pet by giving it small pieces of meat before its system was ready to assimilate meat. He said it should be introduced gradually at the kittens' pace, as the mother does in the wild. If that's the case, then Tom must have been the best brought-up cougar.

Yet on April Fool's Day, incidentally Dave's birth-day, Tom nearly died. As had happened before with Tammy, he got sick without warning. All morning he lay curled on the chesterfield, screaming in what I pre-sumed to be anxiety and pain. A few days before, he had lain in the corner making a lot of growling sounds interspersed with heavy breathing. However, he had stopped growling and started to purr whenever we touched him. But not on the first of April. Before, he had had diarrhea; now he vomited. And always that protracted squealing rang in our ears.

It wasn't quite the multi-noted sound of the female in season that I was to hear Chimo use later. It was a *wow-ow-r-rr-r* call, halfway between a loud whistle-like sound and the controversial scream. It is a sound that means the cougar is desperate and it makes you feel desperate too. Friends of mine have heard cougars make similar sounds in the wild: one from a treed female who was separated from her very young kittens, another from a large cougar who had been treed for a couple of hours in a very small hemlock, and again when a cougar attacked a dog on the ground. Others have reported it from a cougar that had been shot with a bow and arrow, "which dealt him a lot of pain."

Tom's screaming was obvious pain but I didn't know the cause. I turned on the tape recorder and considered what to do. I phoned the zoo. I phoned the aquarium where David was working. There was a ringing but no answer. Being April Fool's Day the staff at both places expected practical jokes and for a period of time did not answer the phone. Driven frantic by the cougar's continual screaming and my horrible feeling that he would die as I watched helplessly and tape-recorded his death cries, I decided to take him to David.

I had no car, so I rushed to the neighbors next door to see if they could take me to the aquarium. Out. The neighbors on the other side weren't too enthusiastic. Then good old Rolf across the street came to my rescue and allowed himself to be commandeered. Tom kept up those frenzied cries for four hours—in the house, in the car, in my arms, as I jostled frenetically through the packed weekend crowds in the foyer of the aquarium, past the tropical display, through the salmon exhibit, and out to the pool where David was just winding up his commentary. I didn't let him finish.

Tom's screams could be heard a quarter of a mile

away. David heard me coming, so he knew something
was wrong. He didn't need to look at my distraught
face. I know he always wanted a wife who could
calmly cope with such crises as a rhino being born in
a bathroom or an elephant having an appendectomy
in the living room, so I half expected him to deliver
a verbal bomb. My entrance into the aquarium had
been anything but unobtrusive.

But he, too, was at a loss to explain Tom's strange
condition. One of the aquarium workers promised to
substitute for him at the next show. We got in the
car and drove quickly to the nearest animal hospital.
The veterinarian couldn't help any more than we
could. That the problem could be a dietary deficiency
was his only suggestion. Perhaps Tom's three weeks
of erratic feeding had caused some disorder. Perhaps
the dog food and pablum he was finally eating did
not agree with him, though they had posed no problem
for the other three kittens. There are a lot of "per-
hapses" in raising wild animals. Even autopsies when
the animal is dead don't always help. Too often they
give the cause of death as "unknown," the patient as
"normal."

Whatever the trouble had been, Tom's screams had
diminished to a moan by the time we got home and
he seemed perfectly all right the next day.

But Tom had another problem, which in the long
run caused us even more anxiety. Where Oola and
Lara and Tammy had growled and lashed out at their
cougar images in the mirror, Tom had not even noticed. Where Oola and Lara and Tammy zoomed between rooms and leaped over the furniture with the
grace and agility of few other animals, Tom of the
pudgy face and awkward gait crashed into tables
and doors. Where his sisters' eyes were blue turning
brown, Tom's were still cloudy opaque, pale blue hol-
lows of emptiness. We long suspected congenital
cataracts but not often did we voice our fears. Tom
had been different from the beginning. Was his physical
disability causing this difference? We kept putting the
answer off because we didn't want to know. But after

Tom's brush with death we invited an ophthalmologist to the house to test Tom's eyes. Our terrible suspicions were confirmed: Tom had been born with cataracts. He might have survived this long in the wild, but not much longer. A cougar kitten stays with his mother for up to two years, but long before that it is killing its own prey, be it grouse, rabbit, or ground squirrel. Excellent eyesight is essential.

The ophthalmologist explained that the lens of an eye with cataracts was like a honeycomb filled, not with clear honey, but with whitewaxy honey. As a result of this opacity of the lens, the eyes appear milky-looking. In trepidation I asked the question that had been in our minds for months. How long would Tom still be able to see? The doctor couldn't tell. What about surgery to remove the lens and then to teach him to focus on the retina? He said it would be a risky operation with only a 50-50 chance of success because Tom probably had other abnormalities of the eye in addition to the cataracts.

My reason told me Tom was one of nature's rejects, that he had probably lived longer than nature decreed, that it was right for him to die. My feelings told me that I had given my heart to this animal, not from a misguided maternal instinct, but from a natural and human desire to protect the weak, the vulnerable. I loved him. I didn't want to take the chance that he might die. We decided to wait a year or two to see how much sight he had then.

Not only was Tom different in the way he looked, the way he walked, and what he wanted, such as his preference for human cuddling over feline frolicking, but he was also different in his development. Except for his first steps into the world as a leader, he had been the last to eat solid food, the last to exchange his long, swirling juvenile whiskers for the short stiff ones of the adult, and the last to molt into his new summer coat.

By the time the cougars were six weeks old, huge patches of thick woolly baby fur came out in our hands, revealing ugly gray bare skin. I thought they must have some disease. Nobody at the zoos I contacted had heard of such a phenomenon, and at that time I knew nobody else who had ever kept a cougar in captivity. David thought it might be a normal molting process and we had only to wait till the new fur grew back in again. The fur kept coming out for more than three weeks and during all of that time I kept wondering at their nakedness.

I still think fur loss is a phenomenon of captivity and doesn't happen so dramatically in the wild, if indeed it does at all. It didn't happen to a second litter of cougars I raised in the house between the ages of three hours and six weeks, nor to a third litter that were kept outside at the age of three months. After conferring with other people, I speculate that fur loss in my first litter might have been due to the kittens being crowded together in a box with Haida in a heated house, to not being licked and groomed in the same way as their mother (with due deference to the dog), to some aspect of diet difference between their natural mother's milk and the milk we gave that was laced with so many additives, or an allergic reaction to some of the vitamins. Fur loss can also be due to feline distemper.

As Lloyd Beebe, owner of the Olympic Game Farm at Sequim, was to put it ten years later, "It never happens when the mother raises them but it happens half the time when the mother does not. Fur has fallen out with the ones we raised on a hot blanket in a trailer and in an incubator. In the wild the mother goes away in wintertime for long periods and the kittens get by. Their hair is long and beautiful, as it is with most of the cougars we raise outside. Nursery-raised cougars don't get their fur licked and groomed as much as they would in the wild, but mother-raised cougars in captivity sometimes get licked too much by their mother's rough tongue and they lose some fur that way because she has more time to groom than one in the wild."

In a reversal of that situation, another of my friends,

Howard Smith, lost the hair from the top of his head when his cougar pet licked *him* too much.

At nine weeks Tammy and Oola started to cover their nakedness in a short summer fur coat with strong enough growth that negated my disease theory. The new coat began underneath, silky and cream-colored. Later it extended to their legs and finally a strong wiry gray, then brown fur clothed their head and sides.

Tom started too, but as with everything else he took a little longer. Lara, despite being well cared for by the capable Barries and on the same diet as the other cougars, was the ugly duckling of the family. To mix the metaphors, she resembled a scrawny ballet dancer, a scared little rabbit with petite face, thin sinewy legs, and long ears sticking up from her tall and lanky frame. At times she looked more like a kangaroo than a cougar. David Barrie was quick to fly to her rescue with "You wait, Mrs. Hancock, Lara's just a slow starter like Tom. Just give her a little more time and she'll beat the three of them in looks."

It was the pleasing part of the experiment that each cougar family thought its own cougar the best. Jack London once said something like this, "When a tame animal loves you, you are flattered; when a wild animal loves you, you are his slave."

Tom grew his new fur coat soon enough to model it at a Domtar Construction display for the same company that Sam had once visited at the Bayshore Inn to help them sell seal joints. We had turned down other commercial opportunities, such as using the cougars in beer and dog-food advertisements, but we did accept the Domtar one. In return the company allowed us to buy a large amount of steel and wire at the wholesale price. David spent the following weekend at Island View supervising its transport and placement for the cougar enclosure.

He returned Sunday night ecstatic again about Tom's tractability. But he floored me with his next remark: "Well, Lyn, you'll have to sleep on the chesterfield from now on. I've got to sleep with Tom. He likes my beard. The folks are quite amused to see how he snuggles up to it all night long and scarcely moves position. It must be because he's molting. It's sure warmer in bed with me than in the box in the bathroom. We haven't solved the heat problems in the house yet. Sorry, kid, but that's the way it goes."

I wasn't really perturbed about my husband's sleeping companion. Long before I thought of writing *There's a Seal in My Sleeping Bag* or *There's a Raccoon in My Parka,* it occurred to me that *There's a Cougar in my Cot* would be a good title for a book one day.

As cougar kittens snuggle together to sleep, closely intertwined, we tried the same strategy that night. Keeping Tom tame and lovable was our most important objective. Being practical, I exchanged our sheets and white bedspread for traveling rugs and sleeping bags.

What a riot! None of us had any sleep at all. Tom purred like a motorboat all night, his head down in the deep cave of the bed with his tail sticking up between us. At 4 A.M. he got up, scratched around the sandbox beside the bed, then, planting his paws on my face, snuggled his way back again.

I mentioned it at school the next day. The children thought it hilarious. The staff looked grim.

The following nights were without incident. Tom had two favorite positions; scrabbling down between our legs at the bottom of the bed and snuggling under David's beard or my neck. In the morning I'd creep out of bed to get dressed for school and leave him there purring continuously. That's how I remember Tom best, warm, loving, and dependent, qualities perhaps due to his impending blindness.

Several weeks later our little idyll came to an end. It was now the end of April and Tom was nearly four months old, about the time cougars leave babyhood behind and enter their teen-age years, which continue till they are about two years old. After two they are adults and ready to leave home.

When Tom was four months old he interrupted our sleep by play. He jumped from the pillow onto our heads, put both front legs around our necks, chewed our ears, and licked the top layer of skin from our noses with his rasping tongue. Too soon the alarm would ring and while I struggled drowsily into my clothes, Tom would then want to curl up and sleep.

My parents in Australia continued to be politely horrified by my weekly letters home. Mum wrote, "Some friends of mine are visiting Vancouver and I'd like you to show them around. But please try to look a little glamorous, dear. Do wear your wig and get out of those jeans. I worry in case there's nothing but animals in your house."

Poor Mum! At a distance of twelve thousand miles her daughter seemed to be living a simply appalling life. My grandmother was even more horrified. "No normal, well brought-up young lady messes about with animals."

My mother's friends arrived at the worst possible time. It was the most hectic week of the year at school. My children were individually involved in singing, dancing, and acting items for the end-of-the-year concert, and as a class were involved in the production of a play, not in English but in French, which made it more difficult. As well as preparing for the concert, we were putting on a display for a special Parents' Night. The classroom was to be transformed into a Quebec village, complete with home cooking. All this meant that I was at school till midnight most nights, usually up a ladder trying to attach something to the ceiling. All four cougars had just come home for a periodic "Seven O'Clock Show" taping. We had just been given notice by the landlord, which didn't matter too much because at the end of the academic year in June we were leaving anyway. But it did mean that we had started to pack, and all available space in the house was taken up by cardboard boxes for the gradual move to the Island. For days David had been suffering from a regular recurrence of his allergy to dust and fur and feathers and was driven to the point of coughing and spluttering, "Let's shoot all these damn animals and have the house to ourselves." That condition didn't last too long as a procession of pets seemed to keep coming.

I did my weekly cleaning on Saturdays when Dave was at the aquarium because he sneezed as soon as I picked up a broom. With our impending departure to Island View Beach he had given up his job as commentator and was making regular trips to the Island to transport our gear, fix up the house, and plan the enclosures for the animals.

In addition, his neighbor and friend Frank Beebe had just announced that Janey, one of the first peregrine falcons to do so in captivity, had just hatched four eggs. I could never get very excited about birds to the same extent as mammals, but this was a first in the bird world and David was keen to get the whole operation on film. David would be going on a ferry one way, then a message from Frank by radio would have him getting on the next ferry going the other way. The phone was constantly ringing and I never knew who or what would be in the house when I eventually got home from school.

Into this confusion walked the Lithgows, my mother's friends from Australia, on their first trip to North America and probably one intended to check up on me on the side. I raced home that day with Stephen, as fast as one can when one walks with a St. Francis of Assisi, and I was just about to move a few boxes when the doorbell rang. Stephen had been asked to clean up the back yard, whose only occupant that particular day was Sam. It was one time I wished the cougars were there to grace the lawns and distract my guests from what I imagined they were doing—drawing circles in the dust. But on this particular day David had just left with Tom and Haida for Victoria, and Oola, Lara, and Tammy had been picked up by their foster parents.

The Lithgows stayed only for three quarters of an hour. I guess it's difficult to enjoy tea when you are perched on a crate. Conversation was uncomfortable.

"Your mother keeps her house so impeccable. What kind of one are you going to?"

I thought of the crowded beach cottage with its lack of heat, lack of water, its coffee-shop entrance, and the three old sheds at the back which still housed the previous owner's junk. "Probably a beach cabin of one and a half rooms," I mumbled.

"Oh . . . What land do you have on the island?"

"Six acres of waterfront on a beautiful beach with a million-dollar view." I brightened considerably, pushing out of my mind that the official gazetteer label described it as "sandy, rocky, poorly drained muck." "What did you do today?" I asked, trying to change the subject till Stephen signaled he had cleaned the back yard and I could safely take them to the garden.

"Oh, we took a bus tour to the British Properties. That's where we would live if we were here. Beautiful homes. So well kept."

One thing about Stephen. He may have been a poet but he was no janitor. He must have dreamed his way through the chores. After almost an hour's work, the yard looked the same as David had left it in his headlong dash to scoop up the animals and race to the ferry. And Sam was not enough to distract attention from it.

"We must write to your mother tonight and tell her everything," the Lithgows promised as I saw them to the front gate.

That was what I was afraid of.

8

Two Go to Hollywood

By mid-May the cougars were over four months old and had begun to cause serious problems. First it was Tammy. Hilary phoned.

"She's a real terror in the apartment, tearing from one end to the other. She doesn't seem to take any notice of me, but then as soon as I stop watching her and go into the bedroom, she sits bolt upright, ears pointed, and with the cutest expression on her face, seems to say, 'Really? Are you leaving? But we were having such fun.' The landlord hasn't said anything yet, so I presume he doesn't know. But I had to confide in a few more people down below. They were wondering what the *kerplunk, kerplunk, kerplunk* was too. Then they came out of their door yesterday just as I was trying to get Tammy up the stairs unnoticed. She's so big now and used to the place that she just won't stay under my coat."

"I know how you feel, Hilary. Our landlord came around yesterday, too, as Tom and Haida were having their usual tug-of-war in the living room. Cats hate anything taken away from them when they lay claim to it and Tom was a regular roaring lion, not the cuddly kitten he usually is. Well, as I told the landlord, it'll soon be June and at least I'm always working on the place to keep it clean and tidy."

"I'll certainly miss you when you go, Lyn. Vancouver will never be the same. I think Tammy is a dear. I'll miss her when she goes. [A slight pause.]

She's getting a bit big for my place. When did you say she was going?"

Prophetic words. Next day Hilary returned home to find a letter on her dining-room table.

Dear Miss Stewart:
I absolutely won't allow cats or dogs in the building. If it's yours and you intend to keep it I must ask you to leave.

The landlord

Ten days later Tammy was returned. Hilary said she was so sweet and affectionate she must have sensed it was her last day. Twice she was picked up and taken to the front door and twice she struggled free to run back to the apartment and hide.

Hilary's problems had ended. Ours were about to begin. Tammy had always been the difficult kitten, nervous and unpredictable. She had built up a friendly bond with Hilary but she snarled at almost everyone else. Having Tammy in the house was really having a cougar and knowing it. She stood on the toilet seat and cleared the window sill. She jumped to a high shelf and sent the clock radio flying. She pulled down all the shirts drip-drying in the bathroom. And during dinner she jumped on the table into David's chicken à la mushroom and wine and broke my salt cellars. That really made Dave mad. He stood up and reached for a rolled-up magazine to teach her not to jump on tables. She sprang straight into his boots and fell unconscious.

Thinking she was dead, I swooped down to the floor to cradle her head. David sat down beside me in sudden remorse. And Tammy got up as if nothing was wrong. She went over to a corner and quietly lay down. I have never run into such a strange cat.

"We won't be able to keep her, Lyn. She's too emotional. To keep an animal tame and trustworthy, you must be prepared to give it much time and care and loving. We have less than two months in Vancouver before we go to the Island without the time and space to devote to such a project. The cougars have already made too many dents in the university year. I can't see myself finishing either my thesis here or the enclosures over there."

At times I resented those cougars. The hordes of visitors. The phone constantly ringing. The dozens of speaking engagements. The stops in the streets and the endless questions. The television programs. The other orphans that kept coming for bones to be mended or feathers to be cleaned or mouths to be fed.

I looked at Barney, a month-old barn owl sitting on a plush red velvet cushion atop the tallest of the lamp stands to be safe from marauding cougars. His bloated pink tummy, sparsely downed nakedness, and grotesque facial discs made him look like some ugly, tired dowager. Barney had been the most miserable of three barn owls brought to the door by two children from a neighboring school. David spent an evening giving the boys advice on how to care for the other two, then volunteered to look after the sick one himself.

So I took the weird-looking bird to school and the children force-fed and weighed and measured and wrote about him. At night and on weekends he lived under a light bulb amid the books and papers and camera equipment in David's study, a room that with the bedroom and living room were now off limits to the other animals. More work and another mouth to feed, but each time I remembered the rapt gazes of the children as they looked at this bird that didn't look like a bird, I thought it might be worthwhile.

And I had only to feel Tom's cheek against mine to the accompaniment of a long rumbling purr or to look at Tammy cringing friendless in the corner, to know that in some crazy way, it *was* all worthwhile.

But time was running out. David said Tammy had to go. But where? A champion of freedom, which may be attributable to my Australian convict heritage, I didn't want her confined in a zoo. So we advertised in the largest newspapers in the States. Knowing Tammy liked women and disliked men, we tried to find a home for her among members of such groups as the Cat

Club of California and the Long Island Ocelot Club. But nobody seemed to want our pet cougars.

The tension tightened between us. We had the first serious rift in our marriage. Tom, quiet, slow, and loving, continued to enjoy the comforts of our kitchen and bed, while Tammy, at least when David was home, spent most of her time locked in a steel cage in the back yard. My reason told me Dave was right. Now at the last minute he had left the problems at Island View Beach and had started to study. He said any time spent on Tammy would be a waste and if she wasn't friendly to everybody she had no place in the Hancock household. But my heart went out to the cougar that nobody wanted. I wanted to lavish the same love and attention on her that Hilary had so she wouldn't run away in fear when anyone approached.

Then Lara came back from the Barries'. Their daughter Joanne, who suffered an acute allergy to fur, had returned to live full time in the house. Nobody in the family wanted to bring Lara back and I didn't want to receive her.

Betty was so concerned that Lara mightn't get along well with Tom and Tammy that she left her claws long so she'd be able to defend herself. She needn't have worried. Lara with the still-shedding fur may have been the scrawniest of the three but when she didn't coolly ignore her litter mates, she was the most aggressive. It was curious that Lara, who used to be the largest of the three sisters, was now the smallest and least developed. And Tammy, who used to be the sick scrawny runt, was now the most beautiful and the best developed. And where Tom used to be the leader, now Tammy, when she was free, became the one to explore.

Sam had now to share his back garden with the burgeoning menagerie. His tactics had changed after that grim reception following the banquet. He now tried to ingratiate himself into the kitchen by sidling up to the porch, twisting his long neck around the door, and swiveling his great goggly eyes that seemed to say, "Please let me in." If he felt neglected when the cougars were in the kitchen, there were probably moments when he hoped to be neglected when the cats entered the domain of his back yard.

The fear that the cougars first felt for his unfamiliar shape in the living room gave way upon closer acquaintance to tolerance at a distance. Only Tom rough-and-tumbled with Sam. When Haida joined in, the trio provided a fantastic free-for-all that amazed all onlookers. Dogs and cougars are habitual enemies in literature and seals normally have no contact with either species.

It was all too much for the poor man who came to read the meter. I arrived home from school one day to find him climbing the walls, literally. He was perched on the top bar of the porch railing. Looking up at him and probably wondering why he'd choose such an uncomfortable position, were one sea lion and three cougars. When I shooed the animals out of the way, he explained what had happened, rather incoherently in his nervousness as he scrambled backward through the gate. Apparently he opened the back porch door to read the gas meter and was confronted by Tom, Tammy, and Lara. Then as he tried to make a hasty retreat he was accosted in the rear by Sam who'd come up for some attention. Sam usually gets what he wants, too, with his intimidating bared-fang charge. It is really a bluff to get someone to run and it succeeds in almost every case. This time with both exits blocked, cut off by the cougars in front and the sea lion behind, there was only one place to go—up the vine-covered porch railing, where he remained till I came along. I expected a letter from the gas company but it never came, nor did the meter reader return. He probably couldn't complain because nobody would believe his story. Well, some people grow pampas grass to cover their meters and prevent them from being read. We don't have to.

Tammy, after returning from Hilary's, was the first to leave the house and investigate her new surroundings; the first to bite at the roses which I had to pin to the fence for their protection; the first to leap up to

Sam's shelf by the garage; the first to find a cubby hole under the dripping bird tank as a hiding place; the first to chase Tom and snarl at Sam.

Lara, upon return, ventured little into the yard. Her thoughts were on Betty and the milk bottle she still had with her meat. Pathetically, she poked and pried into every corner as if hoping her foster family would magically reappear. David Barrie and some of the class came over regularly to play with her, but it just wasn't the same.

All the cougars could have left the yard with a single bound over the back fence, but it was more than a week before they attempted it. As expected, it was Tammy who tried first. She crawled through a hole under the pickets and found herself in the strange new territory of the lane. Seeing the new turn of events from my kitchen window, I ran out to plug up the hole with rocks. I opened the gate and was about to herd her back into the yard when a dog barked. Tammy was so scared she dashed to the hole, found it blocked, and tore at the stones in panic. As she completely ignored the gate I had opened for her, I had to help her unplug the hole so that she could return by the more familiar route. Luckily, it was a long time before she again left the yard.

It was Joanne's allergy that brought Lara back to us and it was David's allergy that sent her to another foster home. With three cougars all shedding fur, David, now at home most of the time trying desperately to do some university work, was in a constant state of sneezing. More advertisements in newspapers had brought no replies. Even our letters to zoos had produced no results. David now wanted to find permanent homes for both Tammy and Lara. But while we were waiting, I had to find them temporary homes till the end of June.

Next day at school I mentioned casually to my science class that I was looking for a foster home for a cougar. A rain forest of eager hands shot upward. Cautiously I stressed that the parents would have to discuss it with me first.

The science lesson ended at twelve noon. At twelve-five on the way to the staffroom for lunch I had a phone call. A delighted father said emphatically, "Yes, we'd be happy to look after a cougar for you. Is it for one or two nights?"

I thought such a quick response was too good to be true. "Well, really, Mr. Harris, it's for a month, till the end of June," I replied lamely.

The voice at the other end was now considerably hesitant. "Maybe we'd better discuss it then. I was under the impression it was for a couple of nights only. Do you think we could manage it? You see, my wife works. She wouldn't be at home in the daytime and . . ."

All lunch hour the phone calls continued. And when I returned to my room at one o'clock there were several notes on my desk.

Yes, Mrs. Hancock, my Nancy can pick up a cougar this afternoon from your room. Yours truly, Mrs. Jones.

Dear Mrs. Hancock, I'll be in your room at 3 P.M. John has permission to bring a cougar home. Sincerely, Mrs. Douglas.

As many as fifteen people came to the house that night to view Lara and Tammy, who sat like a pair of Cleopatras on the kitchen table coolly returning the stares, but spitting and hissing if anyone came near. So, instead of persuading the audience to take a cougar home, I spent the evening listing all the disadvantages of owning one.

For the next few nights I continued to interview prospective foster parents. And although I didn't dare trust the cats to any of them, I got to know the characteristics of the families that wouldn't qualify. It was very obvious that both Lara and Tammy liked women and disliked smokers and people who wore glasses. They were attracted, either playfully or aggressively, to very young children and were afraid of sudden quick movements.

One night a party of teen-agers visited. Their biology teacher had announced in class that Mrs. Hancock wanted a temporary foster home for a cougar. Surprisingly, this group got along with Tammy extremely well. The teen-agers devised all kinds of interesting kitchen games for the cougars to play. The most beautiful jumper of the four, Tammy especially liked leaping to catch a duster swinging on the end of a wooden spoon. She could practically leap four feet from a standing position.

Probably no other cat in the world can equal the cougar in ease and resilience of spring. It doesn't climb up the trunk of a tree but jumps directly to the lowest limb unless it is more than twenty feet above the ground. It can vault high fences, bound down from precipices, and plunge into trees like a flying squirrel. It can even turn somersaults in midair. I once saw a cougar leap cleanly from an all-fours standing position on a limb forty feet above the ground to the same standing position on the limb of an adjacent tree without losing a foot of altitude.

Although I was tempted to try the teen-agers with Tammy if their parents agreed, David insisted when he came home that despite his allergy, we would keep her under close observation ourselves.

The next night a family we had met at a slide show asked to have a cougar. Lara was still the ugly duckling in most people's eyes. Tammy remained the favorite. I winced to see the couple lead in their four-year-old son. As they sat down at the table in the kitchen, Tammy stopped the snarling that was her usual welcome to any stranger and walked slowly over to where the four-year-old was sitting on his mother's lap. She seemed fascinated by the little boy. I warned the mother to keep perfectly still so as not to scare her. Suddenly, never taking her eyes off the child, Tammy leaped to the mother's lap. Startled, the mother jumped to her feet with the little boy on her shoulder while Tammy clung to her dress.

I wiped the slight scratch the child had on the side of his face, deposited Tammy in the bathroom, and took the family out to see comparatively safe old Sam. Even Tom could give a small child a fright though he didn't use his claws. Some time later Dave took him to visit Pat Nagle, then the western editor of *Weekend* magazine. Pat asked, as everybody did, "Does Tom bite?" "Of course not, Tom never bites. Listen to him purr," replied David with the confidence of Tom's experience to date. Pat put down his son on the floor beside the cougar. Tom, still purring and smiling, struck out with his paw. Pow! across the six-year-old's face. There was a stunned silence for what seemed like three days, then Dave joked to the little boy, "See, that didn't hurt, did it? Fancy! You've just been hit by a cougar."

Pat's son had been just as stunned as everybody else, calm and quiet, but at those words "hit by a cougar," he turned on the waterworks and became hysterical. The boy wasn't hurt at all, but he would have to be a lot older before such an incident had value as a status symbol. Tom's reaction could be partially explained by his poor eyesight. He never looked upward. He always looked down or straight ahead on his own eye level. A sudden movement or image appearing abruptly in his vision had caused him to react swiftly. I realized that despite his good-natured exterior he could inflict damage, not with the same intent as the more obstreperous Tammy, but perhaps with the same result.

Since one can't treat such incidents as experiments to test how a cougar sees a child, whether as something to play with or as something to eat, one can never learn the outcome of the situation. But it does seem that the young of all animals have a fascination for each other.

It is difficult to be objective about cougars when you love them. Many cougar owners I met in later years would never admit that their pets could harm a person of any age except after a good deal of provocation. They offered all sorts of excuses: the cougar was playing, it was defending its possessions, it was feeling irritable, the victim was teasing or wearing a floppy hat, long stringy hair, or a fur coat.

"A little kid is just like a mouse to a cougar," Bill

Robb said once. "It is quick and small and something to chase. Of course it can also be damaged easily."

Elaine Foisey, a young mother who raised cougars in Cherryville, British Columbia, said, "They don't know the difference between a human and an animal. When Tanya and Tiger were kittens, they didn't pay attention to babies who were always around them. But when people came with babies bundled in furs in winter the cougars acted very differently. They went hairy, they wanted to grab and hold on to them. I think it's the fur that makes them wild. Another time a five-year-old girl put her hand in their pen, they grabbed it and tore the skin. They thought it was something to play with."

Bill Robb, who also raised cougars with babies, agreed that the animals were not aggressive to his or the neighbor's children whom they saw regularly. "They only got excited if the kid was running around, bending down, or wearing something floppy."

Other cougar owners told me about pets or zoo charges who acted aggressively toward people who were different in some way—in their shape (a very ponderous woman, a man wearing a clown costume or with a glass eye), in their color or smell (a black, an Indian, a girl menstruating, or a woman in a garish dress), in their actions (a very aggressive personality, someone acting fearfully). All agreed, though, that their cougars appeared aggressive to children who were small, unfamiliar, or moved quickly. There are certainly differences between cougars. One friend had a male cougar who was so gentle it would take raw meat from a toddler's hands. Another friend had a female cougar who baby-sat children in the neighborhood like some watchdog.

In my own experience I found a difference between how a cougar feels playing with a duster on the end of a spoon and playing with fur or feathers. The only time I noticed belligerence in all four of my cougars was when they attacked a black bear rug on the living-room floor. Each of them latched onto a section of fur, growled menacingly if anything or anyone threat-

ened their rights of possession, closed their eyes, and
dug in their teeth and claws. In this case the fur was
clearly the reason for the attack. If the black bear
had been alive and within the limit of their power to
attack it, I am sure the cougars would have hung onto
it to the death.

Feathers perhaps hold the same motivation as fur.
Due to Dave's carelessness in picking me up from
school with Tom in the car and mine in opening the
door with Barney in my hand, the cougar killed the
barn owl. Thirty seconds was enough for Tom to grab
the bird by the neck and refuse to let it go.

In describing Barney's demise for the class magazine,
Gordon Kopelow combined both a scientific and literary approach with the directness of the typical eight-
year-old.

> Barney, the barn owl, was hatched April 3rd in
> Ladner. On April 12th he came into our class-
> room. Barney was covered with very, very fuzzy
> white down and had a funny long, droopy red
> face. He weighed 317 grams and he ate 15 pieces
> of horse heart in one day. On April 14th he
> weighed 367 grams. At the time of his death, he
> ate 31 pieces of horse heart a day and his primary
> feathers were half an inch long. He died instan-
> taneously April 19th when Tom, the cougar, ate
> him in one gulp in the car. We are sorry we
> couldn't study his full feather develop-
> ment.

In trying to solve the problem of where to board
Tammy we did test a couple of people. One was a
family newly arrived from Yorkshire, animal lovers
with a huge house and no furniture. They pooh-poohed
the idea that Tammy would trouble their three children, two, four, and six, and wanted to give her a
try. Fortunately, they heeded our warning and brought
Tammy back the next day. They agreed they didn't
like the way Tammy stared at the baby.

We accepted one girl of nineteen as a cougar foster

mother, then discovered she lived with her parents who hated animals, especially cats.

It was funny how nobody wanted to take Lara, the much better tempered of the two. It just goes to show that beauty may be skin deep, even for cougars. Potential foster parents poured through the door for a week, but there was always something that deterred me from making a decision. If it wasn't the people or their children, it was their houses. They were too full of bric-a-brac, their yards were too small or unfenced, they had too many cats or dogs.

Then one day at school Jonathan Griffin offered to take Lara home and I eagerly accepted. Jonathan, a delightful child with dimples and a mischievous smile, had often played with Lara at the Barries'. Nevertheless, I was still astonished that the transfer was made so smoothly. He took her home after school and the next morning in class showed us a Polaroid photograph of Lara spending her first night on the bed, not with Jonathan, but his parents, Basil and Hilda Griffin.

When we let Lara, a cougar, come downstairs into the living room she immediately runs around the couch and sticks her beady eyes out, looking like a detective. She's very funny and curious. She's always getting into the funniest situations such as trying out the toilet for size and falling in, or eating the tulips on my father's dresser while my mom's out of the room. She likes looking out windows and once climbed out on the roof when the window was open. My father stuck out a rag and they had a good old-fashioned game of tug or war. My father won.

Jonathan Griffin

At long last Lara had found a home among people who quickly lost their hearts to her. Theirs was a busy household, with both children and parents coming and going on various projects, but there was always time to enjoy a cougar in the house. Even on nights that Lara threw her fish all over the upstairs!

"We were laughing so hard at her antics and at Bas, who was trying to barge in to recover the fish, that we didn't do a very good job of communicating to her that this was an undesirable activity. We made her think it was a fun thing to do," Hilda told me afterward.

Except with her litter mates Lara was a gentle cat and got along best with gentle people. "She has a great gentleness and dignity," Hilda wrote once. "Even from the moment Jonathan brought her into the house, very frightened at the unfamiliar place and its people, we had only to show her that something like clawing the furniture was not acceptable, and she never did it again. In fact, she was quite upset if she offended us."

The Barries called Lara "lovable, lively, and ludicrous." The Griffins also discovered her lively sense of humor.

"It is our older son, David, that Lara loves most to tease," said Hilda. "He comes in from school and takes her for a walk and they have become good friends. When the family gathers to watch TV Lara strolls in, looks for David, and pesters him by stalking and pouncing on his neck till he gets up and moves. Then Lara takes David's place, settles down comfortably, purrs, and we all watch TV, including the cougar. If David doesn't want to play and moves away as Lara comes in, she simply takes his place without bothering him. But she very much likes company and an appreciative audience."

Our theory that the cougars were far more tractable when separated from each other and in the company of a particular family was borne out by the experiences of all cougar foster parents. Lara and Tammy were never as docile in our house, with its constant hurlyburly of strange people and strange animals, as they were with their respective families. Animals are raised best in quiet, not chaos. It is then that their true personalities are able to unfold.

Hilda commented, "Yes, Lara swipes a paw at people occasionally if she's suddenly frightened or if she's tried to the end of her patience because they're always wanting her to do things that are unnatural to her, like posing endlessly for cameras to be set. Yet she's a very trusting cat and doesn't expect anything bad to happen. She's curious, she approaches life looking for information about it, not trouble from it. So she can be easily startled or frightened. She probably trusts things more in captivity, a comparatively sheltered place than in the wild where she'd be more alert, take less chances, and learn more fear."

Hilda also observed the amazing dexterity and agility of the cougar. "I've been having trouble with my back and I often go to bed and lie flat to rest it. Lara likes to sit on the chair at the end of my bed and watch me. She also likes to leap onto my chest and lick my face. The first time it happened I was reading. The book went flying and Lara crashed on top of me. Now I always keep one eye on her and as soon as she leaps I raise my hand. She stops in mid-air and drops onto the bed. I am intrigued by how she can alter the length of her leap after she's taken off."

A professor from Berkeley was once quoted as saying, "I have seen a mountain lion, when hotly pursued, jump downward and then, while in mid-air, turn almost sixty degrees to one side, so as to make a landing the animal could not have seen when he leaped. I have known even of hawks being caught on the wing, when flying near ground, by a nimble mountain lion."

The cougars had only been full-time residents of the classroom for the week David went to hospital. Occasionally they returned for brief periods so the children could make notes on their development and use them as topics in creative writing lessons. Sandra Lloyd described them at four months:

> Large paws that sneak along quietly
> No more spots but beautiful grayish coat,
> Long black-tipped tail that is held low,
> Sharp piercing claws that still cling tightly
> Large yellow eyes that stare frightenedly at you
> Baby spotted cougar is almost grown up.

Although all cats but Tammy continued to be docile and affectionate, I thought it best to keep them in the more familiar surroundings of their respective homes than the excitable atmosphere of the classroom. I'm sure the staff was much relieved. Jonathan and Stephen kept us informed of Lara and Oola's daily doings in our morning news period.

Sometimes volunteers from the class met me at home after school and on weekends to baby-sit Tom and Tammy. I didn't want the cougars to run around in the yard without supervision, so during the time I was at school I locked them up in Sam's house and that allowed the seal undisturbed freedom to roam his domain. Thankfully, at least one of our animals was not agile enough to jump the fence.

My cougar sitters gave me the opportunity to work on things inside the house, although I always kept a watchful eye on them through the kitchen window. I was happy to see Stephen join in with the other children, not only in the yard at home but also in the yard at school. His poems and stories continued to attract attention in the class magazine and earn for him the respect not only of his peers but also the principal, the staff, and the parents. He didn't write now about cougars, at least not for class consumption. Cougars had provided the initial stimulation and launched him into his present period of productivity. He wrote about a variety of subjects in a variety of ways. If not pressured and allowed to proceed at his own inclination, he contributed not only to the class magazine but also to partner and group projects in other fields. Sylvia was so pleased with his progress on all fronts that she wrote a long letter to the school board and told them so.

This counteracted the ones that complained about my enthusiasm and abundant energy, which aimed at getting everybody to excel at everything. It did seem ironic that whereas most other parents worried that their children weren't working, the parents of my children complained that theirs worked too much. What made it doubly annoying was when the class commented to me that "school is a cinch." Perhaps they were playing the same trick on their parents as I had done on mine. "I can't come with you, Mum, I have to work on school projects or I'll get into trouble," I wailed constantly when I didn't really want to spend Sunday with Aunt Ethel or go on a long drive in the car. The truth was that I enjoyed more the investigations prompted by my teachers. Looking back on it now, I don't think a little discipline and competition did me any harm. My pupils had all been selected for the major work class because of their capacity for achievement, so I continued to see that their achievements matched their potential, despite criticisms that my "questions were too hard." I didn't know all the answers myself, but I think the class appreciated a "let's find out together" approach and I tried to make the learning experience as much fun as possible for both the students and myself, whether our projects were based on animals or not. Fortunately, our room was in the basement so we could carry on our informal learning methods mostly unobserved.

Meanwhile, at home Tammy slept in the enclosed porch at night and Tom still slept in bed with us. But dawn came earlier to Tammy, our lonesome cougar, and at 5:30 A.M. she would wake up, jump to the window leading into the kitchen, tear down the curtains, and cry for company. After several of these mornings I resigned myself to get up and carry Tom out to the porch to be with her. Satisfied, she would lie down and go to sleep again, outstretched and with paws intertwined.

As soon as David and Tom left again for the island I set about trying to make friends with her. There was one good point in Tammy's favor: she was never purposefully destructive. Hilary had trained her well. She had given her a cushion and an old book as playthings and they had seemed to keep her from chewing on the apartment furniture. We did lose our electric clock and a few meals knocked from the table, but these were reactions to fright in unfamiliar places.

Tom, on the other hand, had obliterated my Egyptian hassock and pulled out the stuffing from the chesterfield and two kitchen chairs. Thereafter they were labeled "cougar chairs" and valued as conversation pieces. Another time when Tom was locked in the bathroom, he chewed the toilet cover to a point where it was totally unrecognizable. Oddly enough, when it was finally given to him as a plaything he completely lost interest in it. Then one morning as I rushed off to school I discovered he had played with my briefcase, chewed off the lid, and torn up all the top assignments. When he did the same to my report cards I "did a Hilary" and printed neatly "made by a cougar" on the tears and waited for a bomb to fall from either the parents or the principal. It never came. Maybe they had resigned themselves to the fact that I would be gone in June. Anyway, I like to think those scraggly paw-printed and claw-torn report cards are now the treasured possessions of some proud mother or father reminiscing about the time when a lion, not a lamb, came to school.

The night David and Tom left for Island View Beach I tried the supreme test of tameness and took Tammy to bed with me. I left the light on till 2 A.M. and dared not close my eyes. Realizing she accepted me, all alone and quiet in the house, I finally turned it off and tried to get some sleep. But not for long. Unlike Tom who stayed in one place, Tammy wanted to play with my feet, tear up the blankets, run around the room, throw all the shoes out of the wardrobe, and then scamper after them. She distracted me into playing with her. It was a case of "If you can't beat her, join her."

Strangely enough, she cried continually. Was she thirsty? I gave her water but she ignored it. Did she want out? I left her in the garden till 4 A.M. She didn't use the sandbox and when I opened the door, she just ran inside again, still crying. I concluded she missed Tom, whom she seemed to adore. It isn't the same fun playing with a human who has no protective fur and is always yelling *"no"* and pinching one's claws as it is to rough-and-tumble with another cougar.

It's hard to resist a cute cuddlesome fur ball with blue eyes who begs to be fondled. It's almost impossible not to pick it up, let it lick your cheek, jump in your arms, knead and paw. But when that same kitten with its grown-up teeth, sandpaper tongue, and towering body pins you to the ground and you yell for him to stop or you turn on the water hose or hit him with a two-by-four, he is going to feel frustrated and never comprehend. You have turned on him, not he on you. He has done the same all his life, so why not now? So if you want to be with a cougar when it is older, you must resist the temptation for such physical contact when it is younger.

Elizabeth Guent, a friend of mine from Seattle who has had a male cougar for nine years, puts it this way. "I have taught Loki to respect my body, that it is not a toy to play with. I use balls or tires and I don't let him jump up on me."

"We let the kittens talk and rub against us," explained Bill Robb. "But we don't let them knead with their claws or jump on us. We pick them up in our arms but only when they are tired."

But this advice was given to me several years later. I made all the mistakes of the first-time cougar keeper and, such is motherly nature, I would probably make them all over again. I tumbled with Tom and let him jump on my head. I didn't stop even when I noticed that after several weeks of his playing with Tammy he played more roughly with me, forgetting to sheathe his claws and beginning to bite when he became excited. In his enthusiasm he did not remember the difference between the tactics to be used on me and those he could use on Tammy.

During the time David and Tom were over on the Island and I was home alone, Tammy was quite content to lie purring on my knee as I marked books or prepared lessons or typed. How I wanted David to hear her purr! I found she would even come when called. I grew reckless and let her out in the yard. If a neighbor phoned to say, "There's a cougar at the corner," I had only to call, "Tammy, Tammy!" from the back fence and she'd come leaping back. At the end of the week Tammy trusted me enough that we almost had the same relationship as Dave had with Tom. But also at the end of the week, David returned and so did Tammy's former self.

A knock on the door and she ran to the bathroom or jumped into the sink or snarled if we passed. If anyone opened the back gate she crawled under the bird tank and cowered in her dark den till the disturbance was gone. David insisted on keeping her in the steel cage in the yard while Tom, in contrasting circumstances, spent his time lying on the rug in the kitchen and giving his characteristic squeak of recognition whenever we looked at him. While Tom purred inside, Tammy cried outside. For hours and hours. I couldn't bear it.

Years later Mark Ferrari, from California, whose interest in cougars stemmed from the time he'd seen me take Chimo on a walk through Golden Gate Park in San Francisco, described Maju, a cougar who in several ways reacted like Tammy.

"I got Maju as a two-week-old kitten from a rock star who told me I'd have to blast him as hard as I could whenever I needed to discipline him. This kind of discipline doesn't work, but it took me a long time to find that out. I believe that punching Maju led to his neuroses. Then from being allowed to run totally free over three acres he was put in a cage. He could still see into the house though from his compound and he'd get very jealous if I showed affection to anyone else, whether it was other people or other animals. The first time he tried to kill me I believe he was jealous of a coyote I had been with. As soon as he sniffed my hand and pants he looked up, his eyes totally gazed over like cougars do when they kill, and he jumped up and tried to bite through my skull. After he worked out the aggression from his system he cried and whimpered, as if he'd realized what he'd done and hadn't wanted to."

Like Maju, Tammy was subjected to sudden curtailment of freedom at a time when all her natural instincts were to explore a rapidly expanding territory. Like Maju, she was exposed to a different type of discipline and treatment than that afforded her siblings. She responded to kindness, but her congenital makeup was probably the major factor in causing her to be unpredictable and as a result, untrustworthy.

After David's return to the house Tammy was never really tractable. Sometimes she climbed the back fence and ran off down the lane, and it took me an hour to coax her back again. She was not a cat you just went up to and grabbed. Such an encounter could leave you bloody. My methods of returning her to the house were varied. If I found her on a neighbor's woodpile I would sit beside her until she closed her eyes, purred, and licked my hands. Then I would grab. Once in my arms she usually lay quiet and still. At other times I would corner her on a patio or in a carport. Fortunately, I became so professional in my surreptitious tactics at cat-napping that few neighbors knew I was catching a cougar and there were no complaints.

But as work piled to a climax toward the end of June and retrieving Tammy got too difficult and too time-consuming, I had to leave her more often in the steel cage. The kittens at between twenty to thirty pounds were approaching six months old; our permits to keep them were about to expire as well as our lease on the house. The cougar enclosure at Island View Beach had not yet been built and still there were no replies to our inquiries for permanent homes for Tammy and Lara. David realized he hadn't a hope of satisfying his university commitments before the term ran out, and the first draft of his thesis had been turned down by one of his committee members. Things became tense between us.

Then as tempers reached the breaking point, Pat

and Ted Derby, who kept and trained tame animals for Disney films and commercials such as Mercury Cougar, phoned from the local zoo in Victoria to say they would take Lara and Tammy.

Lara would probably adapt to anybody who was gentle enough, but Tammy needed a woman to bring out the loving qualities that were somewhere inside this fearful and disturbed kitten. Hilary came around to say farewell to Tammy. The two boys, David and Jonathan, no longer laughing on that last day, came to say good-bye to Lara, the pet they had grown to love. The difficult part for me was putting them in the cage I had for so long been trying to avoid. As it was trundled into a truck for their journey to California, I hoped that they would be able to cope with careers in Hollywood and that Pat would treat Tammy well.

We still had Tom and Oola. But my dreams of living in the wild with four romping cougars as companions crumpled with those of the children's. We had learned the heartbreak of "tame" wild animals.

Years later Hilda Griffin reminisced:

Lara never moped but would lie gazing out the window and we would know a great longing to set her free to roam in her own environment. We knew it could not be done, yet we also knew through our own slowly growing awarenesses that Lara would never really be at home in captivity either. Her whole beautiful being was tuned in to an environment she could never have and we could never give her. I don't know if she felt distressed by her foreign environment, but I do know we were. I think such an awareness has played a part in our family's feel about the wilderness and its wild creatures. I am aware of the harmony of life in wilderness, of its balance, of living things existing according to their purpose and fulfilling an overall purpose all intertwined, but I am still uneasy there. Bas and the boys are different. They tune in with the wilderness and feel at home and peaceful there. And for that I am glad.

Lara left and we are left with a great love for her and a great sadness. It was a strange experience for us and in so many ways a learning one. We learned something about animals and quite a lot about ourselves.

9

Oola Makes Headlines

May had brought crises. June brought catastrophe.

Brrr! I opened my eyes abruptly and realized the phone was ringing. 11.30 P.M. I must have fallen asleep over the books.

It was Sylvia Miller and she was speaking from the emergency ward at the hospital. "Stephen let Oola out of the bedroom into the hall where an eighteen-month-old baby was sitting on the floor playing. Oola jumped on the baby."

"My God! Was it hurt?" I felt numb. I imagined the worst.

Sylvia continued, trying to calm me, though I could feel she was tense. "It's just a scratch. Any dog or cat could have done it but it was a cougar so the mother, a stranger—one of the hippies I've been working with at work—phoned her doctor to see what to put on it. Well, when he heard a cougar had caused the scratch he suggested she take the baby down to emergency at the hospital for the doctor to check it. And that's where we are now."

"They probably think the cat's got rabies or something. Don't forget to tell them it's had its shots," I said quickly, fighting the sick feeling in my stomach even though Sylvia had said there had only been a breaking of skin. I'd had far worse scratches myself in tumbling like a tomboy with Tom or Tammy. The nurse at school was always hounding me to have shots

122

for this and shots for that. "Are you going home now?" I asked Sylvia. But my feeling of relief was short-lived.

"Lyn, they are going to keep the baby overnight at the hospital to see if there's any reaction. . . . [then hesitantly] Lyn, the reporters were lined up at the hospital when we arrived. They're trying to get a story, but we're not talking to them. Seems the nurses got it from the doctor on the phone, the police got it from the nurses, and the reporters got it from the police radio. I'm coming over to your house to bring Oola back."

That emotive word "cougar!" Reporters at midnight with a blank notebook would jump at the chance of writing yet another cougar story. Sylvia might not talk but how could she stop the young mother from talking? And why should she? Images of other headlines came flooding into my consciousness from the study we'd been doing of them in the classroom. "ATTACK," "MAUL," "BLOOD-SPATTERED," "KILLER COUGAR." Which would they use?

Sylvia dropped Oola off without too much said. She was as upset as I was. She had always insisted that Oola, the most placid of the females, played gently with everyone, whatever the age. All the cougar parents were intensely loyal to their charges and refused, in the light of their personal experiences, to believe that their cats could do any harm—at least to people. When Stephen told me how Oola, who slept at the end of his bed, often jumped out the window and went walking down the lane at night like any alley cat, or when Sylvia mentioned casually that the lady up the street phoned to say Oola was looking curiously at her baby in the pram on the lawn, I remonstrated and asked that Oola not be left to roam unsupervised. "It's not that she'd hurt anyone intentionally," I said a little testily, "but bare skin breaks easily under the weight of a playful cougar even when it's a kitten less than twenty-five pounds."

It was not advice based on hindsight. Certainly, all

the cats had inflicted a few scratches. But only Tammy had done so purposefully, perhaps even vindictively. Most people who met the kittens marveled at their docility, how closely their behavior resembled that of their own domestic cats. My fears were more grounded in what could happen in the future when the cougars reached maturity or what could happen when damage done in play reached the newspapers. As it had now. All those talks, all those television programs, all the good public relations we were trying to do for the cougar could be destroyed by one headline in the paper, or worse still, a picture.

As usual David was away. The last I heard he was somewhere out on the open ocean near the Queen Charlotte Island in a fishboat after falcons. I lay down but I couldn't sleep. The phone rang again. I shot out of bed to grab the receiver. It was Stephen. His mother wasn't home yet. His story was incredible.

A reporter, not being able to get a story out of the hospital, the mother of the baby, or Sylvia, had phoned the Miller home to speak to someone there. Stephen, thinking it was the doctor as the reporter so identified himself, answered several of the man's questions before he realized his interrogator was a reporter and hung up on him.

It was one o'clock in the morning but I was desperate. I phoned Don MacLeod, the photo editor of the morning paper, an acquaintance to whom I'd been giving some pictures of the animals to enliven his pages.

"They're not the tactics my men use, Lyn," he protested emphatically when I got him out of bed.

"Then if it's the other paper, can you stop them putting the story in? Who do you know there?" I asked helplessly, thinking of the last time I'd tried to suppress something in the paper. Then it had been good for the cougar. Now I feared the worst.

"You can't keep anything out of the papers; it's the freedom of the press," he asserted again. "You're wasting your time. But I'll tell you what I'll do. Let's

TOM,
HIS FAMILY
AND FRIENDS

Here are the four cougars that arrived one
Sunday morning in January 1967.

Top, left: The baby cougars preferred
to be bottle-fed by hand.

Top, right: Haida, the two-month-old Vizsla,
cleaned the cougars after they were fed.

Bottom: Feeding time in the classroom.

Top: David Barrie and Stephen Miller introduce
Gomer the turtle to Lara the cougar.
Bottom, left: Stephen Miller makes friends with Tammy.
Bottom, right: Two sleepy kittens after a busy day at school.

Top, left: Oola, licking her chops in the box of Gravy Train.

Top, right: Playing hide-and-seek in the bathroom.

Bottom: Tom liked to snuggle in bed. (He was shedding his fur at the time this picture was taken)

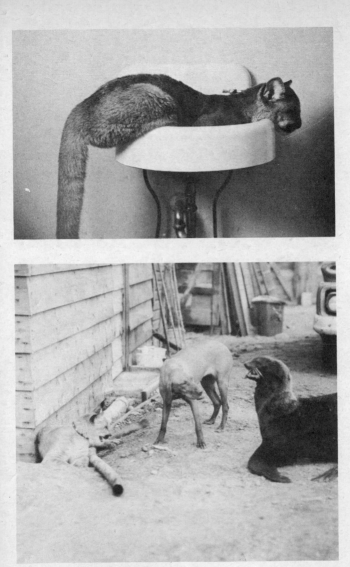

Top: Taking a nap in the sink.

Bottom: Visitors thought that Sam the seal,
Haida, and Tom formed an unusual trio.

Top, left: Tom at seven months. His cataracts
are evident in this picture.

Top, right: Tom gave me a warm welcome
every weekend when I visited him at the zoo.

Bottom: Howard and Dorothy Smith's
cougar, Big Joe. *(Photo by Dorothy Smith)*

Left: Playing leapfrog on our special island...

Below:...and taking an afternoon nap.

Left: When I visited Tom at Rudy's Pet Park, as he had done in his kitten days, he still chased my broom.

Below: Tom came home for the last time at Christmas 1968.

wait till tomorrow. If the story is blown up I'll run a counterstory saying how tame and lovable your cougars are and I won't link it to the previous story at all. Be ready with the Millers to have a picture taken of Oola in your back yard tomorrow afternoon."

I waited till morning. At seven-thirty the phone rang again. Again it was Stephen. "Mrs. Hancock, a reporter and a photographer just came to the door. I got their names but we wouldn't let them in," he said quickly. "They're probably on the way to your house."

Even as he spoke a car was pulling up outside my house. Tom and Oola were playing a lively game of tug-the-cushion at my feet. Feverishly I whipped the pages of the telephone directory to get Don's number. I dropped the book. The doorbell rang again. I ignored it and pulled the curtains.

"Don? They're here at the door, the reporters from the evening paper. What'll I do?" I panicked on the phone.

"Don't tell them anything. They can't write something from nothing. Phone me back at noon," he replied tersely.

Tom jumped up on the window ledge and pressed his nose to the glass. I pulled him back quickly and put both cougars in the bathroom.

The doorbell rang again, this time more insistently. I tried to take Don's advice. I sat on the chesterfield a few feet from the closed door. I heard the men mumbling. Why is it so difficult to stay still and listen to a telephone ringing or a doorbell chiming and just let it ring and just let it chime? I couldn't stand it any longer. I opened the door.

The man smiled. I remembered him. "I'm the fellow who did the picture and caption on Sam over at the school. . . ."

"Yes?"

"I hear you have a problem."

"No, I don't have any problem. Are you trying to make one?"

"About that little kid and the cougar?"

"Oh, that?" I forced myself to sound casual. "A bit exaggerated, isn't it?" And I closed the door again.

They picked up their gear from the steps and walked back down the path. The phone rang immediately. Leadenly I picked it up.

"This is Betty, Lyn. I've just heard the news. Can I do anything to help?" I burst into tears at her voice. It was friendly, concerned, practical. "Heard what?" I managed to say after I composed myself.

"About Oola. Listen, Ramsay will turn the radio up. It's been broadcast on the hour every hour since midnight: '. . . a pet cougar has mauled and roughed up an eighteen-month-old baby in the Point Grey area.' "

No names mentioned. At least that was a relief. Somehow it sounded better that way, even if half Vancouver must have known the Hancocks had cougars. Betty wanted to do something constructive like phoning an open-line radio show or writing a letter to the paper or going on television—anything to show the public how affectionate a cougar can be, that a single scratch was not an attack, that the media exaggerates for effect because that is what people want to read.

Don again advised caution.

I had to go to school. I had to put on an act. I was quivery and nervous and avoided the staffroom. The children were understanding. They knew. Only the Physical Education teacher mentioned it. I didn't know at the time what was written in the paper, but I told him whatever he read was unfounded. He said the staff knew all about it too, but they weren't going to mention it. They didn't want to hurt me. I was glad of that. The day wore on and I left school within minutes of the bell. The Millers, all of them, Sylvia, Stephen, Mary, and Lois were in the back yard by the time I got home.

I phoned Don at the paper and he read the report. "Listen, Lyn, I think you should drop it. It's on an inside page, there's no photo, and it could have been written much worse. To do another story now would only bring the subject up again. Leave it alone and it'll die."

I suppose it could have been much worse, though the writer had no more to go on than the few words he wangled from the police report and the information he had wrested from Stephen in the early hours of the morning and quoted wrongly. Yes, there were words like "maul" and "attack," as I expected. And saying the victim was "in satisfactory condition" made it sound as if he was hurt seriously enough to be hospitalized. And it didn't help our request for scientific and educational permits to house Sam, Tom, and Oola at Island View Beach by announcing we already owned a zoo on Vancouver Island.

At suppertime the doorbell rang again. This time it was the police. Four men in two cars. What now? Oola was splashing in the bathtub and Tom was sitting on the toilet seat intently watching her. It wasn't that I didn't trust them in the yard. I just felt in my present mood that I wanted to lock the three of us in some kind of fortress. I could slam the door in the face of reporters, but it wasn't as easy to do that to the police.

They were quite friendly, even nice. "A lady near the Miller family has complained. She read in the paper that a cougar lived on her street and she's frightened because she has small children. Can we see the cougars?" one asked.

I took them to the bathroom. Oola was now crouching most uncomfortably under the bathtub and Tom, thinking somehow he was safer there than on the toilet, had sprung into the washbasin. As soon as the constabulary spilled through the doorway, both cougars snarled as if on cue.

"I don't think I want to play with them after all," said one of the policeman. "I can see why the lady was upset."

I hoped he wasn't going to press charges for being frightened by a cat trying desperately to get farther down into the basin. He didn't realize it but the cougars were far more scared of him than he could possibly have been of them.

I took them back to the living room and explained the packing boxes. They looked relieved when I said we were leaving for Victoria at the end of the month. This was probably the first time they thought they had to apprehend a cougar and I don't think they knew how to handle it.

A few days later Sylvia and Stephen came over to ask if they could borrow Oola for a few hours to take her for a walk in their garden. It was obvious they missed her. I agreed reluctantly and insisted they keep her at all times on a leash. Not that Oola was rambunctious. She was even more gentle and dignified than Tom. She was all female—light, lithe, graceful, and aloof. Tom was all male, chubby, awkward, and cuddly. Oola would chew on little pieces of fish silently, fastidiously. Tom tore into his food with growls and then left bits all over the floor. I trusted both of them. But I didn't trust people or circumstances.

The Lithgows in town for the day after a sightseeing tour had phoned to tell me the only two items of news chosen in Sydney, Australia, to represent Canada that week was the clipping about Oola mauling a child and something else about grizzly bears. Emotional sensationalism sells newspapers everywhere.

I worried all the time Oola was away. She came back in a few hours, but it was the last time she went walking with the Millers. As soon as the neighbor in the lane behind saw Oola, leashed and walking on the lawn in the Miller back garden, she called her children inside the house and said distinctly so that at least four houses could hear, "Come here, you don't want to end up in hospital, do you?" Then she called the Fish and Wildlife Branch to threaten charges for being disturbed and frightened if she saw the cougar again on her street. The Branch phoned me to say that they realized both incidents were trivial and the truth immaterial, but what really mattered was the extra work involved in answering the phone and making explanations to the public. They, too, were relieved that our departure was imminent.

During the third week of June from being the Keeper of the Cougars I became the Royal Keeper of the Prince's Falcons, and as a result had another run-in with the press.

While I was wrestling with cougar catastrophes David spent the first two weeks of June in the Queen Charlotte Islands with members of the Fish and Wildlife Branch. They were making an annual survey of peregrine falcons and collecting young birds for captive breeding purposes. Two years before, the world-wide decline in peregrine falcon numbers had been widely documented, and attempts were now being made to breed them in captivity as a way of repopulating the wild. While officially declared an endangered species in most places, the peregrine falcon is not considered so in the Queen Charlotte Islands, although in the mid '60s a drastic decline had definitely been noticed on Langara Island.

David's interest in falcons began in his teen-age years when he noticed a wiry middle-aged man tearing madly after a red-tailed hawk in a farmer's field in Central Saanich. The hawk had just caught a duck and was sitting by the ditch guarding its prey. That man was Frank Beebe, one of North America's leading falconers, and now our friend and neighbor at Island View Beach. His peregrine falcons, Janey and Tad, had just hatched the first eggs in captivity in Canada, and almost the first eggs anywhere in the world. Joe Simonyi, from Ontario, another of our friends involved in trying to breed raptorial birds in captivity also achieved success in 1967 when one of his peregrine falcons laid an egg, though it didn't hatch. Joe had gone to the Queen Charlottes with David and was soon to move to the Island as well. The Saanich Peninsula was to become a center for peregrine propagation.

So it was not only cougars that were to blame in

bringing Dave's studies at university to a halt but falcons too. He was trying to capture Frank's breeding successes on film, collect birds for breeding stock, and build enclosures for them on our property. Most of the falcon nestlings went from the Charlottes to Frank's place, where Janey and Tad took over the responsibilities of raising them. It was a strange sight to see both parent birds share their nest ledge with a dozen fluffy white-bonneted babies whom they fed regularly beak to beak.

Four of the birds came to Vancouver where I was given the responsibility of raising them myself. Two I took to the classroom where the children daily weighed them, measured their feather growth, observed their behavior in their math and science classes, wrote poems and stories about them in their language classes, and drew them in their art classes. But we placed our desks far enough away from them in all classes to avoid their evacuation. Raptorial birds keep themselves clean by shooting their droppings far and wide over the edge of the nest and we didn't want to be in the firing line.

As the young in the wild instinctively stay on their nest ledges sometimes hundreds of feet above the pounding sea, and it would be several weeks yet before they fledged, I kept the falcons safe from harm at home by building them a shelf attached to the garage.

Two birds were given special attention: the pair of peregrines for H.R.H. Prince Philip, a gift from the premier of the province. David and Frank had collected a pair for the Prince a few years previously and presented them to him on a royal visit as the official gift from the people of the province. James Robertson Justice, a falconer as well as a movie star, had been keeping them for him in Scotland, and he was also to keep the second pair. But for a week or so, my class and I were Keepers of the Royal Falcons. Or were we Royal Keepers of the Prince's Falcons?

The Prince's birds were real fighters. As soon as we offered them pieces of food they'd wrest it from our hands with their terrible talons—and then take our hands too. No mouth-to-beak method were we going to use! David decided to exchange the Prince's ferocious ones for our tamer pair.

When the time came for the birds to be airmailed to Buckingham Palace by Canadian Pacific Airlines, the real problems began. David had arranged for the morning paper to take a photograph of a CP Air stewardess putting the birds on a plane. The airline was delighted, the Fish and Wildlife Branch was delighted, and the newspaper was delighted. Then a chance remark made by a CP Air public relations man asking if the premier was also delighted threw a real wrench in the works. When David made a routine check the provincial secretary said he knew nothing about it, and the premier when asked said he'd rather not have people know about his private gift to the Prince.

Then began a scurrying around from the top echelons to the bottom to try and get the news out of the paper. Since I had never had any luck either trying to get something out or trying to get something in unless it was some disaster, David tried. Due to his acquaintance with the photo editor, which had deepened somewhat after the last cougar crisis, a compromise was reached whereby the photo went in but the caption read that the birds were "reported" to be a gift for the Prince.

By the last week of June our falcons had gone with Haida and most of our belongings to the Island. I decided to invite the cougar foster families over for dinner. David, insisting that I couldn't pack, clean, and cook at the same time, phoned and uninvited them. Instead of the full-scale affair I'd planned, I baked cakes and cookies and we had just as good a time.

Our common interest was cougars, a source of happy times and a source of sad times, a source of laughter and a source of tears, though for me the time for tears had not yet arrived. As we sat on the porch and watched, Tom and Oola raced around the tree trunk in the middle of the lawn, a tree trunk we'd hauled in from the nearby woods for their exercise. Stephen, David, and Jonathan skylarked among them. For the cougars, too, the sad times were still to come.

At school the class arranged a farewell party, baked a cake, and gave me a Greek-embroidered shoulder bag to replace the one that had been ripped apart by Tom and Haida's tug-of-war.

Hilary gave us a party too, a garden party, but not in the usual style. The guests earned their supper at her apartment by working in our garden first. We mowed the lawns, dug out the dandelions, cut the edges, spruced up the rosebuds, and turned the turf where the bird tank had been. We even cleared the garage of contents left by previous tenants. Inside the house, I scoured the walls, cleaned the ceiling, and scrubbed the cupboards. The object of the enterprise was to leave the place in better shape than it had been before the days of seals and sea lions, sea birds, cougars, falcons, and other assorted creatures. Except for a sill that had been scratched by Tammy in one of her attempts to leave by the window (for which we left ten dollars), you would never have guessed that the house was a place where we'd lived with wild animals.

The last chore was to load the truck. The camera gear had already been packed or we would have taken a photo of the truck's cartoonlike contents as it trundled off—the rest of the furniture, the rest of the books, and the rest of the birds and animals, Sam, Tom, Oola, and the sea birds. Hilary and I took the tortoises on a later ferry.

The problems of moving the animals out of our tiny house in the middle of the city of Vancouver were small in comparison with the problems of moving into our dream property on the beach in the country near Victoria. The sad times were about to begin.

10

Cougars Cause Controversy

My parents were happy to know that this summer their daughter wasn't going off to a Never Never Land of sea-bird rookeries, rain-forest jungles, or alpine mountaintops. Instead she would mix cement, dig ditches, lay pipe, build fences, and paint cabins. Somehow it all sounded more civilized than humping packsacks, bouncing about in a rubber boat, or crawling about on my belly under an eagle nest scrounging for rotting food remains. While my parents-in-law looked after the coffee shop at Island View, I gladly looked after the animals and shared in the construction of the enclosures.

For our personal centennial project for 1967 David and I decided to build a huge cedar plank stockade 100 feet by 100 feet, behind which we would house all the animals temporarily till the log enclosure for the cougars could be completed. Of course as soon as you put up a fence everybody wonders what you are putting inside it, so we decided to put on a party for our neighbors to allay their suspicions. It was a happy affair at which we introduced the animals we'd brought with us from Vancouver, showed slides, and served refreshments. We explained that our property at Island View Beach would be a base for our activities in wildlife conservation. We would be trying to breed endangered species like peregrine falcons and bald eagles, trying to research the biology and aviculture of sea birds like the puffins, murres, auklets, and murrelets,

133

continuing community services like looking after the orphaned, abandoned, or sick animals that were brought to us, and preparing educational lecture and television programs.

Everybody admired the birds, tolerated the tortoises, played with the sea lion, and petted the cougars. Nobody voiced any worries and I felt warmly welcomed. Not yet had I learned the harsh fact of life that what people say to your face is not necessarily what they say behind your back.

Our assistant for the summer was Don Lyster, an enthusiastic teen-ager who had written asking for work after seeing some of our television programs. As construction is not as exciting as explorations into the wilderness, we tried to deter him but he refused to be daunted. He had the right kind of constitution for such around-the-clock activities as ours—polite, hardworking, and cheery. He did get to go on a few short-term expeditions that summer, up in a float plane counting eagles and over to a bird rookery to collect cormorants for Expo in Montreal. He survived such experiences as being air sick, climbing trees, descending cliffs, losing his boat and motor and rowing home, and working from daylight to dark.

As temporary housing for Tom and Oola, we built a sturdy concrete-floored double-wired exercise pen with an adjoining den and furnished it with ledges and logs. So they would feel at home in their new surroundings and because there was nowhere else to store it, I put in our old chesterfield from Vancouver. Tom had already started to tear out the stuffing so I left him to work on the rest. When the job was completed we sent it out to sea for burial.

Not wanting to scare anybody who saw a cougar outside a zoo cage, I used leashes when I took them for a walk on the beach or through the little-used park and farmland that surrounded us. Leashes were more for window dressing than actual control. The cougars would follow willingly or bounce along beside me, but they would not respond to pressure. As soon as they felt the collar tighten, they'd slump to the ground, so I'd be forced to drag them in the desired direction.

Inside the stockade Sam and Haida had a free run, as had the cougars while we were working there. The sea birds were kept in their individual plywood and wire tanks till we had finished landscaping their large walk-in aviary and pool. The falcon pens we built at that time were probably the best on the continent.

Life for me has always been a succession of crises and my first at Island View was losing a peregrine falcon before the enclosures were finished. Unfortunately, Tad, the breeding male falcon at Frank's place, had died and, fearing a disease that might spread to our own research birds, we brought all our falcons home to the stockade. The falcons' white down feathers had now given way to the fine gray plumage of the adult and they were ready to make their first flight. One of the females chose to make hers at the particular moment I walked into the pen to put down her chicken and water. As I opened the snow-fencing door she flew out above my head. Dave's first words were unprintable but when calm was restored, he and Don raced down the track to Frank's, borrowed a live trap, a noose, and one of his male falcons (a tiercel) to sit by it as an attraction. The retrieval system was set up in one of the nearby fields behind the dyke.

By the way that female falcon circled above my head and set off purposefully for the nearest hill, I had little hope of ever seeing it again. Fortunately—miraculously—the trap worked and the falcon was back in the pen within three days. Meanwhile, we built a walkway the length of the pens which served as a second enclosure if a bird flew out of the first. On several later occasions I realized the advantage of this safeguard.

The biggest construction problem was to provide enough water for cleaning all enclosures and for circulating in and out of the sea-bird pool. We borrowed four thousand dollars and tried to put in a pipe and pump system. This involved blasting a channel fourteen hundred feet out to sea, laying a plastic pipe, and then when that caved in through sucking sea water for

too great a distance, laying a metal one. When that was
ripped out in the first storm of the season, we had to
lay a second one weighted down by boulders and
sandbags on a vast raft of beachcombed logs. Even
when the pipe held and we thought our problems
were solved, the valves or the pumps broke down.
Every time the system failed, the sea birds, relying on
constantly flowing sea water for proper waterproofing
of their feathers, were in jeopardy. Long before, we
had given up on the idea of maintaining fish and
invertebrates.

The greatest disaster was the day Don forgot to turn
off the ingoing pump and sea water flowed all night
long at seventy gallons a minute onto the nearest
neighbor's potato fields. These belonged to the Michell
family, who had farmed the valley behind us for a
hundred years. Not that their fields were in production
at the time. They were lying fallow for two years following a plague of golden nematodes, and the Michells
were receiving government compensation. Nevertheless, they didn't want salt water to ruin their chances
of growing potatoes in the future. So we redoubled
our efforts to perfect construction.

While our minds and our bodies were occupied with
providing the best facilities possible for the animals
we had kept in one of the smallest back yards in
Vancouver, those of most of the neighbors were occupied in guessing what we were really doing behind
our quickly erected fence. They just didn't believe
that anybody could go to such trouble for so few animals. The most credible of their conclusions was that
we were establishing a zoo. Certainly David dreamed
of someday having his own wildlife exhibit, where he
could put into practice his talents at interpretation, but
it couldn't possibly be at Island View. Our six acres
weren't enough for even a parking lot; the problems
with water were insurmountable till city water came
to the country, the land on one side was public park,
and the Michells would never sell their potato fields
on the other side. If people had used their minds in-

stead of their feelings, they would have drawn the same conclusions.

A few of them came down after dark to peer through the fence. This was not only annoying but ironic. People were welcome to come in behind the compound any day to see the animals and what we were doing. Mother regaled them with long descriptions and showed them pictures displayed in the coffee shop and Father took them around and answered questions. David, Don, and I spent hours in explanation. Another tack people used was to phone the local municipal council and ask what was going on.

So when the party in the house, followed by daily lectures and demonstrations failed to satisfy everybody's curiosity, we decided to go to the next council meeting, explain our purposes all over again, and ask them to be reported in the local paper.

Thinking the evening would be quite routine, we drove to the council rooms. To our astonishment, who should alight from the adjacent cars but three of the families who lived behind us on the hill. "What's happening tonight that our little piece of the municipality is so well represented?" I whispered to Dave, feeling with some apprehension that we might be involved.

The suspicion was confirmed as Mr. Fowler, the leader of the little group, said, "We've come to follow the Hancock affair," after the Clerk asked the reason for their presence. Even the reeve seemed surprised at the number of people present. My trepidation increased. Councilor Galbraith remarked jocularly that he thought we were going to bring our cougars. Councilor Andrews said that he remembered me from television. Councilor Benn, the postmaster, also jolly, made some comment about all the mail we were getting. The atmosphere appeared informal and our reception favorable. What was there to worry about?

Just the cold, silent stares of Mr. Fowler, Mr. and Mrs. Spooner, and Mr. Worley boring into my back from the seat behind. Why was Mr. Worley there? Surely, living a couple of miles away near the highway, he had no interest in what went on behind our fence! I could guess Mr. Fowler's position. He owned the land directly behind us, was in the process of subdividing and building houses on it, and it was from a well underneath his basement that we got our drinking water, as a result of a complicated agreement undertaken by the previous owners of Island View. The Spooners were there as the Fowlers' friends.

We didn't have to wait till general business to learn of their involvement. The first item of correspondence was a protest letter signed by Mr. and Mrs. Fowler, Mr. and Mrs. Spooner, Mr. and Mrs. Worley, and the veterinarians, Mr. and Mrs. Powell, and a tenant of Mr. Fowler's. They were petitioning council to forbid us to ruin the peace and quiet of the rural countryside by developing a zoo at Island View Beach. They claimed that there would be sanitation problems, health problems, water problems, noise problems, and depreciation of property-value problems. Individually, Mr. Fowler complained that a cougar might escape and kill his children; Mr. Spooner complained that keeping two or three wild animals might be the thin end of the wedge in building a full-scale zoo; Mr. Worley confessed that he was using us as an instrument in his own complaint to council, namely, that it wasn't making its anti-noise bylaw stick by getting rid of the barking dogs that lived in a kennel next to his place.

While I was reeling under the shock of my first bout with politics, Councilor Salt, an elderly woman, chipped in with, "Mr. Reeve, Council, ladies and gentlemen, I have just discovered today on the phone from the Fish and Wildlife Branch that it is necessary to get a zoo permit in order to keep any wild animal, so I submit to you that the Hancocks must be setting up a zoo."

My faith in human nature was severely shaken by her words. David and I had always known that when the cougars were six months old we would have to get a zoo license, the official permit to be able to keep them at all. This did not mean, as the words implied, that we had a zoo; it was the name of the license that allowed the keeping of wild animals in captivity, whether it was one animal or a full-scale commercial development. Several weeks before, David had explained this to Councilor Salt when she had been invited to Island View Beach. I remembered how friendly she'd been, how she'd petted the cougars, how she'd praised our facilities, how she'd invited us to visit her, how much she'd looked like a great-aunt of mine. And I had felt like kissing her. More and more, I was beginning to learn about the world.

David, calm, serious, informed, stood up to reply. At times like these he was the reasoned diplomat and I was the emotional fool ready to burst out rashly in defense of what I thought and felt was right. David negated the first three issues listed by the opposition—namely, sanitation, health, and water—by reading the certificate of approval that our construction work had earned from the health inspector we had invited around. Then he showed our official permit from the Fish and Wildlife Branch to have the animals in our possession and emphasized again we weren't opening up a zoo at Island View Beach. He pointed out that Sam didn't bark, that Tom and Oola so far only purred and whistled, that our sea birds were silent, that our falcons screamed only in the mating season or when very much disturbed, and that our neighbors couldn't possibly hear any noise at all from our property due to distance.

"Ladies and gentlemen, I only need to keep five mammals at Island View, two cougars, one seal, one dog, and one wife [there was a titter from all but the petitioners], so if you limit me to five mammals, this would mean that I could meet a personal obligation to take in any sick and dying animal that comes to my door until its demise or release. Certainly, it wouldn't constitute a zoo or lower property values. The property is zoned commercial and if somebody else bought Island View he would very likely develop it in a far more disadvantageous way than keeping two cougars, one seal, and sixteen sea birds behind a cedar plank fence. And as far as safety is concerned, the cougars are already housed in stronger facilities than any others I know of in the province. A future plan is to house them in a landscaped structure of logs and nine-gauge wire."

A bearded farmer, who had been sitting beside me and making retorts under his breath all through the meeting, finally stood up to speak. Whatever he was mumbling had sounded intimidating and I dreaded the vocal version. To my surprise he was an ally. "Dave Hancock is one of our local boys who has made good. We watch him on television, we hear him on radio, we read his wife's articles. Over the years he has contributed much to our community by his research and public education. We should be proud of him and let him continue his work."

Within a month we would have to apply for official permission for a permit to keep the animals in the municipality so that the one we presently possessed from the Fish and Wildlife Branch could be renewed. With that, the meeting ended.

I plucked up courage to go over to Mr. Worley and ask in wide-eyed amazement how he could possibly use us as innocent victims for his own purposes. I didn't expect much sympathy for anything to do with animals since he'd once said there were three words that one shouldn't use to promote tourism in British Columbia and they were "wilderness," "wildlife," and "Indians." I had to laugh later when a Hollywood film star said publicly on the radio that the best thing he'd seen in British Columbia was a bald eagle.

Mr. Worley at least had the courtesy to speak. He laughed. "That's politics, Mrs. Hancock; it happens all the time." I would have said more, but David ushered me away to the car. "Just don't open your mouth in public. You'll only make matters worse," he warned.

Further post-mortems had to wait till we were home. There was little else we could do except wait for the next meeting at which we would formally present our request for a municipal permit. All the stated objectives to housing our cougars had been covered.

What was difficult to fight were the hidden ones. Mr. Fowler didn't want anybody living in front of him who might affect his million-dollar views. And for all the council's friendliness to us, it didn't want too much change either. It had vetoed a Highways Department sign directing motorists to Island View Beach because it feared an influx of people would necessitate an extension of water and sewage facilities. As it was, we now provided water for campers, collected all the litter, burned all the waste, and set out garbage cans. None of the Hancocks wanted to carry on the coffee-shop business; we provided it as a service to those who came to the beach.

If we hadn't believed so wholeheartedly in public education by firsthand experience we wouldn't have interrupted our work constantly to entertain and hopefully educate beachgoers to a more objective view of predators. After the council meeting I was probably cooler to visitors than before. I was always wondering what the thoughts were behind the smiles. Nevertheless, it was still a joy to stop work and go into the pen and play with the cougars whenever people came. Tom would give that squeak of recognition as soon as he saw me and I'd whisper, "Come on, Tom, give me a kiss and show the people you're not the vicious bad guy of the animal world." He'd then put his front paws around my neck, rub his face against my cheek, and purr so that it could be heard many yards away. Then I'd patiently answer the same old questions.

"Aren't you afraid he'll turn on you when he's older?"

"I've read all about how they attack and kill people? Is he going to do that?"

No, I told them, I was not afraid that these cougars would ever attack me with intent to harm. To them I was their mother. However, just as they could hurt each other, so also could they hurt me, in sheer high spirits, in enthusiastic affection of ebullient instinctive play. I tried to always answer within the limits of my personal experience and not to make the same mistakes as my skeptics who jumped to conclusions at one extreme, as I could so easily have done at the other. Most people gained their convictions about cougars from a lion attack on a small girl in a Nanaimo zoo some years before or bloodthirsty tales of tiger hunting in India. By 1967 there had only been one death by cougar in British Columbia, that of a seven-year-old Indian boy in Kyuquot on Vancouver Island in 1949, after the child had surprised an eighty-one-pound male cougar on its raccoon kill.

David was never happy about me petting and playing with Tom and Oola in front of people. "Listen, Lyn, I don't want it known that you are sentimental about cougars. Don't keep saying you 'love' them or that you are their 'mother.' People will just laugh at you behind your back and think you are a kook. That's just not the way to have a long-term effect on changing people's attitudes."

Although my perspective at the time encompassed little more than a huddle of kittens, motherless and maligned, I was at the same time collecting every word written about cougars by the media, tape-recording every observation made by anyone who has ever seen a cougar, and monitoring Maurice Hornocker's work in Idaho. Hopefully, my gut feelings about cougars would find some support in scientifically analyzed evidence.

We took the cougars out for walks at dusk only when everybody had left, and kept them on leashes, not because they were any less tractable than before but to allay the fears of those who might be peering through their binoculars from the top of the hill. We always followed the same path, a mile-and-a-half run through the bushes to Frank's place.

One night I took Tom to Frank's for dinner to celebrate their catch of a twenty-pound salmon. Vera, Frank's wife, drew the line at having a cougar in her kitchen as a table companion, so I tied Tom to a post in their basement. He kept up such a commotion of piercing calls and whistles that the meal was interrupted several times by me rushing off downstairs to comfort him. When I reached him he expressed his happiness in a succession of leaps and licks and purrs.

After dinner Vera let me arrange her bathroom for photography. I wanted a shot of Tom sitting in her washbasin, a pair of paws dangling down on one side and a long tail drooping down on the other. It was his favorite position in the bathroom, but we never had the camera there at the right time. Photography in a house full of cougars is more talked about than executed. David had infinite patience in the wild but none at all in the house. As a result those shots were left to me.

A hundred times I deposited Tom in the Beebe basin and a hundred times, before I could adjust the camera, he jumped out and into my arms. I finally capitulated and sat on the floor with him till it was time to go home, or somebody wanted to use the bathroom.

We arrived back at the stockade just as the chief of police was getting out of his car. Tom was in my arms but we were still perturbed that our cougar was caught out of his cage, especially by the municipal police. However, Mr. Brownlee had brought his family and relatives from Saskatchewan especially to see the cougars. The visitors patted and petted and didn't think it incongruous that they were dressed in formal dinner attire to do it or that Tom should be behind bars.

On the first Monday in August we spruced up again for the council meeting. We arrived a little late and were surprised to see so many cars in the parking lot. All being quiet, we went inside to find the room packed. There were no chairs vacant. The Hancock affair had certainly rejuvenated an interest in municipal business. There were many new faces, including those of the Michells whose most senior member was on the council. Fortunately, we hadn't salt-watered their potato field again.

I was under Dave's orders to keep my mouth shut

but I did anticipate grunting in the background with Don. Foreseeing this, my husband quickly motioned me to a corner well away from him. Fools rush in . . . so I deposited myself close to the Fowlers and the Spooners on the enemy firing line. I even smiled, but I noticed it wasn't returned. The other three families listed on the petition were not represented, so I realized anew that the whole opposition was really only one man.

While the routine business was being conducted I studied the councilors, the ones who would vote, and I tried to guess their feelings. Councilor Andrews, who kept budgies and wild birds by the hundreds, had visited us only that day. "I can't understand how anybody would beef about your animals," he'd said. Councilors Galbraith and Benn had visited too, brought their families, and said they'd back us. Mrs. Salt, with a nose for publicity, often supported a minority or head-line-getting issue, but she showed me at the last meeting where she stood. Tom Michell, a long-time friend of the senior Hancocks and a fellow fireman with Father, was a real enigma. I couldn't see how we could have been a threat to him even if we did have a zoo. Potatoes don't need a view. There remained the reeve and Councilor Mollard and they both looked and sounded dull. I could read nothing of their thoughts in their faces and that always perturbs me.

During correspondence the clerk read a letter from the municipal solicitors saying that no animals could be kept on the property until it had been rezoned for such special purposes. New bylaws had been passed a few weeks before our arrival at Island View Beach for the summer, listing the commercial activities that could legally function there. As could be expected, none of them designated the housing of two cougars. Another letter was from the Fowlers asking the council to visit us. That was strange since most of the council had already come on our express invitation. The only families who hadn't come to look behind the fence were those on the petition.

The reeve then passed judgment. "The only course of action left to us is to amend the bylaw," he pronounced in a manner suggestive of God. "We cannot vote on this question at this meeting. We must wait till everybody's had time to prepare a campaign and public hearing. I'd suggest this to take place in four months' time."

We didn't have that time. By the end of August our temporary permit to keep Tom and Oola would expire. We had received no further answers to our letters and advertisements made months before in Vancouver. Tom and Oola would have to be killed.

Don put a hand over my mouth. David, a little heated, jumped up. "Sir, if I can keep four cougars in the middle of a city like Vancouver without regulations, and animals of all sorts are kept right now in Central Saanich, such as monkeys, ocelots, and wild birds, why waste the taxpayers' money by putting on a campaign and public hearing sometime in the future when all who might have an interest in the matter are presently sitting in this room?"

"Only domestic animals and horses are mentioned in the act as legally allowed in Central Saanich," the reeve droned on. "There are contraventions to existing laws but people have not found out about them as they have yours."

"Yes, we've done our best to advertise the fact we live with animals," Dave admitted ironically.

The campaign was requested only for Tom and Oola. Everybody turned a blind eye on Sam and the birds. And the maimed and orphaned foundlings, whatever the species, that would continue to find haven at Island View. Right then we were housing a second seal, prematurely born, that we called Susan. The Fish and Wildlife Branch were to busy to be bothered. The S.P.C.A. was inundated with cats and dogs. Educating people to the true nature and function of predators was not seen as a service.

But even if a public hearing was held in four months, what were Tom and Oola to do until then?

The same question also occurred to Mrs. Salt: "We don't want to put the animals out on the street." (Hardly! I thought as I sneaked a look at the Fowlers and Spooners.) "The Michells wouldn't want them on their potato fields either. To shoot the cougars would be the only solution and that might make things nasty in the press." (Not to mention with me.) "We must do something while we are waiting for clarification of the processing of the zoning bylaw."

I felt that Mrs. Salt's motivations were questionable. I think Councilor Andrews meant to be kind. "I move that council allow the Hancocks to keep the cougars temporarily for four months till we have an opportunity to hold the public hearing."

At that moment the Spooners mentioned something dire under their breath and stood up with the Fowlers to leave. As they reached the exit the reeve asked them if they had anything to say. Whatever they were muttering about the four-month extension was not fit for public consumption and they left without a word. Only one other person did have something to say and that was an ex-council member who stuttered some kind of opposition to wild animals in the municipality. In a surprisingly heated rebuke, the reeve accused him of courting votes for the next election.

The enemy left without learning there could be no legal four-month extension period. The rest of the councilors, even the majority who were in favor of the cougars, couldn't officially vote on temporary housing since it would seem they were going against their own bylaws. So the easy way out was just to say nothing. Not to say yes and not to say no. It was fence-sitting that functioned as a negative. As our permit from the Fish and Wildlife Branch was conditioned upon a definite yes, to say nothing became a definite no. Council could blame technicality and technicality had no conscience.

Outside in the parking lot a reporter beckoned us. "You could fight this thing easily. Why don't you enlist the aid of a few influential people, people you know on the papers and in radio stations or at the university or museum? Why don't you get hold of Bob Fortune and Doug Collins and tell them the "Klahanie" and "Seven O'Clock Show" cougars are in trouble? Your neighbors don't have a leg to stand on with their objections; they're totally invalid."

To me the issue was clear. Whether my cougars were love objects, child substitutes, or mere teaching tools, they were worth fighting for. It was no cliché when I said Tom and Oola would be shot over my dead body.

For David the issue was not clear cut. Tom might have been important to him once. Other priorities had now taken their place. In bed that night he gave me the ultimatum. "Look, Lyn, now that the building here is well under way, I'm going to take the folks' camper over to Vancouver, park it at Hilary's or the university, and spend the next four months finishing my thesis. It has to be done this winter or not at all. I do not have time now to go through with a full-scale promotion campaign, to get the press and the people on the side of the cougars. We'll try to find temporary housing for them at some zoo till the university commitments are over and then drum up support for a public hearing after that. So you choose—two cougars or my thesis."

It was really no choice at all. Reason had to prevail over emotion. What was ironic was that we lost not only the cougers but the thesis as well, though I didn't know that till much later.

We had just over two weeks to find a home for Tom and Oola. The obvious choice was Rudy's Pet Park, a few miles away on the other side of the peninsula. But Rudy was trying to phase out his operation by selling all his bigger animals. He had problems of his own. He might sell our cougars but he didn't want to be bothered looking after them. When we arrived to discuss the matter with him, he was trying to tranquilize Flap and Lisa, two of his African lions. He had managed to find buyers for them as well as a cage full of cougars nearby.

This was the first time I had seen adult cougars in a

zoo. I sat down beside them and made the same sounds Tom and Oola did. They acted no differently. They pricked up their ears, came to the edge of the cage, pressed the side of their head against the wire, and purred. I scratched behind their ears. Suddenly another visitor came down the path, broke off a branch, and poked it through the bars. He was trying to stroke the cougar too but with more caution. The stick was clearly seen as a sign of aggression. The cougars snarled and leaped to the safety of their shelf in the corner. They did not come back.

David approached with the man who was buying Rudy's lions: Ted Derby from California. The same man who had taken Lara and Tammy when there were no other offers. I was anxious for news of them. The class had written, even visited several times during the summer to ask about their welfare. But with Tammy being so obstreperous, I didn't want to hear that she had caused problems. I had no worries about Lara. With a little difficulty amid the confusion of men trying to tranquilize two lions and four cougars and then getting them into trailers for the long drive to Los Angeles, I put my questions a little apprehensively.

"Oh, they're in private homes now," Ted mentioned offhandedly. "Tammy had to be declawed but she is now a beautiful animal and is loved by her new owners."

I guess in this business animals are borrowed and exchanged, bought and sold, and the fewer questions you ask the better. I wonder if a wild animal can ever be owned. It seems not that you own it but that it owns you. In the case of Tammy and Lara the animals had been sent south without payment received, so I felt I still had the right to ask about their welfare.

In our search for a home for Tom and Oola, we next drove out to Dick van der Meer's sanctuary twenty-five miles away in Sooke. Dick, a jovial Dutchman, lives in unorganized territory free from municipal regulation and one where the Fish and Wildlife Branch legally could have given the necessary permit. Dick is a wonderful man and lives with his animals on a beautiful piece of property in the hills beside a picturesque lake, but one of the disadvantages of his place was a lack of electricity. He could house the cougars but not their meat.

A third possibility was Jim Oyen's small zoo on the highway near Duncan, about thirty-five miles away. We had found a home for Susan, the harbor seal there. Jim loved her and had made a fine landscaped pool. But he didn't have similar amenities for two cougars. He had fitted his animals to his pocketbook.

Rudy had the enclosures, Dick had the land, and Jim had the heart. Where were Tom and Oola to go? We decided to ask Jim if he had any cage that could be modified for the cougars. It was lucky we did because he was just about to leave with Al Oeming of the Alberta Game Farm for the winter lecture tour. Jim is a very kindly man and like Dick has a good way with animals. He readily agreed to provide an enclosure on his land if we did the work. During his absence, his wife, Tosca, was responsible for feeding and cleaning all the animals as well as manning the entrance gate and caring for three children.

We arranged to repair and extend the enclosure and move the cougars in at the end of the month. I promised to bring them food each weekend and clean out the cage. Providing the physical necessities was a temporary solution to our problem, but I worried about keeping the animals tame and amenable to people with control so remote. Only by constant association and a buildup of mutual trust could we hope to maintain the friendship between ourselves and the cougars as they continued to develop.

Everything was coming to an end. Don was going home to his family in the interior after working slavishly all summer. Mother and Father were returning to their home, which temporary tenants had nearly wrecked during their absence. The visitors were going home from the beach. And our permits were coming to an end.

Four days before the end of August, David and I took Tom and Oola from behind the fence at Island View and ran away with them to sea.

11

Last Days of Freedom

Our final days of freedom on Little Darcy Island, about twelve minutes' fast boat ride from Island View Beach, were the most idyllic ones I have spent in my life.

For some, an island confines. For me, it liberates. It appeals to my sense of romance—exotic, sentimental, optimistic, unrealistic.

There's something about an island that fulfills all my fantasies. An island floats between realities. Like a stage it provides suspension of belief. Physically separated from the rest of the world, one can feel mentally separated as well, drifting in some Forest of Arden.

For the cougars and myself, it was a stay of execution. For David, it was a chance to take some pictures.

We packed the boat with camping gear, camera equipment, and clothes bags, and then went back for the cougars. We had not been taking them for walks lately and once out of the compound, they pulled back obstinately on the leash. While Dave manned the outboard motor and kept the boat steady at the shoreline, I dragged the reluctant cougars down the beach. They protested every step of the way. The few onlookers who curbed their fear of cougars enough to stand around and watch were probably amazed to find that the animals much preferred to return to their prison behind the fence than the new world of water ahead.

When we eventually got to the boat I lifted Tom and Oola aboard. At seven months and well-fed, they were each around fifty pounds, so it was done with much difficulty. With one hand I tried to stuff Oola down in the bilge of the heavily laden boat. With the other I wrestled with Tom's greater bulk to drag him over the edge. Neither cougar showed much enthusiasm for going on a boat ride. David was attempting the impossible as well by lending a third hand to keep the cougars aboard while pushing us all off from shore, jumping in himself, and at the same time trying to snatch some film of it all. At last he put down the camera, started the outboard, and we were away.

Startled by the sudden reverberation of the motor, Tom immediately jumped overboard. Though we had lived by the sea for a couple of months, this was his first swim. With cougars pulling my arms in two different directions, I was in no position to drag his wet weight from the water and still keep Oola in the boat too. David let the motor fend for itself, and with both hands, leaned over the side to haul out a dripping cougar by its neck fur.

I watched apprehensively as our big male cougar unsheathed his long sharp claws and snatched at the inflated rubber sides of the boat. Any second I expected to see the material burst with a sudden puncture. Amazingly, it withstood the pressure from the cougar's huge thumb, the deadly dew claw. There was not even a scratch on the rubber.

We sped away from the shoreline in a cloud of spume from our bows and a cloud of spray from Tom as he shook himself clear of the salt water.

There was an initial restlessness as both cougars tried to find a comfortable place in the bottom of the boat among the cargo. I loosened the leashes that I'd used to drag them away from Island View and encouraged them to lie down beside each other in the bilge. Sitting there produced the inevitable results, as it does for any mammal that puts his feet in cold water or turns on the water tap in the bathroom. We hadn't provided sandboxes in the boat, so clean-up took a little time.

From then on, the rest of the voyage was uneventful. Periodically, I would give the cougars a reassuring hug and every now and then, Tom would lean over the edge and snarl at the sea. I had to laugh. It seemed such an ineffectual way to express his views of this unknown phenomenon.

Within twenty minutes the forested shores of our island loomed close enough to attract Oola's attention. While poor old Tom marveled at things at his feet or under his nose, Oola, ever alert, had seen that land was near.

"Let her swim ashore if she wants and perhaps Tom'll follow," David suggested when we were within a hundred yards.

Believing that cats dislike water, I was surprised to see Oola suddenly lift herself from the gunny sacks, walk along the pontoon, balance neatly on the bow, then dive straight in with the expertise of the professional. With ears flattened and only her head showing above the water, she struck out unerringly for shore. She was brisk and efficient.

Tom scrambled past me to the bow and whistled after her. "Hey, I want to come too," he seemed to be saying. Although he had poor vision, his sense of smell told him there was land ahead and he wanted to be there. This boating was not for cougers. With one ear standing to attention to catch her brother's voice and the other still flat to the water, Oola returned her brother's call. That did it. Tom plunged overboard in pursuit. Reaching land, Oola dragged her dripping fur up the pebbled beach, shook herself like a dog, and then sat on her haunches to await Tom.

Though not well documented, the swimming ability of cougars is considerable. They have been seen to swim four hundred yards across the Nanaimo City Reservoir and one mile across the Arrow Lakes in the Kootenay. One cougar was known to swim five miles between Mitlenatch and Hernando Islands off Vancouver Island. Although cougars while traveling will avoid water puddles like any cat and use deadfalls as bridges to cross small creeks, they will voluntarily swim such rivers as the Horsefly or Fraser in order to find game or elude pursuit.

The reunion of the two cougars was a joy to watch. Oola lifted her front paw and touched Tom on the shoulder. There was mutual nuzzling and squeaking, then Oola set off up the beach. Head down and concentrating on those moving legs in front of him, Tom followed for about fifty yards. Then he stopped and looked back. He ignored Oola's shrill insistent whistle. Oola, the siren.

By this time we had reached the shore and were busily pulling the boat up to the logs. Tom sat on his haunches and whistled as if to say, "Well, come on. When are you coming?"

One would have expected the cougars to celebrate their sudden freedom by dashing off through the undergrowth but such was Tom's attachment to us that he waited. Oola was more inclined to go exploring by herself, but when she found Tom didn't follow, she also came back. While both cougars gamboled around in the grass, David and I set up a crude camp on a grassy knoll by the edge of the trees a few yards above the beach. Since warm sunny weather was forecast we put together a simple lean-to of saplings for a tent frame, covered it with tarpaulin, and lay our sleeping bags underneath. So that we could spend as much time exploring the world of the island with Tom and Oola, we had brought prepared food with us to save cooking. We would eat chicken with the cougars, the only difference being that theirs was raw.

It is hard to imagine a more delightful island than Little Darcy, about the most southerly of the Gulf Islands and close to Victoria. At low tide it is almost two islands separated by a picturesque lagoon. At high tide it is shaped like the cotyledons of a bean. You can walk around it leisurely in about three quarters of an hour to discover endless variety at every bend. With its sandy beaches, pebbled coves, flowery meadows, and rocky outcroppings, it is a mecca for the photographer. Most islands in the Pacific Northwest, if uninhabited, are heavily forested, but on Little Darcy you can stroll through its heart almost as easily as you walk its shoreline. Its vegetation is comparatively sparse and the trails that were cut in the days when it was used as a leper colony are not yet overgrown. These and an old stone house are now the only visible signs of the island's interesting history. Its colorful present is highlighted by a profusion of spring and summer wild-flowers and its many distinctive arbutus trees, whose straggly trunks with their red papery bark lean out from rocky bluffs and look over the sea.

Although we picked up a few old cans and raked over the remains of a campfire, few people frequent this lovely island. Like ourselves, all are trespassers because the island is privately owned by millionaire Americans of Boeing Company fame.

My chief fantasy is that one day the absentee owners will come along and tell me that since I am Little Darcy's strongest supporter, I can live there for the rest of my life for a dollar a year. Or perhaps I shall do some service for my country so that Ottawa will offer me my dearest wish. Then I will build a log house with lots of glass windows and a stone fireplace and roam the island with my cougar companions. Dreams.

We let Oola be our guide. We followed as the cougars chased around the island, as they ran along the beach in long loping strides, as they clambered over the boulders, and as they threw their full weight against our legs to knock us off balance, then jumped on our backs to romp on the grass.

Tom was noticeably less agile than his sister. While Oola would climb up a steeply inclined rock or log, then jump nimbly to the ground, Tom would wait at the top and squeak shrilly till we helped him down. A cougar is graceful whatever it does—whether walking, running, leaping, or just lying down. Oola was the typical cougar, the epitome of easy feline grace, a lovely Cleopatra.

Once I asked a thousand people to describe a cougar and the two adjectives most commonly given were "beautiful" and "graceful," even from those who disliked the animal intensely.

Perhaps a cougar's next most noticeable feature is its tail. It is long and hangs downward in an elegant curve. It nearly touches the ground, then it levels out and curves upward at the tip. Despite gory descriptions in traditional literature the cougar doesn't lash its tail to show fury and malevolence. Nor does it carry it rolled or curled up and always pointed to the left side, as one early zoologist claimed after studying a live specimen in a zoo. But it does often twitch the end of it from side to side, usually before a sudden movement. Although long, about a third the length of its body, the tail is not used for climbing but it probably helps in balance. Some animals have tails that seem stuck on as extra appendages but a cougar's tail is a naturally harmonious extension of its body. It, like the cougar, is the quintessence of aesthetic beauty and practical efficiency.

Because most of the pictures I had seen of cougars in print were of animals in trees, which is how most people see them, I expected Oola to leap instinctively into the arbutus trees. Their crooked trunks and distinctive branches invited climbing and I knew cougars preferred high places in the house after having shooed them down many times from shelves and window sills. However, only once on Little Darcy did Oola jump to a low limb and then she just stood there. She possessed all the strength and pliancy and balance needed to climb to the topmost branches. All that seemed lacking was the desire. Tom, on the other hand, lounged on the ground underneath the overhanging branches. Oola may have looked like Cleopatra, but Tom looked like some regal Caesar.

Wild cougars escape their enemies, such as barking dogs, by leaping into trees, where their relaxed attitudes imply that they feel safe there. Only once to my knowledge has a cougar been described in a tree and not pursued there by barking dogs. On that occasion the cougar was chasing a raccoon. You would expect that an animal with its strength, its jumping ability, its soft pliant body, which gives it a ready adjustment to a comfortable position on a branch, would spend some time in trees apart from using them as places of retreat. Indeed, many observers have noted the strong scent a cougar leaves in some trees, but it has not been determined if at the same time the scent was left by a hotly pursued cougar.

Tom and Oola didn't use trees as safe retreats, but they did use them for other purposes. It seemed they practiced balancing on the driftwood along the beach, just as children do at play. They stretched along the logs and raked their powerful forepaws in long sweeps to sharpen their claws. They stood up against the trunks of trees and scratched deep gashes in the bark. It seemed they reveled in the feeling such movements gave their muscles.

A cougar's claws are long and sharp, strongly curved to hold live prey. They are withdrawn in walking but extended in climbing and slashing. The dew claw or thumb is especially strong and powerful. It can rip out the fur and leave long naked welts in the skin of another cougar. I have seen deep scars made on the forepaws of several male cougars by others of the same sex, probably fighting over females and possibly over territory.

Tom and Oola used their claws to scrape up dirt and leaves to cover their feces both in their sawdust box at home and on the island. Such behavior served the purpose of keeping their surroundings clean and free from smell in the limited area of their enclosure. In the wild it may have been an instinctive action to suppress signs of their presence. Few observers have seen cougars do this in the wild and where they have, it has been done mostly by females at their kill or other special sites.

There are other reasons for scraping up dirt, leaves, and other debris into what is called a scratch pile or scent post. It is thought that such action represents some form of communication between cougars to indicate that an adult is in residence of a particular area, to bring cougars together, or to maintain distance between them. They probably tell one cougar if another cougar is ready to mate or not. Only a fifth of these scratch piles in a sample of eighty-six made by one of Maurice Hornocker's colleagues contained urine and feces.

Skate Hames of the Fish and Wildlife Branch told me once that he counted forty scratch piles in two miles in an area noted at the time for large numbers of cougars. And in another highly populated area he counted nine under an old hemlock. "It looked like a regular post office," he commented with his usual ability to get to the heart of the matter. However, on Hernando Island, which is only four square miles in area, he killed one old male cougar that had lived there alone for a year but had not made a single scratch pile. "Because there was nobody to write to," Skate declared.

Cats, like bobcats, tigers, lions, leopards, and cheetahs, create signposts by deliberately urinating on vegetation or rocks. Cougars do have scent glands and it is believed that they deposit secretions from these glands at their scrape sites, but wildlife workers have not observed them doing it in the same way as the other cats.

As we walked along the almost overgrown trails on Little Darcy Tom and Oola often stopped to sniff, though in most cases we didn't know what it was they sniffed at. They lifted their heads, parted their jaws, narrowed their eyes, and grimaced. This behavior is called "flehmen" by scientists and in some situations it has been seen as a response to another cougar's urine. By the look on the cougar's face you would think the grimace displays distaste, but this is not believed to be the case. I must admit I never saw Tom or Oola do it when they sniffed a flower. To each his own, I guess.

After the initial outburst of bounds and leaps the cougars settled down to a relaxed exploration of the island. They used the trails and strolled the beaches but more often they avoided the open, sunny areas to spend more time in the shady places. As an Australian sun worshiper and camera enthusiast, I found this personally disappointing, although as a student of cougar behavior, I knew it conformed with the usual observation that cover is important to a cougar. On Vancouver Island logging initially opened up much of the dense forest and provided the habitat for an expansion in numbers of deer and consequent expansion in numbers of cougar. Yet cougars avoid crossing over open logging slashes or stump farms and prefer to travel under cover at the edges of the openings.

Though obviously more trusting than wild cougars, Tom and Oola still exhibited an inherent caution, a distrust for things unfamiliar and strange, despite their sheltered life with man in captivity and the love that had always been shown them. Noise seemed to frighten them most. They had escaped the noise of our outboard by diving into the sea, and whenever they heard a motorboat come close to Little Darcy, they dived into the bushes.

During the afternoon I tried to entice them into the sea for a swim. Only Tom, faithful as always, followed me out into the water. Oola stayed by the shore, balanced her hind haunches on a boulder, hunched her forepaws back on the same rock, stretched out her long neck, and lapped at the salt water. Tom, meanwhile, swam around me. I wouldn't say he enjoyed swimming. Rather he came because I called, as Oola had called him to the island in the morning. When he followed me back to the beach, Oola ignored me but greeted Tom at the water's edge with the same lifted right forepaw she had used earlier.

We finished the day by flopping down among the flowers of a lush grassy meadow. Deep rumbling purrs of catlike contentment seemed to shake the ground. The cougars yawned and rolled over till their noses were buried in clumps of vividly scarlet Indian paintbrush plants.

Oola, as one could now predict, kept her distance some yards away from the rest of us at the edge of the grass but Tom, who wouldn't move unless I followed, lay down and rested his head on mine. Though small in relation to the rest of his body, it was too heavy for my comfort so I shifted it gently. Content, he sprawled out on his side, placed his forepaws on my neck, and went to sleep purring. With an island of one's own, such moments could last forever. Tom had given me his complete trust and confidence and it was a responsibility I did not take lightly. Only circumstances far out of my control could ever cause me to betray his gift.

Toward sunset we threw each of them a chicken. In the manner of domestic cats and dogs, they grabbed them in midair and ran off growling possessively to the nearest available piece of cover. Believing that a whole animal provides a more balanced diet than a part, we always gave our cougars whole chickens, many times with the feathers intact. They tore off most of the feathers and left most of the entrails but devoured everything else. Similarly in the wild, a cougar cuts out the stomach of large prey like deer or elk with its teeth and rolls it away from the rest of the meat with its paws. It often eats the liver, heart, and lungs first, then the rib and shoulder area. Most of the carcass is eaten and, contrary to traditional opinion, cougars are seldom wasteful. A predator's meals are few and far between, so there is little reasonable biological advantage for being so.

If the cougar intends to return to its kill it will cover the carcass with snow or available sticks, leaves, dirt, or hair. Tom and Oola rarely covered their food remains because on their diet of mainly fish and chicken, they left little but the entrails. These they would sometimes cover, perhaps in an effort at fastidiousness, though there were no scavengers in their enclosure. Maybe it was instinctive, a fixed action pattern. Howard Smith, of Idaho, took a six-month-old cougar kitten with him when he went to bring home his cow elk kill. "It was cute to see him try to cover up the leg of the elk with snow just like his mother would have done if he had seen her," he remarked.

Several people have noted the cougar's fondness for blood. The animal has been known to puncture the jugular vein of its prey with a neat hole like a syringe, take a drink of blood, and leave the meat. I noticed that Tom and Oola were fond of bloody liver but the food items they were given were too small to test their reactions to similar situations in the wild.

They were very fond of water, as has been observed of cougars in the wild. Oola was even prepared to drink salt water from the sea. Like domestic cats they often ate grass, believed in some way to condition the stomach. Zoo cougars, deprived of vegetation in their concrete cages, can be seen pulling at blades of grass through the wires.

Satisfied with their meal, Tom and Oola groomed after dinner in the manner of all house cats. They licked away pieces of flesh from between their claws and then licked the other parts of their bodies to keep their fur clean and glossy. Now that they were seven months old their spots had all but disappeared, though faint reminders of their kittenhood were apparent on their legs and undersurface. Most of their coat now was a uniformly golden reddish brown that gives the cougar its scientific name *Felis concolor*. Against the dried grass of Little Darcy at the end of the summer, it furnished the same protective coloration that the spotted coat did in earlier days.

Just at sunset David suddenly stood up and put on his parka. "I think I'll go back home and get Haida. It won't take long," he said with sudden inspiration. "She'd enjoy being here and she probably misses her playmates. Give the cats more exercise too."

I wondered if the cougars would be more active at night or during the day. Outdoors on the island would give me more of an opportunity of finding out than at home, where I didn't see them during the night now that they were not sleeping with us.

Traditionally, it has been thought that a cougar is strictly a nocturnal animal. Maurice Hornocker told me that in Idaho cougars hunted almost as much in the day as at night. Of course the movements of the predator must essentially follow those of their prey and also take into consideration possible disturbance from man. So it is more likely that the cougar stalks his prey at dusk or in the early morning and lays up in the middle of the day. In nature, round pupils tend to denote an animal that hunts mostly in the daylight, like the African lion. The cougar has vertical linear pupils capable of considerable expansion, so it seems naturally endowed to be mostly nocturnal.

Since Tom and Oola were not responsible for killing their own prey, their movements depended more upon our own than their instinctive ones. Still, their day had been full of unaccustomed exercise and now that they were well fed, it would be interesting to see whether they preferred to rest as darkness approached or wanted to forage and explore anew. Of course the experiment was hardly a scientific one with Haida as a distracting element.

As soon as the cougars and I heard the roar of the returning motor we raced down to the water. What a confusion of whistles, barks, purrs, and laughter as Haida joyously scampered out of the boat and joined us. It had been a good idea. They could play with Haida far more boisterously than we could ever let them play with us. Even Oola, gradually accustomed to the dog again, joined in.

They went off exploring on their own though Tom was still hesitant about leaving me. Now that it was dark I didn't worry about strangers appearing on the island and getting their guns out at the sight of our wild animals. If they didn't return of their own accord, we would be able to find them easily in the morning.

David and I lay in our sleeping bags under the clear, night sky while the cougars trotted off down the beach, this time with Haida in the lead. Tom and Oola didn't seem to worry now about taking the more open route.

Somehow I couldn't sleep with the animals away. There seemed to be so little time left for us all to be together. And I worried about Tom getting into trouble in his efforts to follow his more nimble companions. After about two hours I decided to communicate some kind of curfew. I sat in the moonlight and called "Toooo-om!" There was no answer. The trio must be on the far side of the island.

Unzipping my sleeping bag, I crawled out and pulled on my boots. Down at the lagoon I called again and this time there was a faint answering whistle. I didn't follow but continued to call to see if he would come to me. Gradually, his whistles increased in intensity. I could hear the rustle of bodies moving through the underbrush toward me. I waited. They were all coming.

The next moment, bursting into the moonlight on the bank above my head, was Tom in the lead. The others straggled up behind and jumped easily down beside me. Tom hesitated. Then as I called again, he landed in a scramble in my arms. I staggered back under his weight and fell onto the sand. He seemed thankful to be back.

We walked back to camp together. David grunted from somewhere down in his sleeping bag. I motioned Haida to a nearby bush or she would have tried to lick him out of it. Oola lay down beside the dog at a sedate distance, not intertwined as in the days of the cardboard box.

Tom knew where he was going to sleep—alongside my head as he had during his afternoon siesta. I had no need of a sleeping bag. Mine was now his warm shaggy fur.

To stroll freely on this Shangri-la of an island with all that one loved was Paradise for me.

Soon we would return to civilization.

12

Imprisoned in the Zoo

I sit here now ten years later at the typewriter trying to describe my feelings as I took Tom and Oola to the zoo. I start a dozen times and a dozen times I tear the page from the machine. I remember the feelings that my upbringing tells me should be suppressed, not expressed—the bitterness, the anger, perhaps the hate. I remember the resentment as we drove away from Island View with the kittens, resentment that intensified as we passed the neighbors on the hill.

Jim Oyen had already left Duncan for the winter film tour with Al Oeming. When we arrived at the zoo Tosca was there with a photographer. We had to allow a picture to be taken as the Oyens were providing a home for our cougars. But I was glad he was from the Duncan paper and not the Victoria or Saanich ones. Then the neighbors couldn't gloat over their success in removing our kittens.

While David put the weeks' supply of chicken, fish, and vitamins in Jim's freezer room, I walked the cougars through the zoo, past the visitors who stared curiously at seeing wild animals on the wrong side of the cage, and down to the last enclosure. I tied their leashes to separate trees to prevent their tangling with each other and worked off my heartache with detergent and muscle power. The previous occupants of the pen had been foxes and vultures. Meanwhile, David came to build a shelf wide enough for them both to sleep on, then we nailed their individual shallow wooden boxes to it to provide something familiar from home. Oola was nimble enough to spring to the shelf in one leap, but we had to lean a tree trunk against it for awkward, bumbling Tom. The floor of the pen was dirt, but because it was at the low end of the zoo's drainage system, we knew we'd have trouble later in the winter.

It seemed ironic that this pen had none of the safety features we had at home at Island View: the double wire, the double doors, the reinforced floor, even the blessing of the Fish and Wildlife Branch. All the Duncan one had was the blessing of the municipality and the neighbors, but for all the wrong reasons.

I placed the sandbox in one corner, filled their dishes with food and water, and let in the cougars. For them it was all new, all exciting, they wanted to explore. They didn't know they'd have months, years, to do it. We left them while they were still satisfying their curiosity.

School started the following week. I had a job teaching grades six and seven at Monterey Elementary in Oak Bay behind the Tweed Curtain in the most traditionally English part of Victoria. I couldn't have accepted a school farther away from Island View and still have been on the peninsula. As David had the only car in the family and it wasn't too reliable anyway, Frank Beebe took me to school. Frank worked as an illustrator at the provincial museum, so after school I hitched a lift downtown to the government buildings and then he drove me home.

I had to wait ten days until the following weekend before I could get to Duncan to see how the cougars were getting along. Finding weekly transportation to the zoo was going to be a problem. That first Saturday Mother and Father drove me up-Island on the way to see their friends in Parksville. Fortunately, Duncan is on the way to several interesting places north of Victoria and I grew quite cunning in listening in to other people's conversations during the week to find out what they were planning on the weekend. The farther north they were going, the longer I had at the zoo before they returned to pick me up.

That first Saturday I hid as I approached the cage. I wanted to see what Tom and Oola were doing undisturbed. A dozen sightseers were standing at the wire staring at them. The cougars were on their shelf lying in their boxes and looking thoroughly bored. I stood behind the throng and whistled. Both cougars pricked up their ears and instinctively whistled back. The crowd turned around en masse as I came forward, excused myself, and pressed my nose against the wire. "Tom, *prrrt!*" I called.

With an excited cascade of squeaks Tom leaped out of his box, ran, almost fell down the log. Purring and squeaking at the same time, he pressed his cheek against mine. Quickly I darted to the back door of the pen and opened it. I wanted to get in before he got out. Not that he would have gone anywhere, but the crowd might have done more than just gasp in horror as they were doing right then. I just managed to get the door closed behind me as Tom, hurling his whole weight against me, bowled me to the ground.

"She's mad, she's gone in with a cougar," I heard somebody say before my hearing was smothered in a shower of licks, a blanket of fur, and a crescendo of chirps and squeaks.

It was half an hour before I could get up. Tom had nearly licked my face away with a tongue, whose sharp raspy ridges are more naturally suited to dressing fur or fleshing deer bones than licking my unprotected skin. To show affection, a cougar is like a house cat but with many times the power. It purrs but with vocal cords that hum like a plane engine; it licks but with a tongue like a rake; it kneads but with claws that are like steel forks digging in and out of your rib cage. The human body just isn't physically able to withstand such loving.

Eventually, when I got a chance to stand up without being knocked down again and Tom let me out of his reach for a moment, I went over to Oola. She pricked up her ears and allowed me to stroke her fur, she even purred, but she was reserved, not ecstatic. She didn't trust as Tom trusted—implicitly—even after ten days of desertion. Why should she?

By this time the crowd, still openmouthed, had expanded to include every visitor to the zoo. Tosca at the admission gate had sent back those who had run to warn her about the girl being attacked by the cougar in the end pen. Now there was a clamor, not from the cougars but from the onlookers.

"Is that really a person in the cage with those cougars?"

"Gee, Mummy! There's a girl being eaten alive by cougars."

"Aren't you brave! Going in a cage with wild animals."

Then:

"How did you ever get them tame like that?"

"When will they grow vicious?"

And later:

"How old are they?"

"How much do they weigh? How big do they grow?"

And much later, when I told them why the cougars were in the zoo:

"Do you think we could put our names on a petition so you can get your cougars back?"

At one point when the crowd thinned out, a lady came up to ask when I would start the next show because she'd missed the first performance!

By announcing to my class that I spent my weekends in a cougar cage and I had no car to get there, I was assured of several months' supply of volunteer chauffeurs. Even if the parents weren't thinking of a drive up-Island on weekends, their children did their best to suggest one. Victoria is a friendly little city, a haven for people who are different. It's the kind of town where a dowager can leave her fortune to a parrot that lives alone in a sprawling mansion and hire a Chinese gardener to feed it biscuits, hard-boiled eggs, and a daily slug of brandy. It's the kind of town where even schoolteachers took weekend drives to

Duncan so one of their colleagues could sit in a cage with cougars.

During subsequent weekends I whistled from the road, even before I got to the zoo entrance, and Tom would whistle back. Immediately, he would start purring and pace back and forth along the wire at the front of the cage. He stood up on his hind legs and clawed the cage wall as my whistles got louder, but though he stopped to stare up the path, he couldn't see through the fog of his increasing shortsightedness until he felt me at the wire. Once inside the cage, his welcome was always tumultuously the same. An hour of whistles, purrs, licks, and kisses, then as many hours of play as possible till the car came to take me away.

By October I began to notice the change that was inevitable. Tom was beginning to forget that there is one kind of play for cougars and another kind for people. Kept at home and in constant association with humans, he had remembered. Now kept in the zoo, Oola was his constant playmate and after roughhousing with her during the week, he expected to do the same with me on the weekend. It was bad enough to be loved by a cougar. It was much tougher to take being played with by one. The more time Tom spent with Oola, the less gentle he became with me.

Sometimes I took Haida to give the cougars the exercise my body couldn't provide. Joyful, affectionate, floppy-eared Haida, long-suffering girlfriend and playmate of a sea lion, mother and then sparring partner for four cougars. She tumbled all over them and they lay on their backs, striking at her with their forefeet and raking upward with their hind ones. It looked to the casual observer (and there were many) that the cougars were killing the dog, but Haida could be seen calmly scrounging food from the ground at the side, in the manner of all puppies, while at the same time, Tom and Oola were hanging onto her throat.

Few hunters can kill cougars without dogs. Their dogs are trained to smell cougar, to keep away from deer and rabbits, to remain on the trail, to make a lot of noise and stay barking underneath the tree when the cougar stops running. It is the noise the dogs make, not their owner with his rifle, that the cougar fears or wishes to elude. Sometimes a cougar doesn't tree but faces its pursuers. Then the classic fighting position is to strike with its forepaw, like any cat, lacerating the dog with its sharp claws or else to draw in its assailant with both forepaws and bite it in the head. The cougar's last resort is to throw itself on the back and to lash out with its feet, as Tom and Oola did in play with Haida. Fortunately, for the adult cougar, it has a very loose hide which often saves it from the snapping jaws of its traditional enemy.

There was hardly room in the pen for all four of us when Haida came visiting. She jumped Oola, who condescended to come down from her shelf to jump Tom who was already jumping on me. Smothered in fur and teeth and claws, I would have to scramble up for air amid the flurry of fall leaves. Once, after nursing a sore ear for a week, I realized I could no longer play with a cougar. As many others had discovered before me, wild animal pets must be taught respect for the hairlessness of the human body.

Time was flying. As the autumn leaves fell, so did my hopes for Dave to ever finish at university. As soon as he locked himself away in his office, I'd have to call him back to fix pipes or pumps, hot-water or cold-water systems, solve the perennial problem of finding enough fish to feed the animals, to give advice on the care of some stranded hawk or otter. When I asked him if he'd finished the first chapter of his revised thesis he replied, "No, but I've finished an article for the local paper." Increasingly, his thoughts on eagles were being supplanted by ideas for summer expeditions, plans for films, schemes for making money to build an exciting educational and entertaining wildlife conservation center, probably in Vancouver, for which Island View was only the springboard. The longer he took to finish his thesis, the longer the cougars stayed in the zoo and the harder it would be to keep them tame. It would have been easier if we just had one.

And then we had three. Tom, Oola—and Natasha.

One night David got an urgent call from a professor of biochemistry at the University of Alberta in Edmonton.

"I just saw your article in *Weekend* magazine about going on a picnic with a cougar and I wondered if you could give a home to my cougar Natasha," Dr. Wolfe explained. "I can't keep her any longer in Alberta because the Fish and Game people are rabidly enforcing their archaic law which states, 'Thou shalt not keep any wild animal in captivity.' They're doling out fines of $500 to owners of skunks and things and then destroying the animals. In fact, vets get in serious trouble here now for even descenting skunks. To top it all, this year is a particularly bad one for rabies in the indigenous animal population and great efforts are being made to contain the disease. Apparently the number of cases is near epidemic and the wildlife people are working hard to prevent people from collecting sick or injured wildlife which may be rabid. I don't know what Natasha, who was born in a zoo in Texas of Arizona parents, has got to do with this, but I guess no individual can be excused. I don't think I can beat the regulations on this technicality.

"The real key to our problem would have been the Alberta Game Farm, where she could have stayed until things blew over and we could have gone out to see her daily; but Al Oeming doesn't want the responsibility of handling other people's pets. We've been trying to find a good home for Tasha for six weeks now and it seems everyone wants her for a rug or something and we will not allow that to happen. The little bugger knows something's up as well because she's been eating out of our hands for the past few days. Can you do something?"

David explained how our own cougars had to be housed at the Duncan Zoo while we were waiting to get

Island View rezoned. Dr. Wolfe sounded desperate. He said he'd send Natasha down on the next flight, just as soon as he'd made a crate.

Natasha arrived at the airport in Vancouver while David was in Victoria. Good old Hilary was given the job of picking the cougar up and bringing her over to the Island by ferry.

David phoned her: "Hi! Are you still planning on coming over this weekend?" he asked.

"Oh yes! I'll be getting the 6 P.M. ferry on Friday as usual," Hilary replied in her breezy fashion.

"Good," said David. "There's something I'd like you to pick up from the airport and bring over with you." Then he added, "Do you think you could come over in the morning? It really can't wait until the evening."

"Yes, I could try and get the day off," Hilary said obligingly. "What do you want me to pick up?"

"It'll be under my name," David continued blithely, "and you go to the Air Canada freight shed. It will be arriving at 6:40 A.M., so get the earliest ferry you can."

"What am I picking up, David?" Hilary persisted, a little less breezily.

"You might find it's too big to get into your little car. If it is call a taxi and have them take it to the ferry for you. I'll meet you at this end."

"David! WHAT am I bringing over? Is it alive?" she asked. "Remember the murres I brought you from the aquarium? I had to sit out on deck freezing to death because it was too warm inside for the birds."

"There's one more thing," he went on. "You just might have some trouble getting it aboard the ferry . . . er . . . if you do, well, I'm sure you can handle it somehow."

"David!" Hilary pleaded. "WHAT IS IT?"

"A full-grown cougar," he finally confessed.

Hilary described what happened next in a story she wrote later for my newspaper column in *The Victorian*:

With some difficulty I managed to take Friday off from work. I had checked with the airline to find the size of cage used for shipping large pets, then measured the trunk of my car. No way! Fortunately Ray Salt, a friend of mine at work, who had a station wagon and lived near the airport, offered to meet me at the freight shed at 7 A.M. to take the cougar to the ferry.

It was a cold, rainy, dark morning in November and I would much rather have stayed in bed. At 6:45 A.M., I checked with the airline to make sure the cougar had arrived. It had. Rain lashed at my windshield as I drove along the Deas Island Throughway and the wipers click-clacked back and forth like a metronome.

As I entered the freight shed a bright smiling lad surprised me by saying, "You must be the cougar lady!" Ray arrived, and between us we loaded the large metal cage into his station wagon, and covered it with a blanket. The animal was beautiful. A light honey-gold colour with dark tipped ears. It weighed maybe 55 pounds and although I knew it to be tame it was now agitated by its travels and strange people.

Ray said he would drive Natasha straight onto the ferry for me so he took off and I followed. At the Tsawassen ferry terminal I parked my car and got to the ticket office in time to find Ray hopping mad. The ferry authoritics wouldn't allow him to drive the cage on board even though he explained the circumstances. So we unloaded it and put it down by the baggage area. Ray had to leave to get to work so I thanked him and assured him I could handle it from here on.

It was now 7:40 A.M., miserably cold and still raining. I headed for the empty coffee shop and sat with a steaming cup of brown liquid they called coffee. The door opened and a lady in a green blazer with a dogwood embroidered on the breast pocket poked her head in and said, "Are you with that animal out there?" "Yes, I am," I replied.

"This gentleman wants to see you," and she tossed her head in the direction of the baggage area. I left my brown liquid to steam alone and went outside. Up came a man in a uniform.

"Is that animal in the cage yours?" he snapped.

"Yes, what's wrong?" I asked.

"The supervisor wants to see you," he growled, "over there."

The supervisor was a large burly man and I sensed trouble. "Does this animal belong to you and what in heaven's name is it?"

"Yes it does and it's a cougar," I said.

"That's not classified as hand-baggage," he exploded, "and we're not allowed to transport anything that isn't hand-baggage."

David had been right, had probably known all along there would be a problem, and I blessed his shaggy beard!

I tried to protest to the supervisor that this was in fact my personal hand-baggage and should be allowed transportation onto the ferry. He listed for me all the items allowed to be termed "hand-baggage" according to the rules and regulations of the B.C. Ferry Authority, but a cougar in a cage was not one of them.

Undefeated, I asked, "Well, can I carry it on to the ferry myself?"

"Yes, there's nothing against your doing that. Have you got someone to help you?"

"No, but I'll find somebody," I said with assurance. I looked out across the rainswept terminal and it was utterly devoid of people, not a solitary figure that I could turn to for help. Now what! I went over to Natasha but she, too, was against me and she flattened her ears back and hissed.

How could I get that cougar aboard the ferry? I spotted a pickup truck in the short line-up of cars. The driver looked approachable so I decided to

approach. Just then the supervisor came and began
to ask questions about Natasha. Perhaps it was my
worried look, the driving rain, or maybe he just
liked cats, but his voice softened considerably as
he said, "Tell you what I could do, lady. I could
hitch the trolly to the back of the baggage van and
the cage could go on that."

Suddenly he was all kindness and help and when
the trolly was duly hitched, he and the driver lifted
the cage on. I had assured him the cougar was
very tame, but when Natasha saw strange fingers
coming through the bars, she lashed out with a
paw and snarled.

"You said it was tame!" he gasped, nearly
dropping the cage.

On instructions from the supervisor, the driver of
the van took it easy, up over the ramp, and
onto the ferry, the cage on the trolly trailing behind. At Swartz Bay he carefully manoeuvred the
ramp and continued slowly toward the gates. I
walked the long walk to the exit and there was
David to meet me.

"Hi!" said David casually. "Did you get Natasha?"
"Sure," I said. "I'm an experienced cougar trans-
porter."

I was at school when Natasha came. David took her
immediately to Duncan. Perhaps he was more concerned about the neighbors' feelings than I was. Perhaps he didn't want me to get too attached to another
cougar.

I saw Natasha the following weekend cringing in
the corner of the pen and far too scared of us all in
such a situation to ever make friends. She had been
traumatically torn from her own family circle and introduced for the first time in her life to animals that
were like herself but not like herself, in that she didn't
recognize them. David had tied her on a long leash in
one part of the pen to enable her to defend a particular
territory, one that Tom and Oola wouldn't encroach

upon. In her fear she spat and snarled as soon as either of them came near and they snarled back. She growled, and I realized this was the first time I'd heard a cougar growl, a real growl, not the sounds that were more like low grunts when Tom and Oola were possessive about a chicken. Natasha growled because she was terrified and alone. I was not afraid of her despite her ferocious face. That was the only defense she knew in this strange new world.

In her life of less than two years she had known only that people represented food, shelter, and affection. She had been kept in a house, she was taken in a car for camping trips, she visited school and had children visit her. People had been good to her. That was all the world she knew.

But now in a few short days that world had changed. She'd been thrust in a box, thrown onto a plane in a place of loud, roaring noises, pushed into a car in a place of still louder noises, a place that heaved underneath her and made her feel sick. Then she'd been shoved onto a truck and when the box opened, four strange eyes challenged hers from the other side of yet another box. The people were more familiar, they spoke with kind voices, they put forward food. But they were part of all this change and they were not the same. She would not eat.

My heart went out to her, but she wouldn't let me come close. She was such a little cougar, a southern species that at maturity was smaller than Tom and Oola, only half grown, were then. How easy it would be to have as a companion a cougar with Tom's disposition and Natasha's size. Perhaps we could keep her as the mate for Tom.

By the following weekend, relations in the cage had settled down to a mutual avoidance situation. Tom and Oola remained on one side and Natasha, no longer on a leash, remained on the other. If their paths met they exchanged ritualistic spits and snarls. It was tolerance, not friendship. But though Natasha acted defensively toward the cougars, she showed a very friendly disposition to people. By the second weekend I spent in the cage, she allowed me to approach and pet her. Complacent Tom didn't seem to mind.

Two weeks after Natasha arrived, Tom Spence at the South Perth Zoo, a few miles from my home in Western Australia, wrote to inform us that at long last, in response to our earlier inquiry, an enclosure had been prepared for two Canadian pumas. But homes had already been found for Tammy and Lara, and we no longer needed his accommodation. David thought otherwise. He insisted that the space at the Duncan Zoo was insufficient for one cougar, let alone three; that Tosca alone in the winter couldn't continue to defend the door daily from three cougars as she went in to feed; that Tom would remain more gentle and loving if separated from Oola, and that he'd not yet had time to organize the rezoning of Island View. And he wouldn't for a long, long time. He was decisive, even threatening.

I capitulated. My mother had just sent me a clipping of Tom Spence, the new curator, walking his pet cheetah on the grounds of the South Perth Zoo. She described how the zoo was to be reconstructed with modern moated enclosures not the old Victorian-type barred cages I'd remembered sickeningly from my Sunday-school picnic days. Perhaps the curator would keep our cougars tame and take them for walks each day with his cheetah. Dreams.

But which two would we send? Tom Spence said he wanted a male and a female. And he wanted them immediately. His next letter was peremptory. My hackles rose at the very suggestion that David send Tom. His cougar? The funny bumbling kitten that he'd picked out as his special pet? The cougar that would soon be blind? *My* cougar.

We prepared the crates for Oola and Natasha. And nine hundred pounds of chicken. They would make a long journey by ship to Sydney's Taronga Park Zoo and a month of quarantine. Then a shorter journey by plane to the zoo in Western Australia. To another world, a hot world with strange accents, something like Arizona and Texas or even Edmonton and Victoria in the summer. Oola's fur would grow short. Natasha's would stay as it was. And they might meet a cheetah.

I talked to them on tape and sent it Down Under with other sounds they were used to. I asked my family if they would play it to them when they visited the zoo so the cougars wouldn't feel so strange. I mailed pictures and a story to the local newspaper to engender in zoogoers a personal interest in the Canadian cougars.

I did my duty and more. But the cougars and I knew that I betrayed them. I betrayed their trust, as once I had said I would never do. I betrayed all three.

On the day the freighter was ready to leave, David and I drove to Duncan to load Oola and Natasha into their shipping crates. It wasn't easy. David placed the two cages at opposite ends of the pen and tried to push the cougars inside them. They wouldn't let him come near them.

"Okay, Lyn, you try," he muttered in annoyance.

I did it but I hated myself. Oola, used to my caresses, followed me into the cage and never looked around till I'd drawn the bolt. Natasha even let me pick her up. I remember the look they gave me as the truck rumbled away to the docks. They would never trust me again.

Three months later they arrived in Australia, still strong and healthy despite their long, cramped voyage. There was some fanfare in the local papers, something about a local girl who gave a gift of two pumas to her home town. Mum sent a clipping about the curator saying he was searching for males for them. But there were no cuttings about their daily walks.

Tom began to scream the moment we left the cage with Oola and Natasha. It was a distress call like the cries he had made in Vancouver eight months before, but much, much worse. It was shrill and piercing, agonized and piteous. Once the hurt had been to his body. Now the hurt was somewhere else. . . . I had no way of explaining and he had no way of understanding. For the first time in his life he was alone, really alone, deserted.

David made me leave. "He'll get over it," he said reassuringly. "He'll be fine by tomorrow."

Next morning, Tosca phoned. Tom was still screaming. She couldn't sleep. "Don't go up there," David commanded. "You can't go running every time an animal calls. You can't arrange your life around a cougar."

When I got to the zoo on Saturday, Tom was still screaming, still pacing. It was not so shrill and piercing now. But it was more anguished. Tosca said he'd been calling for one week, all day and all night. I stayed, but he didn't see me. He hadn't eaten. He walked over the chicken I brought. He walked over me. He gave me no more than a glance and continued pacing.

On the second Saturday he was still screaming but in short, hoarse gasps. He saw me. I stayed again, but he ignored me.

By the third Saturday perhaps he had abandoned hope. Perhaps nature had dimmed the memory of his lost sister. He had no voice. Only a very low painful whisper. Oola wouldn't hear it. But I was there and when he licked my cheek, I cried.

Scientists say cougars are solitary, efficient predators that form no strong attachments and possess no feelings or emotions. They do not understand a world of pain and sorrow, of love and laughter. They merely respond to stimuli like programmed automatons. If that's the case, I don't know how to describe Tom as the scientists would see him. I try, but the words they give me don't seem to fit.

By Christmas Day the ground was so soaked by fall and winter rains that I brought an air mattress to the zoo. It was still raining as David dropped me off at the pen to spend a few hours with Tom. While he joined Jim and Tosca in the trailer to drink cider and wine, I sat on the tarp-draped mattress in the dirt and mud and didn't mind at all.

Tom was almost back to his normal self. What he

lacked in voice, which was still hoarse, he made up
for in affection. It was different than what it was before
Oola left. His actions were now much more pathetic,
much more intense, as if I, in my red sheepskin-lined
coat was the only reason for his existence. No longer
did I whistle at the zoo's entrance. He would hear but
I couldn't bear to know how hard he was trying to
respond. When I got to the wire at the front of the
cage he saw me and started purring immediately. By
now he knew I came in by the back door and he was
there waiting. I sidled in as he pressed his whole bulk
against me and pushed me to the ground. I slid onto
the mattress and leaned my back against the cage
wall. He flopped down on top of me like a fat fluffy
blanket, welcome warmth in the winter cold. Eyes
closed, he stretched his paws under each of my arm-
pits and sheathed and unsheathed his claws, kneading
them as a cat does in pleasure. He pulled my hand
toward him and sucked on my thumbs, wherever he
could find bare skin, and nursed as he had as a kitten.
But now his tongue had such rasping strength that I
had to wear gloves and then later, Band-Aids under
the gloves.

Wearing Band-Aids in a cage with a wild animal
always brought cries of apprehension from the sightseers. They thought the cougar had injured me and
could hardly believe that I wore them so the cougar
wouldn't injure me.

But all the time he purred. And as he purred his
whole body quivered. Perhaps he dreamed. Perhaps
his dreams took him back to those happy days on
Little Darcy. Perhaps he dreamed of Oola.

It was my red sheepskin-lined coat that seemed to
send him into the deepest ecstasies. Once it had been
in top fashion during my single days in Montreal.
Now it told of home and expeditions, of dirt and
sweat, of fish and chicken, of Sam and Haida, of
Lara and Tammy and Oola. I didn't clean it but do-
nated it to Tom on my weekly visits to the zoo. He
clung to the wool and buried his face and slobbered
till both the coat and the cougar were lathered in mem-

ories. When I did eventually wash it, at 3 A.M. in an Oak Bay laundromat when nobody was looking, I realized those memories were too deep to be eradicated.

Bear cubs also suck on an arm and purr, but there's something rambunctious and belligerent about a bear cub, even when it is demonstrating affection. If you dare move away, bears are likely to bat you with their claws for having the audacity to curtail their pleasure. Cougars seem capable of something deeper.

Tom stayed there purring and nursing for three hours that day. Once he lifted his head and tried to nibble at my nose. He was almost a year old now and his new adult canines, which had been growing visibly for the past two months, were now stiff and white and powerful. It was with great care that I extricated my nose from between his teeth and gave him my thumb instead.

I don't know if animals forgive and forget. Perhaps time had dulled the pain. But I do know they feel. They feel the pain of loss and they feel the joy of recovery. And I vowed right then that while the world for this near-blind cougar was just a cage, a chicken a day, and me in my red coat at weekends, I would keep my weekly tryst. While Tom had only me to depend on, I would not let him down again.

13

And Now, Only One

I left Tom with a special Christmas turkey of his own and drove home to David's parents for our own Christmas dinner. Mother had surpassed herself. Her tables were laden with seafood cocktails, jellied salads, green salads, turkey with all its trimmings, chocolate mousse for dessert, and "afters" such as a cupboard full of cakes, cookies, pies, and mandarin oranges. To match the occasion I bathed, groomed, and perfumed, changed my jeans for a cocktail dress and my tuque for a wig. The red coat stayed out in the trunk of the car.

And then fit for polite company, I helped Mother serve dinner. Father snapped a shot of Dave and me at the table to be sent home to Australia to prove to my family there that Canada hadn't completely ruined me and that I still had some social graces. Letters from relatives of late had been punctuated with worried statements like "It is not natural for a girl with your intelligence and gifts to be giving love to an animal," "It is not right you get all mucked up in a cage," "You may get a disease from their germs," and "With your talents and upbringing, you are not leading the life you should."

I had tried to explain that the love you give to an animal is different from the love you give to a man or the love you give to your parents; that, anyway, even in Australia, I was always a sucker for the underprivileged, the underdog, or in this case, a blind "under cougar"; that Tom did his best as all cats do to keep himself clean despite his placement in the zoo; and that I walked through a tray of disinfectant before I cleaned and fed the other animals, in case I brought germs to *them*.

I suppose I shouldn't have sent home my friend Audrey's movie film of my weekly jaunts to the zoo or Hilary's award-winning pictures of Tom flinging his paws around my neck. Still, as I quipped to my mother, "You'd never get the same audiences to your Red Cross money-raising functions with pictures of snotty-nosed kids as you do with films of our animals."

And I suppose I shouldn't have sent two cougars to my family's local zoo and asked my relatives to go and play a tape outside the cage. There are a lot of things I guess I shouldn't have done.

It was some relief therefore to meet that same Christmas another "animal nut." Some time after Boxing Day we left food thawing for the animals, self-service style, and joined Hilary in Vancouver. It was at her brother and sister-in-law's Open House party that we heard of Al Bongard, a Swiss boy who lived in town with a cougar. The three of us excused ourselves from the party and followed a narrow winding road through snow-hung trees to his idyllic log cabin above North Vancouver. Set idyllically amid the firs and cedars and backdropped by the mountains, it was a living Christmas card.

When the door opened I fell back in surprise, not at seeing cougars, but a room full of St. Bernard dogs. There were two massive adults weighing 240 pounds each and about a dozen young ones. The room was literally St. Bernard wherever you looked, and Al warned caution in our movements because the parents were guarding a litter. I feared those dogs more than I had ever feared cougars. These were lions enough.

Al now lived with dogs. But once he had lived with

a family of wolves in the Swiss Alps, another time in an attic with a black bear, and he now contemplated living with wolves in the northern interior of British Columbia. He was a zoologist from one of the universities in Switzerland and studied animals more in the flesh than the laboratory.

His cougar was in an outside enclosure and I recognized it immediately. It had come from Rudy's Pet Park in Victoria and no longer was a good display animal because it suffered from rickets. Rudy was probably glad to sell it. Having a cougar close at hand was a good beginning in the study of British Columbia wildlife (many zoologists never see the animal they are studying in the live, whole state), but I doubted Al would ever get to make friends with it because it had been so long in the zoo. His method of maintaining control in the enclosure was an interesting one. He blew smoke into the cougars face from his pipe whenever it started snarling or looked about to pounce. Our cougars had disliked people who smoked as much as they disliked people who wore glasses.

Hilary returned with us to Island View for New Year's. We declined the usual merrymaking in order to go traipsing around the marshes counting birds with Frank Beebe on the annual Audubon Christmas bird count, watching the ducks and swans that came up from the lake to tap their beaks on Dick van der Meer's living-room windows, hiking our own beach to measure a porpoise that washed up on a zero tide, and then getting the navy and police out in full force to defuse a landmine, only to find, to our embarrassment, that it was a cement anchor instead.

On New Year's Day we caught the Mill Bay ferry up to Duncan to see Tom rather than take the longer Malahat Drive. We didn't stay long. Apart from an initial bout of affection, the cougar took no notice of Haida and very little of us. The haws in the corner of his eyes showed clearly. Tosca said he'd been distracted all week, pacing back and forth, crying and whistling in low gasps because his voice was only just beginning to return. So it wasn't a good time on that first day of a New Year for David to tell me that he intended to drop university work entirely as well as plans for getting Tom back home.

"Lyn, there are things more important than Tom. To win a public hearing we have to fight social, legal, and political battles; we have to get a lot of backup publicity; and most of all we have to get the support of government. They're the ones that make the rules. And one of the names on that petition is powerful. He's a man who is a deputy minister as well as the best friend of the premier of the province. Now how can we fight all that?"

"But you promised," I cried obstinately in my blind idealistic optimism, seeing both the dream and the man together toppling from the pedestal where I'd placed them.

"Well, I've changed my mind," he said abruptly and then began to list so many things that would have to happen first that I knew in my heart the possibility of getting Tom back was more remote than spending a year underground in Antarctica. That was probably the only place, barring the climate, one could roam freely with a mountain lion.

I don't like choices. The cougar or the thesis. The cougar or me. David said I was impossible. Again I capitulated.

There were alternatives. Put Tom to sleep. Send him to South Perth. Mum sent a picture from the local papers of Natasha yawning and Oola panting. Of course the captions read that they were snarling. Physically, they were in excellent condition. Mentally, well, who knows?

And then about the same time Sally Wolfe wrote to ask how Natasha was getting along with me. She told me how much she cared for her cougar. It wasn't easy to explain to her that her pet had just got off the boat on the other side of the world.

But it was much worse six months later. David was away, this time in New York. I came home from school to get a message that I was needed to trap an otter under a house in Oak Bay. I ran to the compound to look for suitable equipment. I pulled down the crate that Natasha had come in from Edmonton and tried to tear off the address slip. I noticed it was an envelope riveted to the plywood. When I ripped it open and deciphered the letter inside, I cried.

November 8, 1967

Dear Dave:

Here is Natasha. She was born April 22, 1966, in the Marseilles Zoo in Dallas, Texas. We acquired her from Pierre Fontine at age about four hours. She was bottle fed on Esbilac till age about three months when she began eating raw liver and beef from a dish. She has seen a lot of the world for a cougar, being transported all over the U.S. by car and she has been with us for several camping trips into the Albertan mountains, where she is always a hit with the park rangers. At present she is eating about three to four pounds of lean meat each day. We simply must let her go. . . .

You will find her very tractable and only a bit rambunctious when people are around, she loves to play. We have noticed that she is partial to women for some reason. She is much less friendly toward men. She will tolerate strangers, but if they are afraid of her she senses this immediately and becomes quite hostile. Generally, she will lie under the buffet and watch what goes on, but anything that can be picked up or rolled on the floor is in jeopardy. She is hell on pillows, for example. We rarely use gloves but perhaps this would be a good idea for you till she gets to know you. She purrs a great deal, usually when she is being stroked. Her typical cry sounds like a small dog's yelp or whistle and she responds to any unknown sounds with this call.

She is regular with urination in the box of sand but on occasion you might find a stool behind the couch or in some other obscure place. I'm not sure why this occurs, she certainly knows better. Please try to understand her at first, she really is a good cat. Most important, loud noises really upset her. I have taken her to the church school ... and when the kids were sitting down or talking quietly she behaved very well, but when about 30 adults came in, all talking at once, she fell apart. I had had her out to various youth groups and my favourite trick is to make a big fuss over her and then leave her alone in the room. She will sit in the middle of the floor making all sorts of plaintive cries, and then is very glad to see anyone return. She is gregarious for being a non-domestic beast.

Warning: she does get a bit carsick. This manifests itself by about 20 minutes of heavy salivation, followed by a small spell of diarrhea. If you travel long distances by car, be sure and take along some towels. Otherwise, she travels very, very calmly. Also she loves to be stroked, but hates to be scratched behind the ears. Whether or not this is a characteristic of the species I don't know.

She has had all the required shots and boosters to date (rabies, leptospirosis, and distemper), but you might wish to continue yearly boosters.

I am very concerned about how she will fare with you and would appreciate . . . after you get to know her.

In the event things do not work out well, please contact me before you do anything towards disposing of her. I feel she will be in good hands with you and I would like to be able to visit her whenever we can get out to Victoria.

Until then, I remain,
Sincerely,
Fred Wolfe

It was difficult to tell the Wolfes that Natasha had been transported to Australia because David hadn't noticed their letter of instructions on the crate that came with their cougar. Fred Wolfe was understanding and forgiving.

Dear Mrs. Hancock:

I was surprised and yet pleased when I received your recent letter . . . and I really appreciate your writing to clear up the problem. I was annoyed and disappointed when I didn't get a reply from you to the letter on the crate and then when we did receive your letter about Perth, I was pretty hot under the collar when you sent Natasha without even telling me beforehand. I contemplated writing you a nasty letter but I am glad now I didn't. . . . In the event that she was not going to work out as a pet for you, I had considered sending her back to a wild animal dealer in Lubbock, Texas, where she could stay until we could make arrangements to leave Alberta. I would appreciate any reports you might get on her welfare and manners.

Fred Wolfe

It was not till three years later that I had a chance to go home to Australia to check up on Oola and Natasha. Their enclosure was a typical zoo cage, stark and concrete and easy to clean. Nobody wanted me to go in with the animals, especially since the TV cameras were recording the reunion, so I called their names and whistled at the wire. Oola pricked up her ears and made one brief pass in front of me. She remembered but remained aloof as she had always done. It was Natasha, still small and delicate, that went into an ecstasy of purring and rubbed her face and neck fur against the barrier between us. Our time together in Canada had been brief. Did she, nevertheless, remember me specifically as the one who comforted her in a period of great stress? Or was she responding generally to anyone who reached out to make sympathetic contact?

I wanted to take her back to the Wolfes, to reunite her to her own family. I promised to get the zoo another male for Oola. But the curator had changed his mind. The two cougars, though both females, were used to the cage. It would be too difficult now, he said, to introduce a strange cougar to Oola.

I had given a gift but I couldn't get it back. Always I want to change life and I can't. Once again I gave in, but not with good grace.

Tom's first winter in the cage at Duncan was a bad one. The dry summer had given way to a wet fall and winter. By January his pen was a lake. Tosca phoned and I hitched a ride up there midweek to help divert some of the runoff water from the inadequate drainage system. Poor Tom waded toward me with his flanks and long tail dragging through the mud and muck. The air mattress didn't float, so we both stood up and leaned against the wire wall. He was so tall now I had to look up at him when he placed his paws on my shoulders.

Then it snowed. At Island View the sea birds tried to eat frozen fish, the falcons' water dishes turned to ice blocks, and with the pipes and pumps frozen, cleaning became laborious. At Duncan Tom weathered the winter better than we did. Snow and ice in his pen were preferable to water.

Dave, a keg of dynamite as usual, exploded back and forth between Vancouver and Victoria planning different projects: to the St. Lawrence to film the harp seal hunt; to the Queen Charlotte Islands to study peregrine falcons; to the Arctic to film the impact of man on the land; to the British Columbia coast mountains to search for a sasquatch. It seemed that every week he deposited on my desk a new work schedule to be typed. And then he was gone again.

The staff at school said one could always tell a Hancock class and I hope they meant it as a compliment. I wasn't too sure when the police started to visit my room regularly to check on a crime syndicate started by some of my eleven-year-olds. The children painted swastikas and Heil Hitler signs on cars, houses, and stop signs with stolen spray paint and wrote such delightfully destructive topics in creative writing lessons such as the various ways they could kill Santa Claus while he was coming down the chimney. I think cougars in the classroom would have provided more constructive chaos.

I still brought animals to the classroom and they still stimulated children to write. Sam, now in his fifth year of occasional schooling, was the most popular visitor.

> Mrs. Hancock, our teacher, said she would bring Sam to school. Weeks went by. Finally it was a week before. I said to myself, "One more week!" Finally the day came. I waited and waited for Mrs. Hancock to arrive at school that morning. Finally her car came. I said, "But where is the seal?" "I'm not bringing him until two o'clock." At last two o'clock came. A knock on the door. It was only the principal. Then it was ten after two. Another knock on the door and the door opened. No seal. It was Mr. Hancock who said. "Sam's out in the truck." He came back in about five minutes. Behind him the seal came prancing in, its eyes were rolling. Mr. Hancock showed us on the map where Sam came from, the Pribilof Islands in the Bering Sea. Sam chased me around the room. I knocked down everything in sight. I didn't go near him again.
>
> Grant Dickson

Jeff Sparks added in his journal, "Sam chased some people right out of the classroom. Boy, I had so much fun!"

Patricia Smith noted that

> Sam sat on a chair in the middle of the room and when the people with food went by he chased them

because he thought they were taking food *away* from him. Even though he chased them we all enjoyed a good visit with Sam the Sea Lion.

Himie, Gomer, and Ludwig, the turtle and tortoises, were now the only animals to enjoy periodic home visits. Being sleepy things, they occasionally got lost. Jane Hoel told about her anxious moments in the class magazine:

> One night I dreamed about the class tortoise running away. We were looking all over the place for it. Then we asked our neighbours if we could look in their yard for it. We were looking in the garden, under trees, under rocks, and under the stairs. The last rock that my sister turned over wasn't a rock. It was the tortoise. We'd found it.

Without a car of my own I still relied on parents or friends to drive me to Duncan on weekends. Heather McIllree recorded her family's visit this way:

> One Sunday afternoon my family and I went to take Mrs. Hancock to see her pet cougar at the Duncan Zoo. The cougar's name is Tom. He is very friendly and lovable. When Mrs. Hancock stands on the hill and calls, Tom whistles in reply. When she goes in the cage he hugs and kisses her. At the end of the afternoon when we have to leave, Tom whistles and cries again.

One of my friends in particular, Audrey Winterburn, chauffeured me most often. Almost every Sunday after church and sometimes on Saturdays too, Audrey and I would visit Tom. Most weekends she dropped me off and then went shopping and sightseeing farther up Island, but occasionally she came into the cage to make the movies that we kept sending home to Australia.

Tom never took much notice of her, or Hilary when she visited, except to rub his head against their legs when he passed. Tosca found him too playful to be able to get her cleaning chores done, so she left them for me to do. On my visits the routine was generally the same. Tom whistled when I came in focus, stood up on his hind legs and leaned his weight against me, which invariably knocked me onto the tarp or the air mattress. For the first hour he was content to purr, knead, and suck my fingers till they got all wrinkled, like they do when I wash a lot of dishes. I preferred to give him thumbs but to save the wear and tear on the same digits, I gave him different fingers in turn.

In the second hour he licked my red coat and then did his own washing. Sometimes he curled up around his tail and I lay my head on his and dozed. Other times he turned on his back and I tickled his creamy smooth tummy as one would a house cat. Occasionally his ears would prick to attention and he frowned in alert concentration at something outside the cage that I couldn't see. His eyes were just hollow caverns. He could hardly see at all at that distance, but he could hear.

By the third hour he became restless. He paced in the typical stereotyped zoo routine. I wrote notes as I watched him. He seemed to have such short legs to be supported by such powerful padded forepaws, legs that appeared shorter because of his flabby paunch and shaggy fur. A cougar has very loose skin, which helps it escape from dog attacks in the wild, but it is not fat. Its natural appearance is lithe and sinewy, despite the quantities of fat it consumes. In carnivores, particularly the cat family, excess fat is excreted by the kidneys and passed out with the urine.

As he paced, sweeping his long muddy brush of a tail into my face with each pass, or standing on top of me as he traversed a corner, he would punctuate his purrs with low goatlike squeaks, a different sound than he had made before he had lost the strength in his voice. He would stare up the path. What worried him? Memories of other times that my presence promoted? Occasionally he galloped like a whirlwind from corner to corner. Did he do this from sudden excitement? Or did he feel a compulsive need for exercise? Did his legs feel soft and quivery as mine do after eighteen hours a day sitting still at the typewriter? Thinking he might be hungry, I'd throw him a chicken. No, he'd only throw it up in the air and it would fall in the mud. Then he continued pacing.

At times he was conscious of me sitting in his path and he'd press his soft hulk against me, stop his nervous cries, and purr contentedly. Then he would gently take my hands, one at a time, into his mouth. I was always careful to place my fingers between his canines along the center of his tongue in case he got the idea to chomp and chew. When I wanted to scratch my nose or my chin I had to do it by rubbing my face into his fur. When spring came, I wore a blue sweater, curious to see if he was responding to me or to my red jacket. He still lathered it to foam, though for not as long.

By the time my friends came to get me, I would be such a mud pile that I'd deposit newspapers on the seat of the car and give myself a whiff of air freshener before I deemed myself suitable as a passenger. The staff at school said Tom and I had a mother-son relationship. David agreed. The association certainly was a muddy one that winter and spring.

Then one weekend I didn't keep my tryst. David had persuaded me to go to Vancouver to visit Al Bongard. I agreed on condition he take me to see Tom on the Monday we got back. It was Tuesday by the time we got to Duncan. Tosca hurried toward me from the trailer to tell me Tom had been sitting in the one spot since Sunday looking up the path just waiting and making that agonized distress call that is somewhere between a whistle and a scream. Even the Oyens agreed that Tom was unique.

That week we were asked to provide homes for another family of cougars whose mother had been shot up-Island, but we turned them down. I didn't think I could cope with the emotional ties entailed in owning any more cougars.

I always took a book with me to the zoo, intending to prepare lessons while I sat for hours with Tom, but usually there were so many interesting people to talk to through the wires that I never opened a page. If David had continued with the campaign in support of the cougars at Island View, I could have gathered hundreds of names on a petition attesting to the tractability of my cougar. In fact, when CBC-TV filmed a segment of our weekly meetings, I wondered if their audiences would recognize my purring cat as a cougar. With the success of the Lincoln-Mercury advertising symbol, they were more used to a snarling cat than a smiling one. Few people know that Pat Derby has to pull on Chauncey's tail off camera before he will snarl for the commercial.

Other would-be budding photographers had the same problem. I arrived at the zoo one week expecting Tom's usual tumultuous welcome, which was to be filmed by a hidden CBC film cameraman. But when I called and whistled, "Tom!" in my usual fashion, there was no reply. Puzzled, I rounded the bend and came down the path in full view of a group of tourists who were swinging on the bars of the cage, pushing sticks through the wire, and leaping up and down in efforts to get Tom to act like a "vicious" cougar and hiss and snarl for their cameras. So instead of running to meet me with enthusiasm, Tom did purr but spent all his time on camera scared and distractedly looking up the path after the embarrassed and retreating tourists. It is difficult to keep an animal tractable in a zoo. Unless you are in control of the situation every day and are on the spot, you have no way of knowing what may be disturbing the animal. Animals, teased and challenged by staring, poking, prodding, and other forms of teasing, may vent their frustrations upon their owners or trainers the next time they get the chance and their owners will never know why.

But there are some people like Donald Cowx who see a little more in an animal behind bars than just a topic to take home in their cameras. And he was kind enough to write and tell me about his own experiences in visiting Tom at the zoo. By the time Donald met Tom, David had come to an agreement with Rudy to board our cougar in a much larger enclosure at his Pet Park about six miles from Island View.

Dear Mr. and Mrs. Hancock:
You do not know me but this letter is to tell you of a nice experience that a friend of mine Bob Sutcliff and I had with your pet cougar Tom last Saturday morning July 6, 1968. We arrived at the zoo after the sun had gone down and it was apparently closed. No one answered our knock on the proprietor's house. Bob spotted a cougar in the cage close to the house. So we went in, not knowing if this was Tom or not. But the cat in the cage came over close to the wire and looked us over. In no way did it look angry or snarling as the bobcats and lynx did. This cougar seemed only curious about us. I said, "Tom," said I saw his ears perk forward. We came up right against the cage and he purred. I felt sure this was your pet, the one we had read about in your articles.
I noticed that his left eye seemed to have a whiteness as if cataracts were developing in it. I hope that he is not going to be blind, for in the time that followed he taught us how wonderful and affectionate a tame mountain lion can be. I have been fortunate enough to have seen two cougars in the wilds and several in zoos but none like yours!! He followed us within the limits of his cage, also wandering off to hide behind his log. Thinking he was hidden, he would leap out at us and repeat the performance as playful as a large kitten. Bob ran around the outside while Tom followed closely on the inside. Tom hooked his forepaws into the wire to stop and turn while he tried to follow Bob. Soon he was panting heavily and I imagine he doesn't get too much exercise except when he is out with you. I know that the cougar is short-winded and will not keep up a hard run for long

but will wander for miles and miles in a night. As it was a hot afternoon we did not try to tire him out, but he came back for more after flopping down and breathing for a bit.

We found that he would nibble and suck on my finger or lick my hand with his rasping tongue. He made no attempt to bite. Bob looked in my car for a bit of meat to give to him but found none. Our own cat likes butter, but Tom didn't take any when we presented him with some.

He puffed his muzzle forward until it looked square as I scratched him under the chin, his black whiskers intermingling with his white, all thrust forward. His purr was deep and rumbling. The wire of his cage did not allow too much of this, and I saw that he did not like the edges of his ears scratched. He turned his head away and shook it. He did like the bridge of his nose and his muzzle scratched. He always wanted to be close to us as if he actively sought companionship. I know that cougars seem to occasionally seek a companionship with man. Wild ones sometimes will follow a person out of curiosity in the woods. At about this time the man and woman from the house came out and the man with a German accent asked us what we were doing behind the log guard rails and what business it was of ours to play with this cat. When we asked if this cougar was Tom, the Hancocks' cougar, he changed his attitude immediately, even told us about Tom and gave me your address. The man and the woman went back to their house and Bob and I thought it best to leave and let Tom rest.

Tom watched us go, his face pressing the wire. When we got to the car we heard three loud, distinct whistles that I knew were Tom's and I like to think that he was calling us to come back. We left, not really wanting to, as we had just seen and done things you just don't do every day.

We headed for the ferry slip but found we had

missed the last ferry. We decided to go back to the zoo to see Tom again. We slept under the stars that night and next day paid our way in to the zoo. As soon as Tom saw us he came over to the wire and we started right in stroking him within the limits of the wire openings. Bob ran him around a bit, then we just sat and studied him as he studied us.

I saw another cougar standing in the doorway of its house beside Tom's, but it did not come close like Tom did. At one point Bob was standing with his sweater against the wire and Tom was standing up with his forepaws gripping the wire, sniffing and cocking his head. As Tom licked the sweater he pulled some of it through the wire because of the barbs on his tongue and playfully locked his teeth in it so that about a foot of sweater was pulled through. After a bit of tug-of-war Bob finally said, "Tom! No!" very sharply and Tom immediately released his grip. We have now the only cougar-chewed sweater in Vancouver.

A couple of old ladies came around and were very surprised to see us stroking such a dangerous animal. I told them that these animals are very rarely dangerous to man himself and that it is usually old animals, with worn teeth or ailing bodies, that may take man's livestock.

Another man came up with children and immediately thrust his hand through the wire to pet Tom. I imagine he knows you, as he knows Tom well enough. He thought a lot of Tom and cougars in general. He told me he doesn't like to shoot an animal unless he has to. He said he used to be a cougar hunter but then he looked at Tom and said, "But you set me straight, eh, Tom?"

Bob or I would hate to see a cougar killed. I know there are professional hunters who take care of livestock killers and trouble making animals but I can't see killing for no reason or just for a hide or horns. I want to see the cougar continue to be part of B.C.'s native fauna far into the future. In areas where they were ruthlessly hunted out in the bounty days they need to be reintroduced and protected to control the deer that multiplied beyond their food supply in their absence. As their main diet is deer, cougars serve as an important check against this.

I have the skulls of six adult pumas which have aided me greatly in my study. A lot can be learned from the study of skulls, as you know. These animals were either cattle killers or curious animals that wandered into towns and were shot. The only male was one that had a broken foreleg and became a livestock killer.

Well, back at the zoo—after at least two hours of being with your pet, stroking him, taking pictures, we left, not wanting to but we had to get back to work Monday. I hope I haven't bored you with this long letter. I've a habit of writing this sort of letter to people about an experience that I have never had before.

In closing, may I say that we had a truly refreshing experience with your pet and that he is guaranteed to throw new light into the minds of people who know little about the big cats. It is a cat such as yours that makes the animal world so much brighter.

Yours truly
Donald Cowx

Such a letter demonstrated a more favorable attitude toward the cougar on the part of the general public than I had encountered two years before in the staffroom at Lord Kitchener School. People were now more willing, in the light of their own or reported scientific experience, to afford the cougar a place in the world. A small minority still think that "every good cougar is a dead one," but the majority even try to find excuses for any damage a cougar might do, whether to pets, livestock, or man. In such situations they say the cougar must be old, sick, weak, diseased, or incapacitated by having porcupine quills in its mouth. And even when it is carrying out its normal function like killing deer, the deer it chooses must be suffering from similar disabilities.

The truth lies somewhere in between such swings of the pendulum. Years later, I rummaged through boxes of diaries in the basements of government offices, collected old clippings from newspaper archives, and recorded dozens of interviews in order to compile a list of man/cougar confrontations since 1900. In doing so, I learned that in North America, cougars have been responsible for only seven confirmed deaths. Of these, four were in the United States and three were in British Columbia. Two of these deaths were thought to be due to rabies as a result of the attack. In all cases it was a child that the cougar attacked. Four of the victims were either seven or eight years old. One child that was thirteen was crawling out of a culvert, a very vulnerable position at the eye level of the cougar. In British Columbia since 1916, there have been twenty additional attacks by cougars which have not resulted in death but which have caused bodily damage. The number for the United States is not known.

In the same period of time humans have killed in excess of 223,485 cougars, a number calculated from available bounty records and obviously a conservative estimate because many kills by sports hunters and farmers were unrecorded. Considering such figures, it is reasonable to say, as Donald did, that cougars are rarely dangerous to man.

Contrary to what he had assumed in his letter, it is not usually the old cougars that do the most damage. From my investigations I found that young male cougars about two years old and just leaving their families to strike out on their own for the first time are the ones most likely to attack people, livestock, or pets.

Regarding not the predator but the prey, Maurice Hornocker found in Idaho that three quarters of the elk killed by cougars were less than one and a half years old or more than nine and a half years old, and as many elk in good condition were killed as those in poor condition. It is a predator like the wolf with its group-chasing technique that kills mostly old, sick, weak, and diseased prey. The cougar with its solitary, stalking method of hunting is as likely to kill prey that is young or in good condition.

The only general statement that may be made is that cougars kill prey that places itself in a vulnerable position. And in situations where cougars impinge on the same territory as man, it is more likely that the predator is a young male, and in the case of direct confrontation the prey is a young child rather than an adult.

I would have to agree from my own experience that cougars are attracted to young children. When they came up to the cage Tom seemed fascinated by their moving feet, their loud cries and shrieks. Oola's reaction was even more striking. She would jump down from her shelf and throw herself against the wire.

Tom and Oola were less than two years old. Bill Robb commented that captive cougars at the Olympic Game Farm settle down in their third year: "They use their teeth and claws less than they did in their first two teen-age years. And then later when they are a lot older their personality changes again. They can't see or hear as well, so they panic. They get senile, cranky, and are touchy to go in the cage with."

So far Tom hadn't shown any crankiness as a result of his increasing blindness, just an interest in things happening actively around him outside the cage. And this could have been less an interest in children and more a natural reaction to relieve his boredom in confinement. His whole world still revolved around my weekly visits. If I didn't come, he refused to eat, he called ceaselessly, he sat staring at the one spot till I materialized. And when I left he acted like a creature gone berserk, pacing, circling, leaping against the wire, whistling.

It was a responsibility, a dependency I could not deny.

14

Day Pass to Little Darcy

And then it was spring again. We celebrated the feeling of freedom that such a season engenders by taking Tom out of the zoo for Easter.

Hilary came from Vancouver and we all drove to Duncan to collect our cougar. Considering it better for the neighbors' nerves to take a cougar past their houses at night, we spent a couple of hours till dusk visiting with Jim and Tosca and the latest guest in their trailer, a rambunctious bear cub. Bears are cute Winnie-the-Poohs till they want something you don't want to give them. I prefer cougars myself.

David and I took a flashlight down to Tom's cage and led him on a leash to the station wagon. He responded immediately to "Into the car, Tom," and settled himself in the back. I crawled in happily beside him while Hilary joined Dave in the front. I don't know which sounded louder, Tom's purrs or the engine's hum during the trip home.

Haida came out the front door with her usual exuberant greeting, but such was the difference in size now between the dog and the cougar, with Tom approaching 150 pounds, that I feared Haida's thin hairy neck might be crushed in a cougar-type "bear" hug. For our own peace of mind more than the dog's, we locked her outside while Tom was in the house.

For Haida, Tom showed only friendliness. For Sam, I was not so sure. This time it was the sea lion that growled and made a fast exit from the living room when

201

the cougar leaped toward him. There was no ears-flattened snarl, but I didn't feel comfortable about it, so Sam was separated too. Tom would have to make do with us. After one circle of the house he chose to squat behind the curtains of the wardrobe recess looking out between the hanging coats. He was content just to sit and purr and watch us. And whenever he caught our eye, he whistled.

But now he was in civilization, there was work to do. Tom had to be cleaned of eight months' muck from zoo living before he was fit for company. Hilary and I spread old blankets on the floor to soak up the expected deluge when the cougar hit the bathtub, and we tried to coax him into the bathroom. Once he had nicely fitted into the washbasin. Now I wondered if he would be too big for the tub.

We managed to persuade him into the room, but we never did succeed in keeping all of him in the tub at the same time. David tried lifting his hind quarters over the edge while I tried ramming in the front quarters. Hilary manned the taps. And how I wish somebody else was taking pictures! I concentrated on keeping at least part of him under the water while David sloshed him with soap as he slipped and slid on the bottom of the tub. We eventually resorted to a sponge bath, mostly of his three-foot-long tail. The sponge turned an immediate brown on each application. I think the whole operation could best be described in terms of my mother's: "a cat's lick and a promise." It says a lot for Tom's calm personality that he purred continually throughout the entire proceedings. Many children in similar circumstances would not have been as well behaved!

Tom followed me out to his old pen in the compound for the night by chasing my kicked-up heels, a method I found more effective than dragging him on the leash. For comfort in surroundings he hadn't seen for eight months, I gave him an old blanket that must have been saturated with "old familiar far-off things" because he sniffed and snuggled into it in the deepest concentration as I sneaked out and locked the door.

Next morning we finished the chores early and loaded the rubber Avon for a trip to Little Darcy. Audrey came around to take pictures for home movies. Hoping there weren't too many telescopes boring into our backs from the people on the hill, I led Tom down to the shore. This time he followed easily as I called. He needed no leash or kicked-up heels. Perhaps he knew he was going on a picnic. He even jumped into the boat without further persuasion. This time with our gear, his greater bulk, and Hilary as our extra passenger, there was little room for comfortable travel. I kept a firm hold on his neck while we bumped our way over to the island in case he suddenly thought that swimming was a better method.

What a glorious day! After the dull confinement of the rainy season in an uninsulated, poorly heated house, I was in a state of absolute euphoria to land on the beach of my favorite uninhabited island, fling myself down in a grassy meadow under a sparkling blue sky, soak up the warmth of the spring sunshine, and breathe in the perfume of the Easter lilies. Wherever you looked, the lush new grass was strewn with flowers, not only white erythroniums but chocolate lilies as well, yellow buttercups, and pink shooting stars. In the unaccustomed warmth everything seemed an effort except lying still, staring at the horizon, or dozing. Tom seemed conscious of the beauty as well. He showed no desire to do anything but sprawl on the grass, rest his head on mine, and purr.

David in his usual fireball fashion had things to do. He had promised to take a picture of Tom in the rubber boat we had been given for the trip. To get the cougar aboard again I used his intense involvement with me by running down to the beach and jumping in the boat. Never letting his gaze stray from my moving legs, Tom soon found himself afloat whether he wanted to be or not.

Once in the boat he concentrated on exploring all the exciting smells in the bilge, now cleared of its cargo. But that was too low a position for pictures of a feline figurehead, so I tried to attract his attention to the bow.

David tried to click the camera before Tom got sight of the shore again and leaped in the water. Since Tom was a pet and not a trained wild animal, such photographic attempts were not too successful, so we soon gave up and went for a walk around the island. Tom never once let us out of his sight.

He maintained oral communication by his usual whistles. Even when I waded into a deep intertidal pool or plunged out to the colder water of the sea, he followed. To quench his thirst after the unaccustomed exercise, he didn't drink salt water as he had on his previous visit but soon emptied the fresh-water pools among the boulders.

It was sad to see how precariously he walked among the rocks, picking his way among the pebbles and stumbling over the boulders. The sharp stones cut his smooth pads, but his awkwardness was more an indication of his increasing blindness. Rather than stroll along the shoreline he preferred to fight through the undergrowth, then flop underneath a mass of foliage. Then David would try to take his portrait. Invariably, the cougar would get up and walk into the lens and give it a lick before rubbing his body against the photographer. And with his 150 pounds, both the camera and the cameraman went flying.

My hectic life at Island View and my daily commuting to school in Oak Bay left little time for sleeping. So on Little Darcy I welcomed the opportunity to doze among the daffodils, especially when my blanket was warm, cuddly, and now cleaned. I'd have preferred to sleep in the sun in the open, but Tom was happier in the shade on the edge of the meadows among the trilliums and lilies. While Hilary and David went looking for Indian middens we slept. And only when he was in the deepest slumber did he stop purring.

The loud report of a shotgun disrupted the idyllic atmosphere. I woke with a jerk to see two boys zooming into shore in a small boat. Tom sprang up and darted into the bushes, the first time he'd ever left me. It is amazing how possessive you can become over something that isn't yours. To me the noisy boat and its occupants were intruders on my island. I had been dreaming that one end of Little Darcy was fenced in for Tom, while David and I lived in a log house at the other, beside our boat and float plane dock.

The boys dragged their boat up the beach and came over to introduce themselves. They were from the University of Victoria and had been collecting ducks for the biology department. They were anxious to see the cougar they had disturbed.

To my surprise Tom was scared, as he had never been in the cage at Duncan, or in the boat, or on the island with us. I had expected him to be suspicious of Hilary, whom he had not seen for a long time, but he had accepted her almost as well as he accepted me. He had not experienced hunters or, as far as I knew, heard guns, so I found his behavior strange. It took much coaxing before he felt secure enough to let himself be approached and petted. And he didn't purr again till the boat had left the island.

At sunset we loaded the boat and left ourselves. It took a long time. Tom had to be literally dragged off the island. It was the first time that I had heard him growl as if he really meant it. I had no way of telling him we were coming back the following day.

As we sped off, Tom started to explore the boat. At twenty-five miles an hour and with his poor eyesight I thought that a perilous pursuit. On the other hand, if he persisted and then lost his balance and fell in, a cold dip might deter him from doing it again. David slowed the motor while Tom was tottering on all fours on the rubber pontoon. Gingerly, the cougar stretched out a paw to touch the water. He pressed. The water gave way and he followed. In less than thirty seconds he was clawing the sides of the rubber Avon trying to hoist himself on board. I whipped out the camera while Dave hauled him in. Hilary grabbed the gear shift and kept us on course. I'm sure the owner of the boat would prefer a picture like that to test the seaworthiness of his rubber than a cougar on the prow.

Tom wasn't nearly as active at night in the house. This time I tried to get shots of him sitting in a chair, lying on a chesterfield, or even—formerly a definite no-no—sprawling on a table. Whether it was lethargy after the day's excitement or his earlier training as a kitten I don't know, but all he wanted to do was to sit in the corner and purr. As a last resort to generate even one other camera location I said, "Into the bed, Tom," and never was there such a springing to life in a hurry. Instantaneously he darted into the bedroom and leaped onto the bed. We laughed about that.

Next day we set off again for Little Darcy. Tom must have known where we were going because about a hundred yards from the island he dived in and swam at tremendous speed for the shore. Obviously, his dip of the day before had been no deterrent. On this day David left Hilary and me to wander with Tom while he zipped over to neighboring Sidney Island to meet the boys from the university. They were going to catch brant together.

The day was dull and cloudy with a promise of rain. As the weather changed, so did Tom's mood. He was far more active than he had been the previous day. Hilary took pictures as he leapfrogged over my back and gamboled on top of me in a free-for-all on the grass, a play technique that I kept telling myself I shouldn't be doing. Not that he had any intention of hurting me, but it was impossible to stay upright under his weight and I didn't want my vulnerability as prey to prompt some wild instinct.

"Let's go for a run through the woods and let him work off his steam," Hilary suggested, gathering up the camera gear.

"Good idea," I agreed.

There had been something strange in Tom's attitude toward Hilary that morning. He seemed to resent her presence as soon as David left. As we walked along the trail he kept batting her leg, at first playfully, then with little nips. It was as if he was telling her to go away.

"Ow, Tom, no!" Hilary remonstrated, waving him away from her legs.

"No, Tom, bad!" I joined in, giving him a clout on

the rump. He glanced at me and whistled but kept on biting Hilary's ankles.

"I think I'll go and look at middens on the other side of the island," Hilary decided finally. "I think Tom wants you to himself."

It seemed strange but true. As soon as Hilary went back along the trail, Tom calmed down and purred. It was impossible to take his picture because he stuck so close to my legs, rubbing against me constantly.

I sat down on the shingle, he flopped down beside me, and I pondered on the meaning of his unusual behavior. Was it some stirring of his wild instincts brought to the surface by a day of freedom on the island? He was almost a year and a half old. Was it the emergence of his sexual instincts? Zoologists point out that hand-raised cats upon approaching maturity relate sexually to their owners and have consequent difficulty in mating with their own species. Was Tom sexually imprinted to me? Did he see Hilary as a rival? If so, why didn't he act jealously or possessively the day before? Of course, he had jumped into the bed when he wouldn't go anywhere else . . . no, that was just a joke. Well, did he regard me as a preferred companion and merely wanted my company alone? Was he trying to guard me from imaginary dangers now that David had gone and I was alone? In short, what went on in a cougar's mind?

I fought against the temptation of interpreting a cougar's thoughts and feelings as if it were a human being, not from any real conviction that there was a vast difference between the two, but because anthropomorphism is severely criticized in scientific circles. Yet these same critics accept anthropomorphisms in regard to their domestic pets. They accept the idea of cats being jealous of their owners, of dogs dying of "broken hearts," so why can't a cougar feel the so-called human desire of wanting to be alone with a mother, a companion, yes, even a mate? Or is a cougar motivated by fixed action patterns entirely separated from those that motivate man? Is love not an accurate word to describe the feelings of Tom for me? I think it an accurate word to describe mine for him.

Anthropomorphisms where humans try to humanize animals may not be scientifically acceptable. Ironically, zoomorphisms where tame animals animalize humans *is* accepted. A tame emu at a zoo in Switzerland tried regularly to mate with its keeper. An otter tried to mate with a man's leg. A ring dove attempted to mate with a human hand. Such acceptance by the animal of man as one of its own species is advantageous in maintaining good relations between the two. But if an animal as large as a moose or a cougar wants to mate with a man or fight off the competition it can be dangerous. I knew that Tom saw me as a mother and as a companion. I refused at that time to believe that he also saw me as a mate.

Who really knows what goes on in a cougar's mind? I stopped speculating, called Tom, and romped off down the beach. He followed, concentrating on keeping upright on the rocks. He moved slowly on the shingle, whistling to me whenever he wasn't sure of where to put his feet next. I had to encourage him one step at a time. He seemed helpless. How could he not pick out pebbles when he could certainly pick out Hilary's moving ankles? And how could he balance on a moving boat when he couldn't balance over rocks? How much of his awkwardness was due to his decreasing sight? I quickened my pace, getting farther ahead of him to see if increased distance might spur him to follow more closely and along the easiest path. Instead, he backtracked up the slope and ran along the grassy verge on top of the rocky cliff. We continued parallel on two levels, Tom on the high road, I on the low one. Suddenly I saw a stone crop flower I wanted to photograph, so I leaned down behind a boulder to get the camera in the best close-up position. Tom must have lost sight of me or thought I had deserted him.

At his shrill whistle I looked up from my flower just in time to stop him from tumbling fifty feet onto the rocks. He had already lowered one big forepaw over the edge and was about to throw himself after it.

I yelled, "No, Tom! Stop!"

His response to the sound of my voice was immediate. He drew back. I wasn't able to stop him biting Hilary's ankles by the same technique, but while we were alone he did respect his early training despite the eight months in the zoo. His quick response to the word "no" had certainly saved his life.

By maintaining voice contact I was able to keep him in the one spot till I had climbed the cliff. The separation had been slight, but his alarm or apprehension must have been great, so joyful was his greeting when I reached him. He purred and whistled and rubbed against my legs so much that I was forced to stumble rather than walk as we continued around the lagoon.

Hilary was busy at her digging as we passed. I looked anxiously at Tom to determine his reaction but was pleased to see he took no notice of her. We exchanged a couple of comments, then she went back to her midden and Tom followed me.

The whine of an outboard motor cut in above the lapping of the incoming tide. It was David returning from Sidney Island. He was surprised to see us separated, but he agreed it had probably been a good move. When Hilary joined us at the water's edge Tom showed no sign of hostility toward her. He seemed to accept her in the same way he had before. However, she wisely decided to remain alert. For the rest of the afternoon we walked around the island together and took pictures of Tom amid the myriad scenic backdrops that the island provided. He seemed quite content.

But when we returned to the boat and packed our gear aboard he must have realized that our odyssey was ending. For the first time he refused to come to my call, even to follow my running legs and kicked-up heels. Again he growled and this time his ears flattened. He wanted to stay on Little Darcy. So did we all. He could never understand.

At last David had to drag him down to the shoreline on a rope. Once there he jumped into the bottom of the boat and worked himself into a comfortable niche at our feet where he stayed till we sped home. Except for a slight seasickness which might have been due to the bumpy water, he looked as if this was his best ride yet.

Back at Island View he followed me faithfully to the compound without further trouble and fell asleep. A couple of hours later on the drive to Duncan I sat with him again in the back of the station wagon. He snuggled his head onto my lap and slept, too tired even to purr. And then it was back to the zoo.

It was a month after this visit to Little Darcy that we went up to Duncan for the last time. Rudy by now had sold all his big animals and was allowing us to put Tom in one of the cleared cages. At this time the cougar was well known on the Island and many people visited him regularly. A Japanese television company had written to ask if they could film a documentary about him. A Canadian man wanted to rent him for a movie showing the cougar's relationship with his wife. A Hollywood company wanted to buy him for use in commercials. We declined all such offers. I hoped one day we would be able to make a film of our own, not just the movies I sent home to my parents, but a film we could share with the world. However, David was always working on eagles or falcons or puffins and never seemed to get around to cougars. I took what I could in stills and kept hoping.

When we got Tom home from Duncan he seemed unusually demonstrative, so although the light was fading I took him down to the beach to take a few pictures. Fortunately, there was no one around and our house hid us from the sight of any who might care. Tom sat on his haunches watching me make sand castles. Only when I dug holes for a moat did he move. Then he followed me around the edge, sniffing at the sand as it fell away in the water. The air was still, not a ripple disturbed the water. His mood matched the placidity of the evening. After supper we took him to Rudy's. He lay on my lap all the way there like some overgrown baby.

When we arrived at the zoo I was glad to find out that

Tom was to occupy the bear enclosure, which was three times the size of his pen at Duncan. Rudy wanted us to first rebuild it where the bears had torn it down, so Tom came home to Island View for the night. Again he was very demonstrative, standing up on his hind legs and placing his paws on my shoulders and licking my sweater with his sandpaper tongue. And it was with great difficulty that I extricated my sweater by distracting his attention with food. His screaming whistle when he noticed I was gone followed me into the house. He must have been very lonely and for the first time I wondered if indeed it would not be kinder to leave him at the zoo, accustomed to the one place and the one routine, than to upset his equilibrium by our occasional forays to islands and nights at home.

Next day we drove him over to Rudy's but again the pen wasn't finished, so we brought him home once more. His attitude on the second night was more worried than loving. He seemed to be concerned about Haida, who was in season in the adjacent enclosure, and Sam, who was pushing against the door trying to reach his canine playmate. The cougar paced restlessly around the pen and when I came in, he even bit my arm deep enough to leave a bruise. Strangely enough, next morning when the pen was finished and we left him at Rudy's, he was his own purring sweet self again.

Although I now saw Tom more often, sometimes two or three times a week, the visits were not as enjoyable as they had been in Duncan. One of the problems was the size of the pen itself. Now Tom could gallop around and build up such speed that if he decided to leap on me at the end of his run, I fell on the cement floor and found bruises under my jeans at the end of the day. Such high jinks on his part would send worried bystanders running to Rudy to tell him to come to my rescue. "There's a girl in the cougar cage and she's having a hard time." By the time they returned, Tom or as much of him that would fit, was lying in my lap, purring.

Another problem was the number of visitors; there were many more in this prime location beside Butchart's Gardens, the main tourist attraction in Victoria, than on the road up-Island. Now for the first time I felt conspicuous sitting in a large enclosure with a cougar flopping all over me, nursing on my Band-Aided fingers. I felt I was in a circus and was expected to put on an act. Somehow at Duncan in the last pen at the end of the zoo among the trees, it had been more intimate and less overwhelming. Tosca or Jim would often sit beside me outside the cage and we'd gossip either among ourselves or with the few people who wandered along.

A third concern was that Tom spent more time in playful activity than in just lying still sucking my thumbs. He still lavished me with affection but for shorter periods of time. This was understandable because he saw me more often, but his times away from my thumbs, when he acted too roughly, became increasingly harder to handle.

His obvious need for affection and company was a consequence of being raised in captivity. In the wild a male cougar is basically a solitary animal after he has become independent of his mother. He has to be in order to survive by his specialized form of hunting. Yet on Vancouver Island and in California, it has been observed recently that cougars do not avoid other cougars or defend territory as much as Maurice Hornocker found they did in Idaho. Near Nanaimo it was discovered that two families with kittens lived within a mile of each other, thus showing surprising territorial tolerance. Perhaps there are times in a cougar's life apart from mating when it appears more sociable.

Comparing a cougar in captivity to one in the wild has limitations. In Tom's case he did not have to lead a solitary existence to pursue his own prey. And at this stage of his life in the wild he would still be with his mother. He was totally dependent on me for everything, especially since the departure of Oola. So I saw his need to lick and suck as natural consequences of his desire to communicate with some other living thing, particularly one whom he depended on for his survival. I was the only constant aspect of his life.

Jim regarded Tom's behavior as a healthy sign of the cougar's affection. Rudy thought it undesirable and sug-

gested I try to train him as a wild-animal trainer would
—forbidding physical contact, teaching him certain
commands, and communicating to him by food rewards.
He warned that I would have trouble at Tom's maturity
in six months' time. I thought it was a bit too late for
such a drastic change of behavior and decided to hope
for the best. I thanked him for his warning and prom-
ished caution. As long as Tom was content to lick and
suck my thumbs, I would be satisfied.

At this time I was receiving warnings in the press
as well. A reporter in the local paper wrote a whole
column on the noises his son had heard outside his
camper at night in a park up-Island. He surmised that
the creature that "yowled, growled and spat" within
earshot of the camper was a cougar and that all such
animals had "vile tempers." His remedy for cougars
that are heard in a park was that they should be trailed
by cougar dogs, treed, and shot.

The phrase I took most exception to was his generality, "all cougars have vile tempers," so I sent in
another anthropomorphic generality to the paper the
next day. This was a portrait of Tom and me asleep
arm-in-forepaw among the lilies on Little Darcy Island.
I added a picture of Tom lying beside me in the rubber boat. Naturally, it was a tongue-in-cheek rebuttal,
an attempt to show the reporter that my exception
to the rule was equivalent to his exception to the rule
and that neither experience was in perspective or could
be called customary cougar behavior. I wanted to
draw attention to the fact that not all cougars were
grouchy. At least Tom wasn't. I even quoted respected
local biologists who shared my opinions.

I'm too forthright for the press and should learn the
lesson that the media always have the last word. In fact,
I was told once by a newspaper editor that you should
never criticize the printed word of the press. In the
columnist's next article he answered me with sarcasm,
anger, and some more exaggeration. He said my claims
were "extravagant," that I had "eulogized" the cat
tribe, and he wondered if his son shouldn't have lured
the cougar heard in the park into the camper and

taken it for a rubber boat ride. He ended by warning me never to turn my back on Tom.

This was something I was concerned about in the larger pen at Rudy's. Whereas at Duncan Tom had to release his pent-up energy by pacing in a small space and running up and down the log that led to his sleeping platform, now he could move like the whirlwind. His activity was stimulated further by a pack of dingoes yapping and scampering in the adjacent pen and the smells of other animals in near proximity and the crowds of little children who ran up and down outside the cage.

In these adolescent years Tom seemed to have an increasing need to use his teeth and claws. Whenever he stopped sucking and started chomping, I carefully extricated my fingers from his molars and gave him an old shoe or coat instead. He always ran away and played with it, so I knew my fingers meant plaything as well as companionship.

One day in order to distract him from communicating with me via his jaws, I decided to clean the pen. As he had done in his kitten days in the back yard he chased my broom, batted my legs, and tore the bucket out of my hands. Since little cleaning could be accomplished this way, I eventually gave him the broom and finished my chores with part of another one I found lying in the corner. Instead of playing with the broom, as he used to do with the shoe and coat, he clasped it in both his forepaws and slobbered over it in apparent ecstasy. When he finally lost interest in it he ran around the pen and leaped at the two howling dingoes beside him. Then turning suddenly, he came running at me. With so many people watching I didn't want to make too much of a show of chastising him. Yet some discipline had to be attempted, else he might continue to think this was legitimate play. I caught him by the head and yelled, "No, Tom," and slapped him down on the concrete. Although he could have mangled me if he'd been so inclined, he lay down, closed his eyes, and purred.

Because of these changes in behavior, which I personally attributed to the change of pen, his new neighbors, my more frequent visits, and his period of adolescence, I wrote to ask advice of Howard and Dorothy Smith, who then lived on Quadra Island. The Smiths had raised three cougars of their own in Idaho and had also brought one with them when they emigrated to British Columbia. They had had dinner with us when we were still in Vancouver. After seeing some of the "Seven O'Clock Show" sequences on television they had shown some of their own film on Bob Fortune's "Klahanie" program. It was the Smiths who confirmed Tom's cataracts and advised us to put him to sleep immediately before we got too fond of him. That was one piece of advice we weren't able to consider. However, I looked forward to receiving their comments on my current situation.

Campbell River,
June 12, 1968

Dear Dave and Lyn:
Of course, only the cougar knows what goes on in his mind, but we can speculate a little after enough experience along certain lines.

In regard to the sucking on your arm or finger, so long as Tom has that much affection for you, you certainly have nothing to fear at any time. The cougar, male or female, gets some sort of sexual satisfaction from doing this, but sexual satisfaction is only a very minor part of this act. The cougar is simply showing genuine affection or love. Even a neutered cougar will do the same thing except that one will not be aware of any sexual arousement in the cougar. Daily association with a cougar will cut the time interval down to about fifteen minutes per session. Each cougar will select an individual for that kind of loving or he may have several people who are dear enough to him to receive genuine cougar love from him. We noticed that each of our cougars had a special friend and the cougar did not want to be separated from that friend for any length of time, but if that did happen, then the cougar would make up for it by an extended loving at the next meeting.

The cougar paces about when he gets excited and if he is in a cage, about all he can do is run back and forth in the restricted area. The nearness of a friend, anticipation of mealtime, or even something which the cougar wants to catch outside the pen will cause him to run around in a cage. If there is anything for them to jump upon inside the cage, they will usually jump up and down as well as pace about.

In regard to growling at people, it depends on the intonation which Tom gives to the growl. It is not serious until the cougar growls very low, that is, deep in voice, loud, and with an exhaling through the nose while giving the growl. Then the stranger should take heed. I have never seen a cougar hurt one of his friends intentionally.

When Tom jumps up on you he is probably wanting you to hold him in your lap as you did when he was younger. Our Big Joe would insist on sitting in my lap even when he weighed 220 pounds—a real lap full.

It is very doubtful if you will ever have to worry about Tom trying to get the upper hand with Lyn but others should be on the alert, especially at his present age. The only outward indications of anything being amiss are ear position and head position. I cannot describe the head position to you but the ears will be turned back about a third of the way and held in what looks like a menacing manner. I don't think there's a time in a cougar's life when he goes wild, the only wild animal that I know is homo sapiens. All the cougar has on his mind is to be the boss man but he can get rough while asserting his authority. You simply must get a little rougher with the cougar than he does with you, something which is a mite easier written than performed. Another change which takes place near the 18 months age is that a cougar will develop a very strong protective instinct at that time. He will protect you from either real or imaginary danger, and if that danger happens to be another person, then things can get out of hand quickly.

The one big problem for you to keep in mind is that you don't know how Tom is being treated when you are not there. It is extremely doubtful that Tom would ever take out a grudge on you regardless of what someone else had done to him but it is something to think about.

Be careful with children. You never know how a child will act and a cougar is a no-nonsense animal.

We hope you continue your friendship with Tom,

> Sincerely,
> Howard and Dorothy Smith

As people continued to speculate on the day Tom would turn on me, I asked further advice from Lloyd Beebe, owner of the Olympic Game Farm at Sequim. "Cougars have given me the most enjoyment in my life," Lloyd said. "And if raised with affection and have passed the play stage they don't try to hurt you. I remember one of my cougars once appeared what you might call wild for a few minutes or so. It was one of my best males too. I used to hike with him in the wilds of Washington. This time I hadn't seen him for about ten minutes. I was just setting up the tripod and readying the camera for a scene of a valley. Suddenly, up comes the cougar from the bank in front of me and looks over the valley. Then he whirls around and starts hissing and circling to within three or four feet of me. He didn't know me, he was somewhere else. He was dreaming. He took about five minutes to forget it. I had several of them like this and all were males, though I don't know if that's enough to mean anything. I haven't really noticed a lot of difference in the tractability of males versus females, though I'd probably lean a bit towards thinking that the females were more tractable. I think it all depends on how they were raised. The biggest mistake is to play with them. Don't rough them up when they are small. If you do, they will want to continue to play rough when they are big and that's dangerous."

Since then I have asked several other people which sex appeared more gentle and they all replied females. However, in my experience of raising a dozen cougars to date, it has been the male who has been more tractable.

I raised Tom in a vacuum of knowledge without any previous experience, either personal or vicarious. I observed but I didn't know how to interpret the behavior I noted. The only people I knew at the time who had enjoyed intimate contact with cougars were Howard and Dorothy Smith.

Then one day Susan im Baumgarten, a local Swiss artist, and her husband, John, introduced us to some California acquaintances of theirs who were writing a book on people and their wild pets. I remember the meeting very well because it was early in the morning just as Dave and I had arrived back from a study trip to the West Coast. Having slept on the side of the road in our sleeping bags the night before, we were dead tired, but enthusiasm waxed and eyes lit up, as always happens when "animal nuts" get together. We took Bob and Lea Leslie around the compound to see the latest batch of puffins, murres, auklets, murrelets and oyster catchers, the resident great blue heron, and some cormorants, then through the eagle and falcon enclosures. Sam coughed his way eagerly between us all and deposited a fishy kiss on Bob's nose while Susan sketched and Lea photographed.

Before we rushed off to another expedition I took Bob to see Tom. I admit to being concerned when Tom, after welcoming me in the usual demonstrative manner, rushed over to investigate Bob. There was a slight curling back of the lips and a bit of a growl as the cougar stepped almost on top of him to get a better look, then he rushed back to my lap. While Bob filmed Tom purred, we chatted about other cougars he had met during his summer research visiting people who lived with wild animals.

When I relayed some of my worries about a cougar's special interest in small children, he told me of ten-year-old Desdemona, a female cougar in Santa Barbara who baby-sat children. In his book *Wild Pets* he describes her in this way:

When we arrived the big yellow-eyed cat—155 pounds—lay flat on her back in the centre of the living room floor with her paws clasped around her head. She seemed to be on the defensive as six small children pulled her ears, crimped her tail, and gnawed her elbows. Two sat astraddle of her chest and pounded her belly. At times she caterwauled bitterly and looked to the adults for help. . . .

Bob then goes on to quote Desdemona's owner:

"Best baby-sitter in the country. Won't let anybody come in the house at night when we go out and leave her with the kids. Helluva lot more authority in her growl than the bark of a dog when she leans on the window sill and stares at strangers.
"She's a good camper too. Loves to swim with the kids but she pulls 'em ashore if she thinks they're in too deep water. . . . You should see the double takes when people pass the microbus and spot that big head among the kids."

It seems to me that heredity plays as much a part of any cougar's given personality and tractability as environment. Tammy and Tom in the same litter were as different as two cougars could be, yet their upbringing was identical. Desdemona, brought up with babies, baby-sat them in safety when she was ten years old, more than middle age for a cougar, and a time when other cougars have become grouchy.

Certain cougars seem unique, or at least rather special. Desdemona. Tom. And Big Joe, the cougar who lived free in Idaho with Howard and Dorothy Smith, the cougar whose story I was soon to hear.

15

The Tragedy of Big Joe

While Tom was staying at Rudy's Pet Park we took a boat trip to visit the Smiths on Quadra Island, about seven miles from Campbell River. As we tied up at their boat dock and they came down the beach to greet us, I wished Tom had been part of our crew. Normally, the Smiths would have met us with a cougar of their own.

"Almost everybody that's fished around here has landed on this sandy beach at one time or another to let Little Joe board their boat for salmon. They'd take pictures while the cougar dragged the fish on the dock and started eating," Howard explained as he helped us haul our gear to the house. "He met all the boats and he sure knew the difference between salmon and other fish like rock cod or ling cod. He'd choose salmon every time."

"Weren't people afraid to see a cougar come on their boats?" I asked wonderingly.

"Most of them were used to the cougar and brought their families specially to see him," replied Howard. Then with an infectious smile: "There were some though that hadn't heard of him. Like the time we just got back from Campbell River with our mail and groceries and met a boat of fishermen coming away from our cove. They could see we were heading into the dock and they shouted out to warn us. 'Oh my God! Don't go in there. There's the biggest damn cat you ever saw in your life.' Little Joe would always wait on the end of the logs till we got back from a trip."

"Some of the women were afraid, though," Dorothy added. "One night a man tied up his fifty-foot trawler at the dock and left his wife aboard. Little Joe went out and climbed through an open window into her cabin. She finally escaped the arms of the entangling cougar and made it to our house."

"Then there were the two fellows who dropped in after dark," continued Howard. "They'd lost their shear pin, beached their boat, and walked three miles in the rain to our place. We gave them supper and during the meal they said they'd heard we had a cougar. I said, 'Yes, I'm surprised you got here without him finding you. Guess he's out eating salmon.' While we were talking, Joe walked in. Well, one fellow almost fainted and the other almost dived out the window. The cougar was about a year and a half at that time and an over-fed 150 pounds. The two fellows said that if they'd known about Little Joe they'd have swum Discovery Passage rather than walk inland to our place."

Unfortunately, although the Smiths are wonderfully hospitable people, they couldn't offer to show us a cougar. Little Joe, the cougar they'd brought with them from Idaho two years before, had been shot by one of the neighbors. As we sat down to supper Howard told us what had happened.

"A farmer who lives on the other side of the island shot him. I can't really blame him as that was the chance we took when we came here with a cougar that roamed free like all our cougars have. Little Joe usually came in at night to sleep on the back porch but one night he followed a female cougar that was in season. It was raining very hard and I couldn't track where they'd gone. Two days later we got word of him. He must have got turned around and wandered to a farmer's house and scrambled into his sheep. The dog came out and started to attack the cougar. When the cougar didn't run the farmer came out and shot him. Like Tom, Little Joe had very poor eyesight. He had a cataract in one eye and an infection from a thorn in the other.

And I think that made him more aggressive than the other cougars."

It seemed ironic that the Smiths should lose their male cougar because he had been led away by a female. They would have been more pleased if the female had followed Little Joe home. Their whole purpose in coming to Quadra Island was to have a friendly female cougar mate with a wild male.

"We want to get a female and tame it so that she trusts us and lets us observe her," Howard explained. "Then when she breeds in the wild and has her cubs, we can be in contact with her without petting the cubs or making them domestic. We want them to live in the wild state, but we need the female to be friendly so we can get close enough to observe her. We want to study how she hunts, how she raises her family, how long they stay with her. We'd like to continue these observations through two or three generations if we could."

"But why did you choose Quadra Island?" David asked. "I would have thought you'd have to go farther afield, some place like Aristazababel Island up north, which is much more remote. Lyn and I have talked about doing something like that ourselves."

"First off, we couldn't use Little Joe because of his poor eyesight and, anyway, he was a male. Vancouver Island should have been a good source of cougars for the project. And then there are a lot of blacktail deer on the Island for the cougars to feed on.

"Campbell River is the last place of any consequence on the Island, so I started looking northward from there. Dorothy and I stayed at a motel near a fishing resort and we heard about a Thor Peterson who had a real estate business on Quadra Island. The Petersons suggested we get advice from Roderick Haig-Brown, who as you know is a well-known fisherman, writer, and magistrate in Campbell River. Haig-Brown said our best bet was the west coast of Vancouver Island but that Dorothy wouldn't like it as it rained too much, it was far from civilization, and we'd have trouble taking decent film. He said conditions were more ideal on the east side of the Island but that the local people probably wouldn't let us carry out the program. Thor Peterson suggested this place on Quadra and we bid till the fellow couldn't afford to turn it down.

"Quadra Island is a pretty good location. There is no habitation from our place north on the west side. On the east there are a few summer homes but they are at least seven miles away. Our nearest neighbor is three and one-half miles by water to the south. And I doubt by the lay of the land that a cougar would wander over to the nearest settlement, which also is three and one-half miles away. Our cougars in Idaho never wandered more than ten miles away if there was plenty of food nearby, and on Quadra there are lots of blacktail deer and salmon runs. Our place has twenty-seven acres and there are no roads in, only skid trails. People that come in by road have to work their way in by four-wheel drive and cross a beaver pond."

"But how did you get into Canada in the first place?" I asked, puzzled that they, strangers, should have got a permit to bring an adult American cougar over the border when we who lived here could only get a permit to keep a cougar for six months.

"When we bought the place we made arrangements to emigrate," Howard replied. "I didn't see the director of Fish and Wildlife, Dr. Hatter, I saw the chief of Wildlife Management, Glen Smith. He said as far as he was concerned there was nothing to stop me bringing in a cougar or a wolf cub. 'Once you get there,' he said, 'there'll probably be some rule but at present there are none.' Still, he advised us for our own protection to contact a particular doctor at the border and have him examine our animals. I called this doctor and he said, 'Sure, I'll be glad to. There are no restrictions except get a rabies shot for the wolf.'

"The day before we arrived at the border the doctor had to go to hospital with appendicitis. I called the customs agent to tell him of our predicament, but he didn't know what to do. I suggested he speak to the hospital to prove that the vet was having an appendectomy. When he hung up the phone the customs official said, 'I suppose we can let you in the country now and get you later if anything is wrong. But you'd better sign a statement that the doctor did tell you that you didn't need any papers to come into Canada.' So we crossed the border by signing our own entrance papers," chortled Howard as he rummaged through his files to show us the document. "Here it is. Our landed immigration papers are typed, but this bit is written in longhand—'Mr. Smith says he doesn't need any kind of papers to bring a wolf and a cougar in to B.C.' That's my signature."

"So you haven't had any problem?" I asked in astonishment.

"Not at the border and not when I checked with Glen Smith at the Fish and Wildlife Branch or the magistrate Haig-Brown. But we weren't here very long when George Taylor, the conservation officer, came over to tell us we'd have to get rid of our cougar. When we asked him why, he said he'd had all kinds of complaints. 'Would you mind telling me one name?' I asked. But he wouldn't name anybody, so I guess he was the only complainant. This made me very angry. I asked him if he was telling me to dispose of my cougar. He said, 'I'm only telling you that you must get a zoo license or else get rid of your cougar.'

"During the conversation Little Joe appeared in the house by way of a hole in the living-room wall where we were going to build a fireplace. The officer was pretty apprehensive, I can tell you. But he could see the cougar was completely free to come and go as he pleased. He wanted me to pay for a zoo license and abide by zoo regulations, but why? I didn't have any animals penned up. Anyway, I got in the boat and went over to Haig-Brown's. He said, 'Howard, why don't you file suit to make them show just cause? It's got to be tried in my court.' Well, I didn't want to get into any kind of litigation. You can't fight government, not a little fellow like me and win. But I did go down to Victoria to see the director, Dr. Hatter, and to tell him what I was doing.

"He said, 'Suppose we have trouble?' I said, 'I'm a responsible person. I've talked to the local judge, the local police, and the neighbors, and they haven't complained to me. They can all use our boat dock and beach and they do. I have promised them compensation if the cougar damages anything. I have sense enough to stay here a year or two to make friends with the people, get to know the island, and do the necessary leg work before we start the program. I'm trying to do something here for the benefit of everybody. And I'm willing to share all my film and notes with you as the program goes along.'

"Hatter asked me, 'But what if a sheep is killed and we suspect your cougar and we send in a cougar hunter to get it?' And I replied, 'Well, I've already told you, I will pay any damage the cougar does.'

" 'But what if that hunter puts his dogs onto the cougar and they chase him to your house?' Hatter continued. 'If that's off limits, it's all right,' I answered.

" 'But what if they chase him onto your property?' he persisted. 'Now who is off limits?' I countered. 'When the hounds cross the property line or the man crosses the property line . . .'

"Hatter didn't wait till I finished. He turned around in his chair and faced the wall and said, 'We do have a problem, don't we?' I said, 'No, we don't have a problem, if we have some cooperation. It's up to you. You have the power over wildlife in B.C. in the palm of your hand.'

"Well, six months after that, Little Joe was shot by a farmer. And since then I've been trying to get another cougar, but now I find from one of the cougar hunters in Campbell River that it is worth the license of any hunter to sell me one. I could get one from the States but I'd still have harassment from the Branch if I continued the program. When you have an extremely difficult project to begin with and then harassment on top of that, the odds are too great to get anything done."

"You still have a wolf, don't you?" I asked, suddenly remembering the cub that came across the border with them.

"No, Little Joe killed her. She was a charming thing but she teased the cougar unmercifully. It was so bad that I had to build a containing pen for the cougar while I was training the wolf to heel and obey commands. Otherwise she wouldn't pay attention. One day I put the cougar in the pen and took off with the wolf. But she abandoned me and went home to tease the cougar. Little Joe jumped right through the fence, grabbed the wolf, and killed her," answered Howard.

Some people have stated that a pack of wolves is one of the cougar's few enemies. Felix Michaud, a hunter and naturalist, writing at the turn of the century, describes graphically how wolves may chase a cougar into a tree:

> "Should the quarry succeed in gaining a tree its fate, in bitter cold weather, will still be very uncertain; for the wolves, unless called off by an earlier chase, will watch, in a restless state of action which keeps their own legs limber, until the cougar's feet are frozen, and the animal powerless to cling falls into their waiting jaws. Thus the lion has been killed minus tail, ears and several of its toes, lost in standing such a siege."

Another observer noted that when four male wolves broke out into howls in a zoo, a captive cougar, a couple of cages away, stopped its pacing, lowered its ears, and slunk to a corner in obvious alarm. I wondered how much of Tom's increased excitability at Rudy's was due to his placement beside the dingoes.

By this time we were enjoying not only coffee and conversation in the Smiths' living room but a beautiful view over a shimmering sea as the sun set behind Campbell River. The tranquillity of the scene was in sharp contrast to the turbulent tale Howard told us when I asked him for details on living with cougars in Idaho.

"Dorothy and I are backwoods people. We lived in a log cabin on my mining claim fifteen miles from the nearest post office in Elk City and seventy-five miles from the nearest incorporated town of Stites in Idaho. Most of the people who live there are friends; they are there because they want to be left alone, because it is still the freest place in the world. Idaho County is the only place in the States that has no building inspection, no land planning. It's in the books but they don't dare come and do it.

"All of the people there are outdoorsmen, so it was nothing out of the ordinary for us to have cougars. At the time we got our first one, Big Joe, a cougar was classed as a varmint, it wasn't big game and subject to regulations. The bounty was off, so I didn't have to worry about bounty hunters—just trophy hunters who might want the head or hide. We put up signs, 'Please don't shoot our pet cougar,' and hoped for the best. Hunters sometimes got a surprise when Big Joe popped up beside them to help in the cleaning of their kills. In the beginning we had no trouble."

"How did you get Big Joe?" I asked apologetically. "I know you told me back in Vancouver, but there were so many other things happening that night I can't remember the details."

"Two of our South Texan friends came for a visit in August 1961. We accidentally stumbled on a young fellow that had just shot a female cougar. The hunter thought he'd keep the one male kitten that survived as a conversation piece, but when he ran out of beer money in Elk City, he sold it to an elderly man who lived alone, but the man couldn't get it to eat. So our Texan friends bought it for twenty-five dollars and gave it to us as a present.

"Big Joe was pretty little when we got him, three and one-half pounds and less than two weeks old. Dorothy fed him on Pet Milk with two parts of water and a few drops of Karo syrup. He couldn't tolerate fresh cow's milk. When Dorothy wasn't looking after him, Torrey, our part shepherd, part sheep dog, did. The dog and the cougar became good friends. The only time they were separated was at night when Big Joe slept in his own cot next to our bed. He was always free to come and go as he liked. He never learned toilet training but he did learn to open the door. He put his mouth right on the knob and twisted it."

"How did you discipline them?" I asked.

"Dorothy taught all our cougars to sheathe their claws so they wouldn't hurt people. She trained them to the word 'no' and if they still didn't mind her, she slapped them behind the ears and that got their attention. I'm sure the cougar mother would do the same. Sometimes a cougar determines he's going to be boss man. I've broken the bones of my hand disciplining a cougar if I found it necessary."

"But they have a real sense of humor too," Dorothy interjected. "That Big Joe was a big tease. He would come into the house and steal a roast off the table, then run out the back door. I'd chase him with a broom and take it off him. He let me do it too. Of course, the roast wasn't fit to eat by that time so we'd give it back to him later. He did it for devilment. He'd steal my broom too and run to the woods with it. I'd have to keep a spare one up on top of the cupboard almost at the ceiling so he couldn't reach it.

"I remember one day it was freezing cold. I had done my washing and hung it on the line. Of course it froze stiff. I went out after dark to bring it in. I'd forgotten about Joe. I had both my arms full of clothes when Joe came up behind me and hit me in the middle of the back. Of course the clothes went this way and I went that. Then the cougar just sat back and laughed." Dorothy giggled.

"He teased me too," broke in Howard. "Many times when we were in the woods nature would call and I had to relieve myself. I'd dig a hole like any woodsman. The cougar also dug a hole and then covered it up afterward. He'd dig with his front feet. Well, one day I dug a hole and just as I turned around after unzipping my trousers, there was Big Joe sitting in my hole. I kicked him in the rear end and made him dig his own hole. I wish I'd had my movie camera there then!"

We all broke into laughter at that story, so Howard had to wait until we settled down again before he could continue. "Little Joe had a sense of humor too. He sure got in the way when Bob Hall of Campbell River tried to help me log the old fir off my place here on Quadra.

As soon as Bob got in his tractor, there was Little Joe in the driver's seat with him, trying to help him start. When we tried to pull the choker cable to skid the logs, the cougar would grab it and as he weighed 170 pounds, we had to get him loose first before we could pull it. Bob thought it was cute at first, but then he got mad and said he wouldn't work with a cougar on the line."

Always conscious of the practical consequences of living free with a cougar, I asked, "I know you lived a long way from people but how did the cougar behave toward visitors?"

"All cougars are different but Big Joe was the most gentle cougar we raised. He showed no aggression at all. I could give raw meat to toddlers and Big Joe would take it from their hands. If I had a cut hand he'd lick the blood off. We lived in a remote area, but the word soon got around about the remarkable cougar at Elk City, and hundreds of people came knocking on the door. Some Sundays the three of us had to leave and go up to another cabin we had in the woods and sleep there for the afternoon to avoid them."

As Dorothy got up to pour us more coffee, Howard reminisced further about Big Joe: "He sure frightened a lot of visitors but he never hurt them. I remember when he was sixty pounds, a Forest Service engineer had occasion to come over to the house to get me to repair a radiator. I left him in the yard and said I'd be back with some solder and a torch. Joe left the house by the back door, saw the visitor, and slunk up to him. Now the engineer was new to the area, he came from Washington, D.C., and the local boys had done a good job of indoctrinating him about cougars that eat children. When Big Joe got into his stalking position he lost his nerve, dropped the radiator, and started to run to me at the garage. As soon as he moved, the cougar bounded out to him and had him down in the snow with his front feet, though his claws were sheathed. He was looking that engineer right in the eye when I came out. As the guy wasn't hollering I didn't pay much attention. I went back into the garage, but then when I came out again, he was still down in the same position. It dawned on me the fellow was in shock. His eyes were glassy, he was tongue-tied, and sweat was pouring off his face even though it was 17 below. I told Big Joe to get off him and then I had the engineer try to hold the radiator so I could repair it. Well, St. Vitus dance must have set in—he was incoherent and he couldn't stay still. Half an hour later, over at the ranger station, he was still incoherent. When word got around next day as to what happened, his wife and child came over to the house to pet Joe and nobody would believe his story of the night before.

"Then there was the elderly fellow that came up one night with his sleeping bag and pitched camp near our cabin. I went over to warn him that a cougar would probably be down to see him. He didn't seem to be a bit afraid, Big Joe showed up while I was still talking to him. I told the fellow that if the cougar gave him any trouble, he should not try to fight back but just come up to the house and I'd take care of it. I told him to come to the house anyway in the morning and have a cup of coffee with me before I went to work. At that time I was working for the Forest Service, the only big employer in the area.

"Next morning I asked the old man if he'd been visited by a cougar in the night. 'Yeah,' he said, 'he came down and I offered him a bit of bacon. He didn't like it but he reached behind me and bit a hole in my sleeping bag and air mattress. It just went *choo-oo* all the way down.' I offered to replace his equipment but he said, 'No, I've got a conversation piece here I can talk about forever.'"

I found Howard's tales amusing, but I wanted to know how he and the cougar went hunting together. To me, that was why Big Joe was something special.

"I took Big Joe hunting with me while he was still on the bottle and when the snow was so deep he had to walk in my tracks. When he was about a year old he started catching a few grouse and squirrels for himself. He'd go hunting with Torrey, the dog. People would tell me they'd seen a cougar and a dog wandering together and I wondered if I should pen the dog, give it away, or even kill it. It's kind of serious to have a cougar and dog hunting together. There's little worse than a domesticated animal going wild. And if dogs are seen harassing big game, whoever sees it kills it, down in that part of the world. I talked it over with the local law enforcement officer and he said, 'Don't you kill that dog. It's the most fascinating thing this country has ever seen.'"

"Did you ever worry about the cougar killing the dog?" I interjected, thinking of Tom's behavior toward Haida and Sam now that he was growing up.

Howard guffawed. "Hell no, less chance than a calf killing its mother. And it wasn't only the dog that went hunting with Big Joe; it was the hunters too. During the season hunter after hunter would come to the house and ask, 'Can I go hunting with your cougar?' Then in the summer young person after young person would come and ask us if we would let Joe go and shoot squirrels with them. Big Joe thoroughly enjoyed it. He would be perfectly satisfied to let you shoot your quarry but if you missed and it got away, he would reprimand you by knocking you down and giving you a good going over. And if he was going to get himself a deer and I made a noise and frightened it off, he would do the same thing. Once when he scared off a deer I was going to get, I lay my gun down, went up to him, jumped on him, and pounded him with my fist all over the shoulders and chest and face as hard as I could. He just lay there grinning as I got my own back."

Dorothy interjected with a hunting story of her own. "I went for a walk one day with Big Joe and a grouse jumped down from a tree. Big Joe saw it. I raised my gun to shoot it and the cougar stepped back. I fired a shot but missed and the grouse flew up in the tree. All the way back home Joe kept hitting me with his paws, first on one side, then the other. He was really aggravated with me for missing that grouse."

"Did he get all his food himself or did you feed him too?" I asked.

"We always provided food because we thought he

would get into less trouble with the neighbors that way," Howard replied. "And he was lazy, he didn't do much killing on his own. But we knew he was getting some on his own when he either stopped eating at the house or was eating less."

"Did you ever see him make a kill?" David questioned.

"Yes, he must have been about 180 pounds at the time. He went through the whole procedure. He was just like a human hunter. He lay down on his stomach and deliberately scanned an area. Then he moved over and stared at another area, at each individual tree or bush or rock, just like a hunter does with binoculars. And as he glassed it, his ears would take in every sound like radar screens. He knew if it was big game or if it was a dog or a squirrel dropping cones. If he heard an elk or deer break a twig he took a line to intercept where the animal was going. He seemed to be able to determine its direction from one sound; at least that's all I could hear.

"A cougar is naturally very quiet. Even at thirty miles an hour Big Joe could spread those big paws out on the ground and go over downed timber without making a sound. And very efficient too. I'd lay a scent trail down or blow a wounded prey call. I could see him leave the house and the next thing I knew he was there licking me on the back of the head.

"Anyway, on the day I saw him make his first deer kill, he stalked it as it was moving downhill. Seems that just before he made the kill, his tail twitched. Then he sprang, hit the deer on the shoulder, and knocked it off balance. Then he grabbed it by the back of the neck and bit into its vertebrae with his jaws. At the same time he had his back feet over the deer so that it couldn't kick him loose."

"How much of the hunting procedure do you think was instinctive?" I wanted to know.

"I don't know anything we had to teach Big Joe for his survival," Howard replied. "He was a natural stalker like all cats. On the other hand, he could have learned from the house cats and the dog he was raised with.

And then he was free to roam in the woods in an area with lots of game to practice on. He seemed to play at hunting till he was about two, but from then on it was strictly business."

Although deer is the kind of prey most commonly killed by cougars, it doesn't appear that this choice is an instinctive one. In Arizona, 60 per cent of the prey taken by cougars in one survey was white-faced calves. In Idaho, in the summer months cougars fed almost entirely on ground squirrels. In a third survey undertaken in the central interior of British Columbia at a time when the varying hare population was at its peak, cougars fed more on hare than deer. Cougars are opportunists that take the prey that is most easily available.

Perhaps young cougars have to actually eat the carcass before they recognize it as food, as something to hunt when they come across it in the wild. Rich Poelker, a game biologist from Washington, put it like this: "I don't think cougars catch sight of a deer and associate it immediately with the bloody mess they were chewing on the night before with their mother. I think deer are commonly around where they are and when they get close enough to get one down and then to smell it, they say, 'Hmm! That's food, Mum.' So they run and hit it in the butt, maybe get kicked in the chops, do a few somersaults in reverse, bounce a lot, and soon learn what prey is."

Rich agreed with Howard and me that much of the hunting procedure is instinctive, but must be refined by practice. He stated his opinion a bit more colorfully than we did: "A cougar doesn't get taught by his mother what to do, but she does provide the opportunities for learning and she protects him while he makes mistakes. Cougars stalk a lot of things instinctively and instinctively they want to hunt, but they have to learn from trial and error what to catch and how to refine their stalking and hunting techniques. Mother get them in on a hunt or two, but when they do it by themselves, she's not there saying, 'You put one paw here and another there.' The kittens have to get out and work at it till they find the right combination. Now cougars don't go around dragging animals by the rear haunches, they grab them by the front end. They all finish up doing the same thing, so there must be a certain amount of instinctive behavior. And I think that's why so few people get killed by cougars. Cougars just don't know what to do with prey that's straight and tall and two-legged. They've had no experience with that kind of prey."

Very few people have ever seen a cougar make a kill in the wild. Even when you live with free-roaming cougars as Howard and Dorothy did, the opportunity is rare. However, the Smiths knew when Big Joe was going to make a kill and sometimes they found the kill afterward.

"Big Joe seemed to get restless just before sundown and he'd leave the house. He'd come back to sleep, then leave the house again an hour or two before sunup. When I got up I'd find his kill dragged to a shady tree or windfall and opened up, I believe, to let the animal heat out."

"Was it covered up?" I asked.

"He didn't cover it up during the night but he'd do it the next day. Then the following night he'd uncover the kill and start eating. I guess a cougar thinks that covering his kill is like putting it in a safety deposit in the bank, that it is perfectly safe till he returns."

"Remember how mink would steal Little Joe's kills?" broke in Dorothy.

"Yes, we'd give him a salmon, a hindquarter, or something, as he couldn't kill his own like Big Joe, and if it was small enough, a mink would drag it away to its hole. Little Joe would get so angry he'd scream and holler and I'm sure he was cursing. Then he'd follow the scent trail, reach as deep as he could into the mink's hole to get that mink out of there. He hated mink—every time he saw or smelled one, he tried to get it."

"What's the most interesting thing that happened while you were out hunting with Big Joe?" I asked, bringing the conversation back to the Smiths' special cougar.

"That's an easy one," answered Howard with a smile. "It was in June a few years ago. I was out hunting for a shootable animal at a time when some of the deer are just getting fat enough to be edible. The folks around Elk City all lived off the land and in the summertime one of us would kill a deer and share it with everybody. Nobody tried to press charges and you can bet your bottom dollar if it wasn't permitted somebody would have been after someone. We had a ranger station right by us. Anyway, on this particular day, the cougar, the dog, and I made a five-to-six-mile hike, one which cut the various game trails that led into our area. On the way back about a mile from home, we came on a cow elk with a calf probably four or five days old. The dog was on heel, but the cougar bolted through the bushes and caught the calf elk. I couldn't see anything for about ten seconds but I could hear the calf hollering like a wounded jackrabbit. It was a pitiful sound and I figured Joe was playing with it as a cat plays with a mouse. I hoped the cougar would kill the calf because it was probably too late to save his life. But when I reached him, there was Joe with the calf down and licking it profusely, just like he licked the dog. As soon as he saw me he thought he was going to get reprimanded for killing the calf, so he turned it loose. The calf got up and bolted through the woods. Joe took off again after it and caught it again. I thought I'd better check if the cougar had broken the calf's leg, so I made Joe and Torrey both go away. The calf was thoroughly wet from the cougar's licking but nothing seemed wrong. When I released Big Joe he came over, put his forepaws around the calf's neck, and continued to lick and wash.

"By this time the cow elk came along with her hackles up. I got the gun ready in case she struck me. I really thought Big Joe would take on the elk because he was so protective he wouldn't let anything bother me. What I could picture was the cow striking at me, the cougar jumping the cow, and with it all happening on a side hill, everything coming down on top of me. But the elk sized up the situation, her hackles lay down, and she moved away. Big Joe went back to loving that little calf again.

"I made the cougar leave the calf, though it followed us around a bit, then I called Big Joe and Torrey. We slid down off the bank to home and I locked them both in the house. Then I went back to check on the elk. There he was getting his dinner, so everything turned out fine. That was the only time I saw Big Joe catch a fawn or an elk. He used to go for larger animals."

"You lived in the wilderness but you did have some farms a few miles away. What about trouble with Joe and domestic animals?" I asked.

"Big Joe was a strange cougar. He loved pups, kittens, that calf elk; he even let a parakeet pull his ears and whiskers and he never bothered any of the livestock that grazed near us. You should talk to Leonard York in Elk City. His cattle range was close to our cabin and he's got some stories to tell."

Nine years later I accepted Howard's invitation. By then the Smiths had sold their place in British Columbia and were back living in Elk City. Dorothy met me in Stites and we bumped along the South Fork of the Clearwater River to visit again the places she and her husband had lived with cougars. Leonard York lived in a palatial log house at the turnoff to the Smiths' cabin. If any of their cougars had taken a liking to beef they wouldn't have had to go more than a mile to find it. Leonard was a kindly old bachelor, hospitable and independent like most of the Elk City people.

"I knew Big Joe quite well," he reminisced during an afternoon visit Dorothy and I made one day. "He came down to my ranch often, but he never bothered my cattle. One day I was sitting on the couch there. Joe was sitting beside me. Then he got up and put his forepaws on my shoulders and licked my face. It took the skin off, mind you, but I couldn't move away as he well and truly had me.

"Tina was the one, though. That was the Smiths' second cougar. She came down to the cattle and it did scare me for a while. I watched, and did those calves go, running to the bottom of the hill with the cougar after them. Then they'd take off up the hill again as fast as they could. Sometimes it seemed that the calves chased the cougar. Tina could have killed them in a second if she'd wanted to. But I was never worried about Big Joe or Tina. They'd get hold of me more than the calves. How'd you like a big cougar to hold you by the knees and take a great big mouthful?" He chuckled at the memory. And having suffered through such embraces many times ourselves, Dorothy and I laughed too.

Back on Quadra Island, it was now practically midnight but none of us had any desire to go to bed. The blackness of the sea and night sky was relieved by a silver shaft of moonlight and the lights of Campbell River twinkling on the horizon. Dorothy came around with coffee again and cougar talk resumed.

"Howard, what about wild cougars?" I asked. "Did you run into many of them when you had Big Joe?"

Both he and Dorothy looked at each other and laughed. "Well, yes. . . ." Howard smiled and I wondered what was coming. "I used to leave Big Joe home when I went to work. At that time I was a welder, about fifteen miles away. I was coming home one particular night when I saw this cougar sitting beside the dirt road about two miles from the cabin. I thought, well, Big Joe's got tired of waiting for me and has come looking. I'd better give him a lift. So I stopped the truck, went over to him and put my arm around his neck. I was just about to pick him up when he said something like, 'Keep your cotton-picking hands off me.' He looked at me straight in the eye and said, 'Don't touch me.' I remember saying two or three things that Joe was used to but it still didn't dawn on me that this wasn't Joe. I thought, 'Maybe a hunter came into the yard and chased him, so he's a bit excited.' I scolded him a bit, threw a rock at him, and tried to get him well off the road in case he got run over. Every time I threw a rock he snarled and threatened me. Anyway, I gave up trying to get him in the truck but I did get him off the road and into the bushes. As I drove off I thought, 'He'll be all right in a while.' I got home and there was

Big Joe asleep on the couch. 'My God,' I chortled to Dorothy. 'I've just wrestled with a *wild* cougar!' "

"He was almost a year old then," piped up Dorothy with a smile. "You wouldn't have mistaken him when he got older because he developed very individual qualities."

Howard is not the only person to have met a wild cougar and thought it was a tame one. Another friend of mine went to take pictures of Elaine Foisey's pet cougars at Cherryville, British Columbia. When he arrived the Foisey family was out, but there on the porch to greet the visitor was a cougar. Two more were behind an electric fence within a few yards of the house. My friend took close-up pictures of the free-roaming cougar and then left. Next day he phoned back to the Foiseys to thank them for the experience of visiting and photographing three cougars, especially the one that was walking around the house. "Three?" echoed Elaine in surprise. "We only have two and they're behind a fence." The cougar he had been photographing at such close quarters was a wild male that had been attracted to the female in season in the pen.

Mating a tame female cougar to a wild male was exactly what Howard and Dorothy wanted to do in Idaho and later on Quadra Island. He explained his program in detail.

"It became evident by the time Big Joe was over three years old that in order to do a good study on cougars we needed some kind of income to replace my work. We wanted to get a young female, raise it to be friendly, and have it bred to a wild male—the same program we tried to do here on Quadra. We also wanted to make a film of the cougar's growth and development. So, as a control, we built a den close by in the woods that could be floodlit in case the birth took place at night. Now it takes money to buy good camera equipment and devote all your time to making observations, so I joined up with a partner from California, a Mr. Leadbetter who came hunting in our area. This was two years before Lincoln-Mercury's Cougar car came into production. When my partner found that

Ford's new car was to be called a Cougar, he arranged with their advertising agency to make a pilot film on 'The Cougar as Companion.'

"We bought a cub from a local cougar hunter who had killed a female and this was Tina who, by the way, had cataracts. But she could get along by holding her face in a certain way. She could see downward but not upward. She could see her feet and she could run and play. Big Joe mothered Tina. They were friends a year together. Then we got two males. One had a congenital hernia and developed adhesions and died. The other was Little Joe. We started teaching the cougars commands to jump in and out of the truck and up and down onto the hood. Everything was going well when Big Joe was shot, followed by Tina and Torrey."

A strained, uncomfortable silence pervaded the room. Our eyes were drawn to a huge portrait of Big Joe that hung from the wall above the fireplace. You didn't have to be a cougarphile to appreciate the regal head, the distinctive face, the soft brown eyes, so different from the pictures or the heads of cougars that usually hang painted or stuffed on cabin walls. I glanced at Dorothy. It was for her that I felt most sympathy.

"Yes, cougars are a lot of heartache," she said very quietly.

Howard continued the story of Big Joe, Tina, and Torrey, an incredible and complicated story of political intrigue, jealousy, rebellion, attempted murder, and murder, with cougars as the victims. The story from Elk City made mine at Island View seem more like a fairy tale.

"The then supervisor of the Nez Percé National Forest was a Yugoslav Communist who was trying to see how many regulations he could implement against the people," Howard began. "The people of Idaho County don't like being run over roughshod and I rebelled immediately. I started making public speeches and writing articles in mining journals. I tried to tell the people what was happening to them, how they were being manipulated by government. I tried to get the magazine *True* to do an exposé on the Forest Service. They promised to send out a reporter if I got three affidavits that could be used in litigation, beside our own. I got two. One was from a man who staked a mining claim on the Salmon River where everything had to be backpacked or boated in. He and his wife were schoolteachers. They were disgusted at the school system, which was allowing immoral things like free sex to go on. So they decided to raise their six children on the Salmon River. Well, the Idaho and Nez Percé school boards joined forces to try and stop them. The supervisor went to order them out of the National Forest. But the answer he got was typical for that area. 'Not unless you want to leave your dead carcass here.' He didn't make the arrest anyway. He couldn't. Only the sheriff could do that. Of course, now the Forest Service has its own special agents to keep down dissent.

"Well, I was called on the carpet at the Red River Ranger Station and told by the then ranger that the supervisor had given orders for my dismissal. There were no good grounds as I had always done my work well. But there was no chance of promotion either because a system was organized where nobody but a graduate in forestry could hold down any kind of responsible job. After 1965 there was a rapid deterioration in the quality of the kind of worker they got. They put a bunch of inexperienced young people, college students, in jobs that needed experience.

"Then the Yugoslav Communist bribed my immediate neighbors, two Forest Service workers, to destroy my cougars and the dog. And straight after that, my neighbor, who could hardly read or write, got to become one of the Forestry Management personnel, the only time an undegreed person ever received a promotion of that kind."

"But, Howard, how can you be positive that they killed your animals?" I persisted, a little bewildered.

"Big Joe was killed first about three hundred yards from the house on the last day of hunting season and they were the only people on the road by our house at the time. When Big Joe first came up missing, I went to them and asked if they knew anything. 'Will you please let me know if you do?' I said. 'Oh, yes, we'll let you know. That's terrible,' they replied. Then they went on and on about how terrible it was that the cougar was shot."

"You know, I trusted them," broke in Dorothy, obviously upset. "The wife always said she didn't like cougars but they still came to the house to see Big Joe and Tina. We weren't their friends. We weren't used to the life they led but we were cordial. We said hello and Howard, being the shop foreman who went to the post office every day, picked up their mail and delivered it.

"I guess things cooled a bit when she accused Leonard York of stealing their meat from the deep freeze they kept at his house. He was the only one that was plugged into electricity at the time. I told her Leonard would never take other people's stuff. He's the most honest person you could meet.

"Anyway, we found out for sure she'd killed Big Joe from the sheriff himself. The woman even admitted it. 'Sure I killed him,' she said one time when she was intoxicated. And then they were the only ones in the neighborhood when Tina and Torrey were shot too. I met her returning from the woods a few minutes afterward on the only trail she could get in and out of the woods. No one else was in the woods that day but ourselves: I could tell by the tracks."

"You're getting ahead of the story, Dorothy," Howard intervened calmly. "One day Tina didn't come home. We thought she was coming in season, so we went out to look for her. We made circles from the house to see where she was. A mile from our house I met the neighbor lady coming off the hill and carrying a gun. She had always been cordial before. This time she was cold and wouldn't speak. I walked up the road and fifty feet from where I'd met her, I found Torrey shot."

"The dog's front leg was severed and her back leg was hanging from the skin. She had shot the dog and left her there to die. Howard had to destroy her because she wouldn't have been able to walk again,"

Dorothy added heatedly. "Later, we found Tina's body on the Forest Service dump."

"Didn't you go and tackle them about it or see the sheriff?" I asked, ready as usual to spring to the defense of the defenseless.

"No, there's no legal redress for shooting a dog or a cougar," Howard explained. "After we learned from the sheriff of her admission of guilt when she was drunk, it was a real touch-and-go situation. Once they knew we knew, they tried to frighten us out of the country.

"They drove up below the cabin one day and shot a big bore rifle over our house top. There was no way they could shoot into our house from the road down below or they probably would have. I stepped down over the bank with the full intent of killing them. I came within a hair-breadth of killing all three of them, the man, the wife, and their boy. Somehow I didn't but I did shoot close to them to let them know I had seen them shoot. They jumped in their pickup and left.

"Shortly thereafter we got word about it to the sheriff of Idaho County, who was our chief law enforcement officer. He drove to our place in an hour and a half, which meant he had to risk his life to get there. He told us they were real no-good people and he'd known of them for about ten years. Then he went to their house. He came back again and told us we could file charges if we wanted to, but there was no other way he could protect us. 'I can just tell you privately,' he said, 'if I was in your shoes and encountered them in the woods, I wouldn't turn my back on them. I would shoot them first rather than have them kill you.'

"It was shortly afterward that I came home from work to see Dorothy deliberately stalking the wife. We had established a boundary at Ryan Creek and Dorothy was hoping the woman would cross the boundary onto our claim."

"I think I just about went off my rocker," Dorothy interrupted. "The worst part was that she was a neighbor, that she lived next door. They had nothing against us. We were never unkind to them or anything."

"Dorothy at the time was understandably very angry

and upset," continued Howard. "Killing her two cougars was just like taking her children away from her. A woman has a different nature than a man. A man's nature with a handicapped child is that it shouldn't live, it is better to put it to sleep. But a woman's nature is to do everything in the world to save its life. And when a woman raises something, whether it is an animal or a child, she becomes overly protective, especially if it is a dumb animal or has a disability and can't protect itself. She raises it to trust other human beings and then when another human being comes along and destroys it, she will get much more involved emotionally than would a man. It's just the nature of things."

I knew. I had trod part of the same path and I was to continue it alone, long after I left Quadra Island.

"What did you do then?" David brought us back to the story.

"It seemed best both to preserve my sanity and to preserve my family that we go to Texas for the winter and then look for somewhere else to do the cougar study," Howard told us. "We went to Brownsville and waited for my partner, Mr. Leadbetter, to return from Tampico, Mexico, which we thought might be a good place to continue with our program. We still had Little Joe. But then we learned that the Mexican who was *his* partner had killed him, so obviously Mexico was too risky for such a project. See, you can't buy property in Mexico outright unless you are a native of the country, so in this case a gringo—my partner—had gone into partnership with a Mexican to buy it. Then after the deal was made the Mexican killed him, and everybody divided the spoils. So Dorothy and I decided to go north to British Columbia and start again. And here we are."

Dorothy came around with more coffee as we sat digesting the turmoil of the Smiths' story.

When we went to bed in the early hours of the morning only Big Joe remained calm and serene from his position over the fireplace. As Dorothy had remarked, "Joe made us feel so inadequate. He was so much more alert, so much smarter than us. Yet it was through no fault of his own that he died. I don't mind accidents that you can understand, but not deliberate attempts to destroy an animal when there is no way you can fight back on their behalf."

I think David and I were in a state of shock or at least bemusement. Our own story might be a fairy tale compared to the Smiths' grim drama, but unfortunately it was to have no fairy-tale ending.

16

And Then There Were None...

Most people who came to visit me at Island View really came to visit Tom. Some wanted to buy or rent him, others wanted to film, sketch, or write about him. But most, like the families of schoolchildren who still came from Vancouver, wanted just to say hello. Taking visitors with me to the zoo and the increased number of visits helped to relieve Tom's boredom. He was now approaching two years old, the time that in the wild he would be foraging farther afield, leaving his family and approaching sexual maturity.

The larger cats, like lions and tigers and cougars, kill infrequently—perhaps only once every ten days. As a result they are inactive much of the time, and so they probably don't suffer in confinement as much as smaller cats, who are kept very busy hunting smaller prey daily. Yet the cat family as a whole is intelligent and accustomed in the wild to encountering new sets of stimuli and solving new problems. Some zoos, advanced in their thinking, are doing away with empty, easy-to-clean concrete boxes, and designing structures and experimenting with techniques that allow the captives more exercise, reduce their boredom, and satisfy their natural ability to learn. They don't want complacent fat cats that look stuffed. They want alert predators with sharply honed hunting instincts.

For this reason, the cougars in the Brookfield Zoo

in Chicago no longer get their meat handed them on a plate by a dependable zoo keeper at a dependable hour. They now have to work for their supper. In each of their cages there is a "stalking branch" about seven feet from the ground. When the animals climb on it, their weight activates an electronic device hidden out of sight that starts a tape moving. Sometime during a twenty-minute period after the tape is activated, a mechanized plastic marmot scuttles out of a hole in a rock and makes a frantic eight-foot dash into a hole in another rock, about thirty feet away from the stalking branch. The cougars have only one and a half seconds to pounce to the area where the marmot vanishes into the hole. They then must root about with a paw or with their noses in the hole and press a lever. The lever rings a bell in a small nearby cave and if the animals have acted swiftly enough, they will receive raw meat that is pushed into the cave from a conveyor belt. If they are too slow to pounce they get no food and must try again when prompted by hunger pangs. Such naturalistic devices allow educative viewing for those outside the cage and more natural activity for those inside.

Meanwhile at Rudy's, Tom had to make do with me. To keep him from engaging in too many activities with me, I brought him old shoes, balls and other playthings. I wrapped them in my sweaters for a week beforehand to get them saturated with my own smells, but after the first few sniffs, he took no notice of them. He continued to race around the enclosure, leap at the dingoes, tear at the woodwork, and roughhouse with me.

As summer gave way to fall and school resumed, both Rudy and I noticed that Tom bumped into things more often, missed his footing after a jump and stumbled off the ledge that led to his sleeping platform. He held his head down to the ground and I knew he couldn't see.

We decided to take him out of the big bear pen and put him in another pen, which, though smaller, allowed him less room to hurt himself. It had previously housed cougars and had no distracting dingoes next door. His nearest neighbors now were chimpanzees several yards away on the other side of the path. Perhaps their humanlike characteristics would be more familiar to him.

On the day of the move I merely slipped a choke collar around his neck and strolled with him on the leash to his new accommodation. As he accompanied me meekly, I smiled a little at the deserted zoo. All visitors, even Rudy and his family, were taking the precaution of staying indoors.

The quieter pen, surrounded on three sides by trees, seemed to suit him better. Certainly it suited me. With less of a runway to build up momentum, Tom's welcoming ceremony no longer sent me plunging to the ground.

By now I had given up hope of David's ever doing anything to get Tom back. He was always buried in his own work, planning a dozen projects, or darting about the country trying to execute them. It seemed I only got his attention when some crisis occurred, like the day a mink chewed through the wire of the sea-bird enclosure and killed eight of our oyster catchers. As a result, I was beginning to feel resigned to preparing a permanent and familiar place for Tom so he could grow old and blind with dignity. Like Big Joe, Tom was special.

But as fall turned to winter and Christmas approached, Tom began to get noticeably thinner, so much so that visitors to the cage commented on his condition. Now when he came leaping at me, it was not to put his forepaws around my neck, it was to knock the bucket of chicken from my grasp. He seemed ravenous. And sometimes he regurgitated his food.

I didn't like to disturb David with my worries because he was immersed in preparations to go on the road with our first full-length movie, *Coast Safari*. If it was a success we were going to hire an assistant to look after the animals, buy a house nearby with central heating, running water, and insulation, and think about raising children. But as Rudy continued to make plans to close down the rest of his zoo and my concern for

Tom grew, I eventually broached the subject. To my surprise, David came out with "Okay, kid, I'll get him home for Christmas and you can fatten him up."

The Christmas of 1968 was both the best and the worst I have ever spent. It was the best because Tom came home for the holidays and the worst because of weather and its aftermath.

I came home from school one day in mid-December to get my Christmas present, the new wildlife regulations that allowed the Fish and Wildlife Branch to give us a permit to keep Tom at home. This was ironic after I'd just resigned myself to Tom's lifetime imprisonment. Although we had no intention of opening either a private or a public zoo at Island View Beach and we did not charge admission when visitors came to see our animals, David decided to pay for a commercial zoo license in addition to the scientific and educational permits we already had. We no longer needed one permit from the municipality to get another from the Fish and Wildlife Branch. However, we were not sure how the councilors viewed the situation or the neighbors who had documented their opposition eighteen months before. That was a problem we could face in the New Year—although by then there would be no need.

We collected Tom from the zoo on the morning of Christmas Eve. To allay the fears of those who might be perturbed at seeing a two-year-old cougar peering at them from the windows, I played our usual game of crouching down on the floor of the truck whenever we passed people. Tom was pathetically glad to see us and this time lathered me with his usual affection and not the chicken bucket.

We decided against continuing our plans for a large landscaped enclosure in the back field with our helicoptered logs, and designed instead a sixty-foot pen running the length of the compound with an off-the-ground log cabin den and a huge tree lying diagonally across the enclosure for climbing exercise. While we dreamed, Tom nosed around for old familiar things. He wouldn't be having Sam and Haida for playmates any more. Tom was one creature Sam could not herd into his harem now that the weights of the respective animals were so diverse. Haida had gone to friends in Kamloops. We didn't like to keep Haida penned up and when her affectionate nature expanded beyond us to every dog in the neighborhood and her howls in season awakened their owners, we knew she had to leave.

The climax came on the day Frank Beebe, our neighbor, wearing hipwaders, stormed into my kitchen and told me I didn't know anything about sex.

I seem to be able to cope with wild-animal problems much more than the domestic kind. There have been many waifs left on our doorstep, but the one that caused the most trouble was a black German shepherd dog. I phoned various animal-control and protection agencies, but it seemed that Island View escaped being in anybody's jurisdiction but our own. I tried to ignore him as much as you can when your unwelcome guest lies under your feet as you step past the door. I tried not to feed him, hoping that hunger would make him look for another home. But he stayed. Frank, the volatile type, suggested I shoot him and then made comments on the way to school in the morning that suggested he might shoot me if I once more stepped over a black dog when he came to pick me up. Haida was in season again so I locked her up in the compound to avoid a litter of German-Hungarian pointing dogs.

But one black Saturday she escaped over the back fence and went looking for love and romance with our doorstep visitor. She came back alone half an hour later, but I spent the rest of the day worrying if she was pregnant. According to the nearest pet hotel she probably was. I didn't know where her companion was and I didn't care.

That is, not till suppertime, when first Vera Beebe came in to ask if I had seen Bubbles, their noisy little Peke, and then Frank raged in to inform me of my ignorance of the birds and the bees. When I emerged from his screaming tirade I found out what he meant. During the half hour that Hilda had been displaying her wares around the countryside, Bubbles had left home to answer our dog's call and become embroiled in a vicious triangle with the black German shepherd which, to my horror, had left the little dog dead. "And it's all your fault," were Frank's parting words as I burst into tears. "You should have known they'd get together."

Mother came to administer tranquilizers. David came to tell me I should handle things better. The police came to collect the black dog, who had returned to his unwanted position on our doorstep. Frank came the next Monday to drive me to school as usual and, thankfully, talked not about dogs but sasquatches. And the Davieses came from Kamloops the following week to take Haida, still lovelorn but fortunately not about to mother either part-Pekes or part-German shepherds.

It was a bit cramped that Christmas. The director of one of the zoos in the United States had just brought us several parrots, one macaw, a Malaysian otter, and a gibbon, all of which were warm-weather species and had to be kept in the house. The Christmas tree brought home from the school party just managed to fit in the front door beside a sixteen-foot dinghy that had been made for us by the woodworking class at the local high school. While I hung presents on the tree, Mike, a teen-ager who was staying with us for a time to help with the chores, painted the boat. Tom, in his new winter coat, sat as far away from our one heat outlet as possible and contentedly watched the proceedings.

He was not so contented later when on Christmas Day I got dressed up for dinner. Instead of smelling of old sweaters, jeans, and a red cougar coat, I was freshly bathed, perfumed, stockinged, and formally gowned. I popped out of the bathroom and patted Tom in passing. For one nasty moment I felt fear. He didn't recognize me. Startled, he snarled and swiped at me with a paw, claws unfurled, on the defensive against the unknown. I realized then that his blindness was becoming more of a certainty with the passing of each day. He detected people's presence more by smell than by sight. Except for Dave and me, who smelled more familiar, strangers were probably just a blur. I grabbed his forepaws and called his name. As I came into focus he purred.

On Boxing Day it snowed. Not the usual white stuff which disappears before the novelty wears off. But it snowed in December. And January. And February. Victoria lost its Christmas image of greenery and red roses, and the disaster area that Island View became because of heavy snow and cold weather was a portent for the tragedy to follow.

As the mercury plummeted, lower than it had since 1880, the pipes and pumps froze solid. To get drinking water for us all, I boiled the icicles that obliterated our view of the snowdrifts that piled up outside the door. To keep the birds and Sam from eating ice blocks, I brought their herring into the house to defrost in the electric stove. Later, I brought in the birds. When a sudden two-day thaw cracked the pipes and sent a deluge through the ceiling, David called a plumber and escaped to Hilary's in Vancouver where he was organizing the last-minute arrangements for the film tour.

As soon as the new pipes and pumps were in, they froze solid again and remained that way for the winter. When the driftwood from the beach, the propane from the gas man, and the logs from the supermarket all ran out, I lay down with Tom and used his warm fur as my blanket.

There was no need to worry about neighbors. Nobody came to the beach, and the house and compound were hidden under blankets of their own. Tom and I went for daily walks in the snow—if walk is the word for tumbling and stumbling amid the snowdrifts. And with a wind-chill factor that reduced the temperature to 20 below, it was warmer to play games like angels in the snow than run up and down the beach beside the steaming sea.

Frank and Vera and the falcons had now left the rented beach cottage for property of their own on the other side of the peninsula, so David bought me another clunker of a car to get me to school. When classes started again, I had lots of opportunities to run the car —into snow dunes, ice-edged ditches, even other cars when blizzards or an accompaniment of parrots, gibbons, or otters en route to school blocked out my visibility.

While I was away Tom stayed out in the compound in his old pen. The new one, which Mike was helping to build, wouldn't be ready till David returned from the film tour. When I was at home Tom seemed perfectly content to sprawl on the floor. He never rough-and-tumbled over the furniture now as he did in his kittenish days. He was much more placid.

Except the night he defended me against Mike. As soon as David left for Vancouver in early January, a change came over Tom. Mike and I were the only people in the house. Tom growled whenever somebody came near me. I try not to be anthropomorphic, not for any villainy I can see in the term, but because I strive to keep things in perspective. However, jealousy and a desire to protect me while I was alone are the only reasons I can give to explain the cougar's strange behavior.

I was sitting at my typewriter in the living room as close as possible to the potbellied stove when Mike came in to give me some papers. He strode briskly up to my desk, brushed past Tom who was sprawled on the carpet near my feet, and deposited the letters. As he leaned over my shoulder for a signature, Tom jumped up from behind and leaped onto his back. Mike, bent under the cougar's weight, threw his arms over his head.

"Tom!" I yelled. "No! Get down!"

Instantly the cougar dropped to the floor. Mike straightened up and backed slowly to the door. Apart from being a bit shaken and wearing a torn shirt that had borne the brunt of Tom's claws, he had survived his unexpected encounter with a cougar without further ill effects. As soon as he had left the room, Tom lay at my feet again, purring. I deemed it prudent, however, to keep Tom in the outside pen for the rest of Mike's stay while Dave was away.

Dorothy Smith had also remarked on how Big Joe guarded her jealously if there were too many visitors. He had growled, nudged them away, or clamped his jaws around their arms. Usually the owner of the arm hadn't waited for a further demonstration of the cougar's feelings.

By the end of January David returned from Vancouver with all arrangements completed for the film tour. Halls had been rented, school lectures organized, advertisements placed, licenses paid. Now all that separated us from repaying our debts and having a more normal life style was the size of the audiences. Would people leave their cozy chesterfields in front of their television sets in the worst winter on record and skid or stumble through snow and ice to the local school auditorium to see an outdoor film?

"I'm going to take Tom with me up north," David said suddenly a few nights before his departure. "He'll help to draw attention to the film and when the audiences see him they'll realize that not all cougars are the vicious monsters that most people think they are. Predators need a better image, especially up north. Tom'll be good for public relations."

"No, Dave, don't do it!" I hurled the words like a fusillade. An arsenal of arguments inflamed my mind. Tom had only just come home after a year and a half in zoos. His equilibrium was still disturbed by being moved from cages to house and compound. Neither of us had spent enough time with him lately to ease the change-over. I'd been trying to cope with the horrendous conditions at home and the end-of-year activities at school. David had never spent enough time with Tom, not since he was a kitten in Vancouver.

"That's what's wrong," he burst out angrily. "You spend too much time with that cougar anyway."

"But, Dave, he needs me," I pleaded, and then hesitantly as my eyes clouded over, "and you don't. You only need me when you want some work done. . . . He's blind. He's got nobody else. You do."

I clenched my fists and shut my eyes tight to stop the

tears. Dave hated weakness. He was used to winning. And he would win this round too. I knew that further argument was futile.

"Where will Tom live while you're traveling?" I asked dully through a blur that was as much in my heart as in my eyes.

"I thought I'd make him a cage on the back of the pickup," Dave replied blithely, as usual with an answer for everything. "I'm taking Scarlett too. People up north have probably never seen a tropical bird like a macaw. She's one the kids can touch too."

"It's the worst winter on record. How'll you keep her warm?"

"I'll put her in my parka. No need to worry about Tom. He's got his own fur coat."

We went out together to the compound to take Tom for a walk. His paws were bleeding from the sanitary cement floor of the pen. He wouldn't be able to use his luxury pen till he came back from the tour. Then he would be able to roll in sand, munch grass, claw logs, and jump over trees. And for company I would only be a whistle away.

But until then how would he adapt to the pace of Dave's rigorous schedule—the daily radio, press, and television interviews, the daily checks with janitors, fire marshals, rent collectors, the free daily school lectures, the paid evening performances, the nightly cleanups, and the early morning drives to get to the next town, where it started all over again?

I prepared packages of chicken and fish for Tom's meals and persuaded Dave to arrange extra meat for him en route. Rationally, I knew our future depended on the success of the film tour. Emotionally, I was still upset. I felt a loss I could not explain.

The macaw was happy as the truck was loaded. She had Dave to herself, very intimately, inside his parka. Now she could share his shoulder and pick peas from between his teeth and croak, "I love you," without interference from me.

I gave Tom my old red coat for reassurance and

snuggled my cheek against his purring face. He put his head on the side in obvious puzzlement and squeaked as if to say, "Aren't you coming too?"

"Be good, Tom," I whispered and brushed away tears so I could better slam the back of the truck. "Please be good to him, Dave. He's only just got home."

I went to school when I could. When the car would start. When I could shovel out the drifts that piled against the front door. When the snow plow came and cleared and sanded the hill behind. The staff was always surprised to see me. And when I hurt my eye by bashing ice for water, some of them even came home to thaw out fish, unplug drains, or clean up birds.

My colleagues, friends, and a few neighbors might worry about me at Island View, but I was worried about David and Tom in Kitimat, Terrace, Smithers, Prince Rupert, Vanderhoof, Prince George, Fort St. James. Driving conditions were disastrous. People were being warned to stay indoors. Elderly citizens were dying. Few could remember it being 50 below before. David phoned most nights. He made it sound like fun. "Everybody's talking about the film and those who've seen it are raving. We got a standing ovation in Rupert."

"And how's Tom?" My mind was constantly on the cougar. I had feelings of foreboding I could not suppress.

"People love him," David rattled on. "He even shares the microphone with the macaw. Can't get him off the stage though. He wants to stay. So I get Gordon [our assistant] to go down on all fours on the floor and get Tom to chase him out of the auditorium. I'm not sure Gordon appreciates this as part of his public relations job but I don't want to leave Tom on the stage during the film because he's too distracting. I think in future while I'm narrating, I'll bring him onstage when the movie's over."

But in the tiny settlement of Fort St. James the audience insisted on seeing their first live cougar before the show. This time Gordon didn't have to kick up his heels and lead Tom on and off the stage. In this school hall there was no stage. David had to lead him in through the front door on a leash. When everybody was seated, David and Tom walked in to meet Gordon at the ticket table at the entrance to the hall. Scarlett, the macaw, was sitting on the back of a chair beside him.

Suddenly, a seven-year-old Indian boy, his two younger brothers, and some other friends left their seats and ran to the entrance before the show started, for a last look at the macaw and probably a first look at the cougar. . . .

I was in bed when it happened. I had come from school so exhausted by months of late nights, early mornings, and harassed days that I lay down under an electric blanket in the snowbound house. I intended to get up later to do the chores. I must have been asleep for several hours. The phone ringing raucously at 8:30 P.M. made me jump. Dave was terse and serious.

"Tom's just grabbed a little Indian boy. The kid brushed past him and he took a swipe at his jacket. He smelled moose blood on it and tried to rip the sleeve off. You know what a cat's like when it's got something you don't want it to have. It took Gordon and me a while to get the boy out of the jacket with the cougar hanging on. The boy needs to have some stitches. The doctor is fixing him up now. The audience is fine, they want the show to go on. Two R.C.M.P. were in the audience and they're not worried. They didn't get up . . . but, Lyn, I'm going to dispose of Tom later tonight."

I didn't say anything. I couldn't. I was numb. The receiver dangled. When I lifted it again it was dead. I felt very cold and put on another sweater under the electric blanket. I felt the ultimate loss. The thesis. The cougar. The man.

I was told later that the audience enjoyed the film. They gave Dave a standing ovation at the end. For two hours his talk had been punctuated with tears—perhaps because Tom represented one battle he had not won.

And in the third hour a bullet ended Tom's life.

It was the final capitulation.

I knew I had to go to school. I knew I had to face the friendly inquiries. I knew I had to say something when I heard the "I told you so's."

The next day it thawed and I got to school easily. They were waiting. The teachers with their coffee in the staffroom. The children with their clippings in the playground. I adjusted sunglasses, piled up papers, and walked as steadily as I could to the classroom. I shut the door. I didn't want to let anyone in. The bell rang and it was time for news.

"Mr. Hancock's in hospital. I heard it on the radio."

"Mr. Hancock's been killed by a tiger, my mother read it in the paper."

"This one says the boy needed two stitches. But this one says he needed fifteen."

"This one says the cougar attacked while its owner was trying to promote an appreciation for native wild-life. That's pretty funny."

"Tom's on the front page of the newspaper. And on the radio. And on the TV."

Tom had hit the headlines. Hilary said she tried to stop it at the studio, but there just wasn't anything much happening that day. Just "COUGAR ATTACKS AND MAULS BOY."

And then the question that none of the media had asked: "Mrs. Hancock, *why* did Tom do it?"

I told them about his blindness, how he couldn't see but he could smell, how he reacted to sudden shapes that flashed past, about the running boys and the moose meat their mother had been cutting up for supper, about Tom's long stay in the zoo, about how he'd just got home only to be taken away again, about his long journey in a very cold winter in a cage at the back of a truck, about the new faces and more new faces and still more new faces, about prodding and poking and patting.

"Mrs. Hancock, what's going to happen to Tom now? The paper says he has to be kept in a cage."

I told them about the new pen with the logs and the grass and the sand and the trees that was meant to be his home for the rest of his life.

And I tried to tell them why it couldn't be. But the words were wrung from my mind, not my heart. I told them that people expected cougars to attack people and if Tom had remained alive, people would remember and ask if he was the cougar that had scratched the little boy. I told them that if Tom had remained alive my neighbors on the hill would never let him live at home in the pen at Island View. I told them if Tom had remained alive, people would remember our film because of him and not for what the film was about. I told them our film was the story of a man and his wife studying animals in the wild, that it was trying to make people like animals and care for the land in which they lived. I told them that reporters don't find that kind of story interesting enough to put in newspapers or to talk about on radio and television; they prefer stories about the damage that animals can do. But those were David's reasons why it couldn't be . . . not mine.

I couldn't tell them then that a year later, when the little Indian boy was eight years old, he ran up to me in the same hallway of the school in Fort St. James and asked with bright eyes alight with anticipation, "Did you bring my friend Tom?"

And I didn't tell them that for David, Tom was just too much of a friend to me.

That once there was a marriage. . . .

And once there was a cougar called Tom. . . .

ABOUT THE AUTHOR

LYN HANCOCK was born and educated in Australia. After completing her university studies, she set off in search of high adventure—and found it—living in Southeast Asia, hitchhiking from Cape Town to Cairo, banana-boating around the West Indies, and mountain climbing in Mexico. But the greatest adventures began after she married David Hancock, who proposed to her while they were making an aerial census of bald eagles along Vancouver Island's west coast. In addition to her two previous books, *There's a Seal in My Sleeping Bag* and *There's a Raccoon in My Parka,* Lyn is the author of many articles about wildlife. She now lives in Burnaby, British Columbia.